EXOTIC
STYLING

HUMAN BEHAVIOR
THE ART OF SEWING
THE OLD WEST
THE EMERGENCE OF MAN
THE AMERICAN WILDERNESS
THE TIME-LIFE ENCYCLOPEDIA OF GARDENING
LIFE LIBRARY OF PHOTOGRAPHY
THIS FABULOUS CENTURY
FOODS OF THE WORLD
TIME-LIFE LIBRARY OF AMERICA
TIME-LIFE LIBRARY OF ART
GREAT AGES OF MAN
LIFE SCIENCE LIBRARY
THE LIFE HISTORY OF THE UNITED STATES
TIME READING PROGRAM
LIFE NATURE LIBRARY
LIFE WORLD LIBRARY
FAMILY LIBRARY:
    THE TIME-LIFE BOOK OF THE FAMILY CAR
    THE TIME-LIFE FAMILY LEGAL GUIDE
    THE TIME-LIFE BOOK OF FAMILY FINANCE

THE ART OF SEWING

EXOTIC STYLING

BY THE EDITORS OF TIME-LIFE BOOKS

TIME-LIFE BOOKS, NEW YORK

TIME-LIFE BOOKS

FOUNDER: Henry R. Luce 1898-1967

Editor-in-Chief: Hedley Donovan
Chairman of the Board: Andrew Heiskell
President: James R. Shepley
Group Vice President: Rhett Austell

Vice Chairman: Roy E. Larsen

MANAGING EDITOR: Jerry Korn
Assistant Managing Editors: Ezra Bowen,
David Maness, Martin Mann, A. B. C. Whipple
Planning Director: Oliver E. Allen
Art Director: Sheldon Cotler
Chief of Research: Beatrice T. Dobie
Director of Photography: Melvin L. Scott
Senior Text Editor: Diana Hirsh
Assistant Art Director: Arnold C. Holeywell
Assistant Chief of Research: Myra Mangan

PUBLISHER: Joan D. Manley
General Manager: John D. McSweeney
Business Manager: John Steven Maxwell
Sales Director: Carl G. Jaeger
Promotion Director: Paul R. Stewart
Public Relations Director: Nicholas Benton

THE ART OF SEWING
SERIES EDITOR: Carlotta Kerwin
EDITORIAL STAFF FOR
EXOTIC STYLING:
Assistant Editor: David L. Harrison
Designer: Virginia Gianakos
Assistant Designer: Robert McKee
Text Editors: Don Earnest, Gerry Schremp,
David S. Thomson
Chief Researchers: Wendy A. Rieder,
Gabrielle Smith (planning)
Staff Writers: Sondra R. Albert, Carol I. Clingan,
Michael T. Drons, Marion Gordon Goldman,
Angela D. Goodman, Marilyn Kendig,
Wendy Murphy, Sandra Streepey,
Reiko Uyeshima
Research Staff: Rhea Finkelstein,
Nancy Jacobsen, Ginger Seippel,
Vivian Stephens, Jean Stratton
Art Staff: Sanae Yamazaki (art coordinator),
Angela Alleyne, Penny Burnham,
Patricia Byrne, Catherine Caufield,
Jean Held, Jill Losson
Editorial Assistant: Kathleen Beakley

EDITORIAL PRODUCTION
Production Editor: Douglas B. Graham
Assistant Production Editor: Gennaro C. Esposito
Quality Director: Robert L. Young
Assistant Quality Director: James J. Cox
Copy Staff: Rosalind Stubenberg (chief),
Mary Orlando, Ricki Tarlow, Florence Keith·
Picture Department: Dolores A. Littles,
Jessy S. Faubert, Carolyn Turman
Traffic: Feliciano Madrid

THE CONSULTANTS:
Gretel Courtney taught for many years at the
French Fashion Academy in New York City. She
has studied patternmaking and design at the
Fashion Institute of Technology in New York and
haute couture at the French Fashion Academy.

Annette Feldman is a knitting and crocheting designer, both for clothing and interior decoration.
She is the author of several books, including *Knit,
Purl and Design; Crochet and Creative Design;*
and *Beginner's Needlecraft.*

Tracy Kendall has for many years designed sets
and costumes for commercial films and advertis-
ing. She is presently a fashion stylist.

Julian Tomchin is a textile designer who has been
awarded the Vogue Fabric Award and a Coty
Award of the American Fashion Critics. A grad-
uate of Syracuse University's Fine Arts College,
he has been chairman of the Textile Design Department at the Shenkar College of Fashion and
Textile Technology in Tel Aviv and now teaches
at the Parsons School of Design in New York.

Portions of this book were written by Michael
Durham, Richard Oulahan, Keith Wheeler and
Edmund White. Valuable assistance was
provided by these departments and individuals
of Time Inc.: Editorial Production, Norman Airey;
Library, Benjamin Lightman; Picture Collection,
Doris O'Neil; Photographic Laboratory, George
Karas; TIME-LIFE News Service, Murray J. Gart;
Correspondents Maria Vincenza Aloisi and
Josephine du Brusle (Paris), Lois Armstrong
(Los Angeles), Steve Hughes (Rabat), Lucky
Marmon (Jerusalem), Ann Natanson (Rome),
Laverne Lane Praeger (Beirut), Mahamet Ali
Kislali (Ankara), John Riddle (Cairo).

CONTENTS

1
FARAWAY FASHIONS

xotic. The word stems from the Greek *exō*—outside. Anything out of its place is exotic. But in fashion, the exotic is more than something just out of its place. It is the imaginative and innovative use of colors, materials, accessories and design to suggest, rather than copy, the look and spirit of another place, another time.

It is the evocation of Japan in a kimono's gracious flow; of ancient Persia in a caftan's

THE HIGH ART OF ADORNING THE BODY

long, loose lines; of West Africa in a dashiki's bold, square-shouldered cut. It is a sunburst of saffron for a turban, a broad stroke of embroidered silk for a sash, a net of filet crochet for an evening gown and a maelstrom of color in tie-dyed cotton for a robe.

Paradoxically, the construction of these garments does not require infinities of fuss. "To dress a woman is not to cover her with ornaments," said Paul Poiret, the designer whose style revolution in the early part of the century laid the foundation for today's exotic fashions. "It is to underscore the endowments of her body . . . to reveal nature in a significant contour which accentuates grace. All the talent of an artist consists in a manner of revealment."

For the most part, therefore, only the simplest sewing techniques—such as the plain seam and hem—are required to construct the basic garments shown and described on subsequent pages. And with a few other, more advanced skills, it is possible to create special effects with the collars, necklines, halters, slits and hems, or to enhance the exotic mood of a garment with trims, braids, beads, sequins, tassels, fringes, fasteners, embroidery and crochet.

The appeal of the exotic in fashion is as ancient as Greece. Alexander the Great scandalized some of his tough Macedonian troopers by adopting the sumptuous robes of the Persians they had conquered. Later when the Muslims invaded Europe in the 8th and 9th centuries, Christian generals began to emulate the bright robes and turbans of their Moorish foes. The Crusaders themselves were not immune. The closer they got to the Holy Land, the less they looked like their brothers at home.

In succeeding centuries, Western dress was further enriched not only with new fabrics but with new fashions. Mmes. de Pompadour and du Barry posed for portraits gowned as sultanas. Wives of ambassadors returned from Eastern capitals with wondrous wardrobes, and inspired other ladies of the court to dress à la Circassienne or à la Turque. Marie Antoinette made popular a gown of Levantine inspiration by wearing it during her first pregnancy.

Until the first decade of the 20th Century, however, exotic styles and fabrics remained for the most part the exclusive privilege of a tiny minority of the rich and titled. Then came revolution in the rotund person of the dark and dapper Frenchman—Paul Poiret.

In the late 1890s Poiret père, a Parisian draper and a solid petit bourgeois, had become increasingly dismayed by his son Paul's fascination with the world of art: his predilection for bright colors, his way of sneaking off to museums and to the theater, where he avidly sketched the costumes of the actresses. When, in 1896, Paul presumed to question his father's conviction that the controversial Jewish army officer Alfred Dreyfus belonged on Devil's Island, that was the last straw. Father Auguste apprenticed 18-year-old Paul to an umbrella maker with instructions to work the boy hard. The prescription failed. As he trudged around Paris delivering bundles of umbrellas, Poiret dreamed of turning bright fabrics into beautiful gowns. A display of Oriental rugs in a department store sent him into ecstasies. "A fresh breeze from the countries of the sun," he wrote in his diary.

Poiret began offering some of his sketches to fashion designers, and soon landed a job with one of the greatest, Jacques Doucet. Doucet's new apprentice admired him not only as a designer but as a patron of the arts and supreme dandy—each of Doucet's innumerable pairs of patent-leather shoes was varnished daily and dried in an oven between wearings.

The youngster absorbed some of Doucet's grand manner, and his own dress designs began to show some of the master's elegance. Poiret rose rapidly with Doucet; soon he was designing costumes for a distinguished clientele that included famous actresses like Sarah Bernhardt. But the imperious Sarah got the outspoken youth fired when, while attending one of her rehearsals, he commented disparagingly on some of the other actors. After a 10-month hiatus for military service, however, Poiret bobbed up at another great fashion house, that of the brothers Worth.

Here again he triumphed. Though brother Jean, the chief designer, shuddered at some of Poiret's unorthodox creations, brother Gaston, the manager, beamed over their sales figures. Some clients sided with Jean. When Poiret offered the aged Russian Princess Bariatinsky an Oriental-looking coat cut like a kimono, she snorted: "In Russia when serfs pester us, we cut off their heads and throw them into sacks that look like this thing!"

Poiret and his exotic modes were fascinating to most fashionable women, however, and after he left Worth and set up his own salon, it became so packed with customers clamoring for his clothes that within two years he had to move to larger quarters. By now he was openly attacking the very foundations of fashion, beginning with salvos and volleys of arresting colors. As he later recalled: "At that time, lilacs, sky-blue hortensias, straw, anything that was cloying, washed out and dull to the eye was held in the highest regard. I hurled some hellbent wolves into that sheepfold. The reds, the royal blues and the oranges and lemons made all the rest take notice, and my sunburst of pastels brought a new dawn."

The new dawn of color was just that —a mere beginning. Poiret's untrammeled imagination envisioned changing the look of the female figure itself. "I like a plain gown," he once said, "cut from a light and supple fabric, which falls from the shoulders to the feet in long, straight folds, like dense liquid, just touching the figure and throwing light and shadow over the moving form." With this in mind, he produced subtly provocative, tunic-like dresses reminiscent of the ancient Greek statues he had studied intensively at the Louvre.

But such a gown could not possibly fit the then-fashionable S-shaped figure, imprisoned by a corset that cinched in the waist while accentuating the stem and stern. Poiret's daring solution was to abolish the corset, which for centuries had molded women to its whalebone whim. He substituted instead a thin, lightweight rubber sheath, the girdle. Shortly thereafter he invented the *soutien-gorge,* later to become known as the brassiere.

As intrepid in propaganda as he was in design, Poiret one Sunday escorted to Longchamps racetrack three of his young mannequins. They were uncorseted and wore full-length Hellenic gowns, slit *à la Chinoise* from the knee down—*tiens!*—and disclosing not proper black hose but —*zut alors!*—colored stockings. Women screamed and dragged their husbands to the exits, while Poiret warded off attackers with swings of his tasseled cane.

The Parisian press was scandalized.

"Those gowns are, beyond any shadow of a doubt, the worst of the recent insanities," said *Le Figaro.* "To think of it!" fumed *l'Illustration.* "Under those straight gowns we could sense their bodies!"

But the critics seethed in vain. Before long some of those outraged Longchamps ladies were wearing Poiret skirts slit to reveal knee-high, skin-tight boots of brightly colored Morocco leather. To complete his long, columnar silhouette, Poiret also ordered his subjects to reduce their bouffant hairdos to more closely cropped tresses, bound with Greek-style bandeaux. For evening wear he added delicate aigrettes of spun-glass filaments. "They are hideous, barbaric!" raged his old boss Jean Worth. "They are really only suitable for the women of uncivilized tribes." But to stay in business, Worth and all the other couturiers had to follow Poiret's lead.

Poiret's gaudy conceptions received an enormous boost on May 19, 1909, with the Paris première of the Ballets Russes. The repertoire of this brilliant Russian dance company was like nothing ever seen or heard before in Western Europe. The dances they performed were vigorous, erotic displays, as far removed from the formalized patterns of classical Western ballet as the Volga is from the Seine.

Not the least part of the total effect was

Costumes that the Russian impressario Sergei Diaghilev commissioned for the 1909 Paris debut of his Ballets Russes made fashion—as well as dance—history, and set off a generation of exotic couturier designs. The Ballets reached a sartorial crescendo in these costumes for Scheherazade. From the left are a pearl-draped dancer, a richly bedecked sultan and his sultry favorite, and a pantalooned costume worn by the great dancer Nijinsky.

the costumes. They blazed with audacious colors, with veils and jewels and feathers, and they revealed flesh in quantities never shown before to a respectable Parisian audience. For Poiret, the event was an open invitation to expand his exotic revolution.

A Paris exalted by the Ballets Russes fell eagerly upon the fantasies Poiret now introduced: turbans, kimono blouses, tunics over sheaths, caps sprouting antennae, huge tassels. He revived the kimono coat that had so affronted the Russian princess, adding an extravaganza of embroidery over the shoulders and down the back. His harem gown featured filmy chiffon pantaloons and a gossamer, gold-fringed top. His dresses and evening wraps shone with beading, brocades, embroidered leaves and flowers, gold and silver arabesques, and metallic bands encircling hemlines and cuffs.

In an arrogant but enormously successful aside, conceived perhaps to show that he could enslave women as easily as he had liberated them, Poiret briefly thrust women into the hobble skirt, a sack gathered at the bottom that forced the wearer to totter about with tiny steps. Women obediently flocked to buy them and caused traffic jams as they minced slowly across boulevards and clambered laboriously into and out of vehicles. Pope Pius X denounced the garment and ordered priests to refuse absolution to any woman wearing one.

Happily, Poiret soon tired of the conceit, returning to his Eastern look. To publicize it he invited 300 people to a party billed as the Thousand and Second Night. Guests were to come dressed as ancient Persians, and Poiret provided costumes for any who neglected to dress the part. He himself was the sultan, clad in turban and caftan and seated on a throne. By his side in a golden cage was his wife, Mme. Denise Poiret, impersonating the sultan's favorite, in harem pantaloons under a short hoop skirt.

The gardens of the complex of buildings where Poiret lived and worked had been turned for the night into an Oriental bazaar right out of the narratives of Scheherazade. Ibis, flamingos and a white peacock wandered over the lawn. Parrots, macaws, herons and monkeys were chained to trees. Bare-breasted young girls tended braziers of incense and myrrh. Orchestras hidden in the shrubbery filled the air with music and a young "slave" girl danced in nothing but gauze. The evening ended with a display of fireworks that caused terrified birds and monkeys to break their chains and flee into the Champs Élysées.

The party was as successful commercially as socially. Next morning, Paris could talk of nothing but Poiret's exotic fashions. To make sure the city kept talking, Poiret took some pantaloon-clad mannequins to Auteuil racetrack, where he achieved a replay of his Longchamps scandal. Again, outraged onlookers assailed the girls until they fled. "It is vulgar, wicked and ugly!" harrumphed old Jean Worth—again, while Poiret raked in orders on a scale never before achieved by any couturier.

Poiret went on to give even grander parties, leasing the former hunting lodge of Louis XV for the purpose, and outdoing even Louis XIV's fabled "Fête of Bacchus." Dressed as Jupiter at one extravaganza, he entertained an Olympian assortment of guests costumed as gods and goddesses. He gained even wider publicity for his creations by costuming, first, leading actresses like Ida Rubinstein, Mata Hari and Mistinguett, and then entire stage shows. Orders for gowns like those worn by the stars followed every Poiret-dressed opening.

Through his prosperous years, Poiret lived magnificently, up to and even beyond his vast income. His inability to hold onto money scarcely seemed to matter; there was always more where that came from. But after World War I, a combination of spendthrift living, business mismanagement and his unwillingness to follow the skimpy styles of the '20s eventually did him in. He lost everything but pride and hope. After years of struggle, he died broke in 1944 while planning still another comeback.

Others continued Poiret's exotic revolution and helped to spread it beyond the Atlantic. His influence was evident in the movie attire of the vamps, a series of sultry sirens with foreign-sounding names like Theda Bara, Pola Negri, Anna May Wong, Lenore Ulric and Greta Garbo, who writhed across the screen swathed in feathers, sequins, beads, veils and lamé.

The vamps faded out with the '20s but Poiret's ideas continued to mark the work of other designers. The three Callot sisters, Parisians like Poiret, covered their dresses with Chinese colors and motifs. Italy's painter-turned-designer Elsa Schiaparelli added to her collections dresses with a hint of an Indian sari, a North African butterfly design embroidered on a lapel, a Balkan coachman's pocket treatment on a jacket. The costumes of Javanese and Balinese dancers who appeared at the Colonial Exposition in Paris in 1931 inspired a host of exotic touches in the designs of Alix, Mainbocher, Marcel Rochas and Schiaparelli.

Exotic costuming languished in the war years. But the occupation of Japan, and the arrival in the United States of Japanese war brides, revived interest in the kimono. In the '50s and '60s came the West African influence. Americans both black and white discovered the lure of bold, bright prints and easygoing garments like the dashiki in which African delegates to the United Nations made such stunning appearances.

The year 1970 also marked the apotheosis of the caftan. The American designer Roy Halston Frowick (known just as Halston) added a few deft touches to this ancient Persian robe and sold it for as much as $800 a copy. Under the general label of "caftan," one variant or another of practically every North African outer garment became a basic item in the collections of Mollie Parnis, Victor Costa and Oscar de la Renta.

The '70s also brought a rediscovery of Chinese styles. Designers such as Giorgio di Sant'Angelo, Oscar de la Renta and Bill Blass began turning out evocations of both the new and traditional: Mao jackets, mandarin coats, flowing robes and slit skirts.

With these additions, the exotic revolution had reached a new phase and a new prominence to the point that Paul Poiret received at last the kind of tribute he would have cherished. His garments were the feature attraction, for fashion designers and for casual visitors alike, at a 1974 show of styles of the 1910s, '20s and '30s at Manhattan's Metropolitan Museum of Art.

A fashionable encounter of East and West

Nowadays fashion ideas travel not only far but fast, creating rapid turnovers in style concepts wherever they touch down. Shown here are three elegant and exotic shapes, all traditional in their own Eastern lands but offering the Western seamstress tasteful departures from more conventional silhouettes.

The saffron-gold evening gown *(left)* borrows its provocative one-shoulder wrap from the ancient Indian sari. The tie-dyed black dress *(center)* plays a delightful old Chinese trick in its cut: on top it is all long-sleeved, but on the side the skirt is deeply slit for a provocative glimpse of leg. The evening pantsuit *(far right)* also honors its distant Chinese ancestry in the flared cut and narrow stand-up collar of the richly brocaded tunic.

Exotic tones in Third World textiles

Fabrics and tints derived from the handicraft traditions of Africa and the Orient give these eye-catching costumes their particular panache. The airy caftan at far left is created from a rectangle of Japanese silk, tie-dyed and hand painted in a one-of-a-kind design. The two-piece cotton halter dress *(center)* shows a Nigerian folk motif in two intensities of indigo. The short wraparound jacket, left, has been fashioned from the rough-textured tussah silk of India, and its brown and gold tones intensify the natural texture of the raw fibers.

The allure of ornate detail

Ornamental trimmings, audaciously oversized, animate this collection of dresses. Functioning like pieces of exotic jewelry, the bold embellishments offer counterpoints to clothing of basically simple styling. Shown at far left is a striped cotton caftan, dramatized with gold embroidery banding and a parade of round gilt buttons down the front panel. The crochet dress below, with its extravagantly flared sleeves, reflects a dash of see-through intrigue in its diagonally patterned openwork. The regal shawl (*opposite*) combines a large square of silk paisley with a swagger of color-coordinated fringe for a smashing cover-up.

2
FABULOUS
FLIGHTS
IN FABRIC

During the year 2640 B.C., the Emperor of China, Huang-Ti, affronted at the havoc an ugly caterpillar was wreaking among the mulberry fruit trees in his gardens, began watching the creature closely. He noted that in early summer the worm whipped its head about in frantic figure 8s and exuded from its jaws a fragile filament with which it completely wrapped its own body, as if making a do-it-yourself coffin. In husbandly fashion,

THE QUEST FOR WOVEN TREASURE

Huang-Ti sought advice from his 14-year-old wife, the Empress Hsi-Ling. He asked if she could please devise some use for the material spun by this nuisance worm.

The young Empress took the worm's cocoon—tenderly for fear the spirit of some revered ancestor might live inside it. When it accidentally slipped into a dish of hot water, she was aghast. But then, before she could retrieve the cocoon, its filament began to unwind. Tugging on it, she discovered that it formed a long, continuous strand of lustrous thread. Several strands of this thread could be twisted together to form a fiber strong enough to weave. And the result was spectacular: a light, sleek, truly exotic cloth. Inevitably, the very practical Chinese domesticated the worm to assure a steady harvest of the precious filament, which came to be called silk. Almost as inevitably, Hsi-Ling came to be deified as China's "Goddess of the Silkworms."

For more than two thousand years the Chinese guarded the exotic fabric jealously. Not until about 100 B.C. did the outside world get its first tantalizing samples of silk, when the commerce-minded rulers of the Han Dynasty began to send camel caravans laden with cloth westward on one of the most arduous overland journeys ever undertaken.

The caravans, with as many as a thousand animals, each packing 400 pounds, left the last protection of the Great Wall at Tun-huang fort and struck out into the cold desolation of two terrible deserts, Gobi and Takla Makan. From these wastes the route rose up to the passes of the Pamirs, above 15,000 feet, and finally down the other side to its western terminus at Samarkand. When the journey went well it consumed eight months, and no mile of it was safe from cold, thirst and wild Hun tribesmen.

Greek and Syrian merchants came to Samarkand to bargain with the Chinese, and to transport the exotic new fabric to caravansaries with names as exotic as the cloth itself: Baghdad, Damascus, Jerusalem, Antioch and finally Athens and Rome.

These early silk cloths from China were generally smooth, close-woven fabrics with the sheen of satin. But when the unloomed fiber was sold in other lands, it was woven in a fascinating variety of other ways, to produce the exotic range of silken fabrics still prized by the needlecrafters of the modern world. Persians turned the lustrous fiber into heavy brocades, ornamented with seemingly raised figures of real and mythical creatures, enriched by threads of gold and silver. The pure metal was hammered out into thread almost as ethereal as the silk filament itself. The craftsmen of Baghdad perfected velvet, a dense pile weave as smooth and soft as a caress.

Indian artists, meanwhile, had begun to weave their own brand of exotic cloth from the cocoons of wild silkworms. Unlike the long, smooth filament of domesticated worms, these fibers were short and uneven and they made up into a type of fabric with a number of variants which now go under the generic name of tussah, or raw silk. Tussah was also the particular term for the heaviest and roughest of the raw silks, most often left in its natural rich brown. Pongee, on the other hand, was a lightweight raw silk which could be dyed or used in its natural creamy color.

Classical Europe was enchanted with all the varieties of this mystical fabric, and Roman grandees bankrupted themselves to pay for the costly stuff; undyed silk fetched the equivalent of $52 a pound. When dyed purple, the Imperial color, silk sold for $500. Among the most prized cloth was the airy silk woven on the island of Kos off the coast of Turkey, and imported for the delectation of Roman matrons and their admirers. These costly vestments, Pliny the Elder scolded, were much too flimsy: "While they cover a woman, at the same time they reveal her naked charms."

The Roman Senate prudishly agreed, and passed an ordinance outlawing the sale or wearing of diaphanous silk. The ladies of Rome, however, refusing to be ordered about so summarily, picketed the Senate and won a repeal—to the approval of many powerful Roman males. Among them, quite obviously, was Mark Antony, whose Cleopatra rode in a barge with sails of purple silk, while she lolled about dressed in silk so filmy that it was called the "woven wind." Alas for the silk trade, Mark Antony, Cleopatra —and ultimately Rome itself—came to grief. And after the Empire had finally fallen to the invading barbarians, the silken treasures of the East were nearly forgotten.

Silk returned to Europe to stay, in 1295 A.D., when a Venetian named Marco Polo came home after a 20-year absence spent in the lavish court of Kublai Khan in Peking. While there, Polo claimed, he had seen 12,000 warriors completely outfitted in silk battle dress, and 5,000 elephants blanketed in similar astonishing luxury. "I tell you, no day of the year passes that there do not enter the city gates one thousand carts of silk alone," he declared.

At a dinner party, Polo put on what was probably the first great Western show of exotic fabric since ancient times. He changed costumes before each course, wearing first crimson brocade, then crimson damask and, for climactic flourish, crimson velvet.

Shrewd observers in the awed company noted that Polo's damask was of a unique silken weave, since adapted to many other fibers but then entirely new to Europe. By altering the number of threads of weft over and under the warp, the weavers had found a way to bring out a reversible pattern or figure in the finished cloth. The pattern, often loomed all of a single color of thread, appeared to be formed by alternating areas of dull and lustrous surface.

Polo's stories of the wonders he had seen during his journey, and the splendiferous garments he displayed, sent the merchants of Venice scurrying to reopen the trade with the Orient. This time the camel—and later ship—routes stayed open. And over the following centuries a cornucopia of exotic silks spilled out of the East to the delight of Western ladies—and merchants.

When Anne of Brittany chose a white satin gown for her marriage to Charles VIII of France in 1491, it was such a remarkable silken confection that ever afterward the brides of France wore white instead of traditional red for their weddings. In 1498, Anne set another apparel precedent by wearing a black-dyed dress, also incidentally of silk, at Charles's funeral. During the next century, Lucrezia Borgia was similarly entranced by silk. And when she was married for the third time at age 20, to Alfonso d'Este, the eldest son of the Duke of Ferrara, 150 mules were needed to transport her silk, satin, brocade and velvet trousseau.

Henry VIII, one of English history's fanciest dressers, splurged so on lavish silks that he had the sleeves of his incandescent doublets slashed to show off the embroidery on the shirts he wore underneath. And when

Henry's daughter, the formidable Elizabeth, was given her first pair of knitted silk stockings she wore them four days in a row —and then demanded more.

"For indeed," she said, "I like silk stockings so well...that henceforth I will wear no more cloth stockings." So saying, she forbade all other women to wear silk, perhaps for fear that some lady in waiting might show a better-turned ankle.

In pursuit of more silk—and any other marketable treasures that might be lying around—on December 31, 1600, Queen Elizabeth granted a charter for trade with the Orient to the British East India Company. To everyone's surprise the real financial bonanza turned out to be not silk but an array of new varieties of cottons, which ultimately changed the basic textile tastes of the entire Western world.

Like souvenir collectors everywhere, the captains of Indiamen, as the company's ships were called, at first picked up Indian piece goods in village ports and brought them home simply as curiosities. Company directors took to grabbing these cottons for themselves, excusing this minor piracy on grounds that "they serve more to content and pleasure our friends than from any profit that ariseth in sales."

The directors soon realized their error. Indian cottons were far more finely woven,

James H. W. Thompson, shown here in a Thai silk weaver's house, was an American Army officer who stayed on in Bangkok after World War II. Struck by the bright beauty of the native fabrics, he organized the local weavers and helped to sell their goods around the world. Although Thompson disappeared mysteriously in 1967, he left behind a multimillion-dollar cottage industry that is still based on hand-dyed silks woven on ancient looms.

more brilliant in color and varied in pattern than anything that the English weavers could then produce. Britons were especially fascinated by the curious squiggles on prints from Kashmir. To the native craftsmen these may have been fertility symbols stylized from the flowers of the date palm, but to British purchasers they were simply appealing patterns. A colorful imitation, known as paisley after the Scottish city where it was manufactured, became a favorite design with customers throughout the Western world.

Equally intriguing were the vegetable-dyed plaids and stripes from Madras. At first Britons were put off by the tendency of Madras colors to bleed when they were washed. But soon, in a classic bit of reverse chic, this blending of colors became accepted as the stamp of genuineness—and thus a certificate of value.

Other new and exotic favorites were the striped fabrics from Bengal that made splendid cravats in regimental colors. And from an Indian port called Calicut came a plain-woven, printed and magnificently durable fabric called calico —destined one day to descend from the pinnacle of exotica and become the all-purpose dress goods of American pioneer women.

Of all these imported cottons the most striking was the bright and splashily patterned fabric produced in the Ganges valley. The Britons came to know it as chintz (probably from the Hindu word chint, which means "spotted cloth"). Although the cloth originally had "sad red grounds," its colors were printed on white to the East India Company's orders and became the rage of the West. Samuel Pepys indulged himself in a chintz dressing gown in 1661 and two years later saw fit to buy "a very noble parti-coloured Indian gown" for his wife. The winsome way that identical flower or foliage motifs marched in serried rows across such chintzes prompted one poet to liken the pattern to "a parade of virgins performing a rhythmical and holy dance."

Taken all together, these cottons from India dominated the fabric markets of the world for 200 years until the English learned how to weave copies of many of them mechanically—whereupon India lost a huge slice of its fabrics business, and some of the fabrics lost their exotic cachet.

Other fabulous cloths, however, were arriving from different corners of the Orient. In Java, traders of the Dutch East India Company discovered a technique known as batik—after the Javanese word tik, which describes the dripping sound of the wax used in this method of decorating the cloth. The Javanese were devout Muslims, and most batik was patterned with highly formalized and repetitive geometrical figures that abided by the Prophet Muhammad's prohibitions against the portrayal of any kind of living creatures.

For all their complexity and variety, Javanese batiks can be classified into at least eight distinct types by connoisseurs who study them carefully. Among the most familiar types are the kawung, which is made up of interlocking four-petaled ovals; parang, which is made up of diagonal stripes, often scalloped on the edges; tjeplok, or checkered arrangements of circles, rosettes or squares; and semen. This latter type of pattern features gracefully sprawling arabesques in which flowers and even birds are nearly recognizable—close to a violation of Muhammad's taboo.

Preparing the basic cotton cloth to create a true batik is an exhausting process. First the undyed cloth is subjected to successive washings in water; then comes a soaking in oil while the cloth is kneaded; next a boiling in water with rice-stalk ashes; then starching; and finally the cloth is rolled into a bundle and beaten with a wooden hammer to soften the fibers and render them more receptive to the dyes.

Creating the pattern to finish the batik is even more painstaking and delicate. The artist begins by tracing out the basic pattern in hot wax with a sort of inkwell pen made of bamboo and called a *tjanting.* The cloth is then dipped in the basic dye, which will color the material wherever no wax has been applied. Next the wax is scraped off or washed out. Then this whole waxing, dyeing and scraping procedure may be repeated again and again—sometimes as many as 10 times—to fix the additional hues into other sections of the pattern.

Dutch traders took the fabrics back to Holland, copied the patterns, simplified the process and adapted batik to mass production. Then during the last decades of the 19th Century they developed a new market for their modified batik in another part of the world—west and central Africa—among the peoples of such nations as Nigeria, Ghana, the Upper Volta.

At the same time that the Dutch introduced their Java-style batiks to Africa, they discovered a kind of native cloth dyed by a similar process. African batik, as the West calls it, evolved independently and utilizes indigenous materials. Starch made from cassava roots serves like wax to resist the dye—typically a shade of indigo. In addition, the Yoruba people of Nigeria developed a special color-patterning technique known as tie-dyeing, by which areas of a fabric are reserved from dye baths by stitching or tying up pinches, folds or pleats of the material with raffia or thread.

Batik or tie-dyed, Nigerian or Javanese, silken or nubbly cotton, all these fabrics carry an undeniably exotic air and a few still carry their places of origin in their names: ornamental damask, for example, was introduced to Europe through Damascus; shantung was created in that Chinese province; crepe de Chine came from China; filmy gauzes came from Gaza in Palestine.

After centuries of the cross-pollination of trade and taste, however, most generic cloths have become hybrids from everywhere. And stuffs that once were products of enduring patience, woven thread by thread on hand looms and colored by clever fingers, are now turned out in thousand-yard lots by high-speed machines.

Though the allure of the genuine article still remains, many of the machine-made and synthetic copies qualify as exotic in both their look and feel. Thus the tastemakers, and dressmakers, of today make use of both the imported handmade versions and their mass-produced imitations. In fact, some of the copies are so good that even Cleopatra might have envied the silken fabrics that are spun now out of the jaws of machines instead of worms.

A spectrum of fibers and weaves

The bazaars of Africa, Asia and Asia Minor are treasure-troves of richly textured silks and cottons that can give even ordinary clothes like shirtdresses or A-line skirts a flavor of faraway lands. The textures come from the nature of the yarns in the fabric or from the way the fabric is woven.

Raw silk, for example, taken from cocoon to loom with a minimum of processing, is a stiff yarn that produces rough fabrics like the two tussah multicolors from India shown below *(top and bottom)*. The Indian cutwork cotton gauze *(below, center)* has a raised pattern made by filling in an open mesh with soft nubby thread. At right, clockwise, are Ghanaian kente cloth, a patchwork of patterns woven in narrow strips and sewed together; a tussah silk using two yarn weights; an Indian gauze highlighted with loose squares; and a heavier tussah silk.

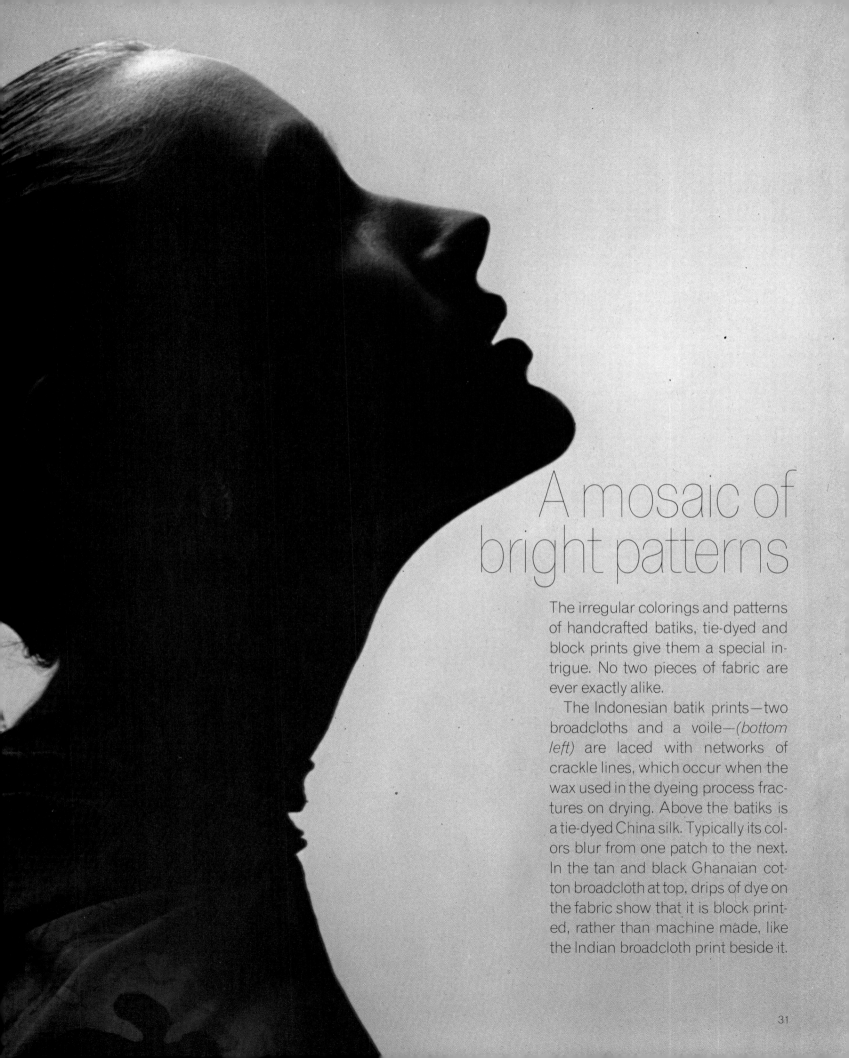

A mosaic of bright patterns

The irregular colorings and patterns of handcrafted batiks, tie-dyed and block prints give them a special intrigue. No two pieces of fabric are ever exactly alike.

The Indonesian batik prints—two broadcloths and a voile—*(bottom left)* are laced with networks of crackle lines, which occur when the wax used in the dyeing process fractures on drying. Above the batiks is a tie-dyed China silk. Typically its colors blur from one patch to the next. In the tan and black Ghanaian cotton broadcloth at top, drips of dye on the fabric show that it is block printed, rather than machine made, like the Indian broadcloth print beside it.

31

A galaxy of shimmering metallics

Brocades, laced with gold and silver and rich with symbolic motifs, make elegant evening wear for American ladies—just as they have for sultanas and maharanis. The silk turban at right is a case in point: a sari cloth, it is highlighted with stylized pine trees and pomegranates, Indian emblems of fecundity.

Also shown here, from the top down, are a Japanese red brocade strewn with silver camellias—traditional symbol of spring; a Japanese silk embroidered with silk chrysanthemums (the sun); an Indian silk decorated with talismans—a parrot, a horse, an elephant and a peacock. And finally, an Indian brocade, whose paisley is an abstraction of a date palm flower. The maiden and fawn within are figures from some unknown garden of delights.

Selecting and sewing dramatic fabrics

At right is a descriptive roundup of exotic cloths to help provide the basis for deciding which fabric may be most suitable for making a given type of garment. Besides indicating the texture and look of each fabric, the roster includes special tips for cutting and seaming, as well as for marking, pressing and cleaning.

Composites and synthetic counterparts are available for almost all of the natural fibers listed. Depending on the manufacturer, these are either entirely of artificial fibers or a combination of naturals and synthetics. All are sturdier and more crush resistant than the 100 per cent natural fabrics, and almost all have the additional advantage of being machine washable. There are certain other ways—some subtle and some more obvious—in which a particular synthetic can vary from the natural fabric. These distinctive differences could well be the determining factor in your choice of natural versus synthetic cloth.

BROADCLOTH: A fine, closely woven fabric with a firm, soft finish, most frequently made of cotton. Broadcloth is excellent for hand-dyeing techniques such as batik, tie-dyeing and block printing. Because of the striking and often complex designs that result, such broadcloth pieces should be used for garments with simple lines. When sewing this fabric, use cotton thread, and set the machine at 12 stitches to the inch. Finish the edges of the seams with pinking shears. Press with a steam iron set for cotton. Broadcloth generally launders well, but if the fabric has been hand printed it should be dry-cleaned to help prevent the designs from running. No matter how carefully treated, however, the colors will gradually fade.
Synthetic broadcloth: Simulated hand-dyed designs of the machine-made cloth will never run, and will retain their original brightness for the life of the garment.

BROCADE: A sumptuous, richly textured fabric characterized by a raised floral or figured design simulating embroidery. Brocade is frequently made of subtly colored silk or cotton threads interwoven with metallic or tinsel yarns, and is most suitable for elegant evening and at-home clothes.
Finish off the seam edges with a zigzag machine stitch or an overcast hand stitch (Appendix). Mark with tailor tacks rather than a tracing wheel to avoid damaging fabric. Use silk pins and silk thread, and stitch with the machine set at 12 stitches to the inch. Always line brocades that have metallic threads. To avoid crushing the raised design, do not press down hard with the steam iron, and use a pressing cloth to protect the fabric. Dry-clean only.
Synthetic brocade: Colors tend to be more intense than those in genuine brocades.

CALICO: A relatively inexpensive fabric made up of coarse cotton thread loomed in a plain weave. Calico always has a small-scale design that usually is printed in the traditional soft colors. The resulting old-fashioned look makes calico especially suitable for informal long skirts and casual at-home wear.
Sew calico with cotton thread, setting the machine at 12 stitches to the inch; finish the seams with pinking shears. Press with a steam iron set for cotton. Hand launder.
Synthetic calico: Available in several different blends, the synthetics have the same old-fashioned designs as the natural fabric, but they are often made up in brighter—and hence more modern-looking—colors.

CHINA SILK: A fragile, almost transparent, plain-woven fabric with a lustrous finish; best used for showy lingerie, delicate blouses and luxurious linings for any garment.
Cut extra-wide seam allowances and finish off the seam edges with an overcast stitch (Appendix). Use silk pins and silk thread, and stitch with the machine set at 14 to 16 stitches to the inch. Press on the wrong side, with a dry iron. Dry-clean only.
Synthetic china silk: The synthetic counterpart of this fabric appears to be just as fragile, but it is easier to sew because it has more body.

EMBROIDERED SILK: A lustrous, medium weight silk that is ornamented with machine-embroidered silk floss, and makes dramatic evening gowns and sumptuous blouses.

Since embroidered silk tends to fray, wherever possible cut wider-than-average seam allowances and finish off the seam edges with a zigzag machine or with an overcast hand stitch (Appendix). To avoid damaging the fabric, mark with tailor tacks rather than a tracing wheel. Machine stitch with silk thread, with the machine set at 12 to 15 stitches to the inch. Press on the wrong side with a pressing cloth and a dry iron set for silk (a heavy iron may crush the raised design). Dry-clean only.

Synthetic embroidered silk: Even synthetics should be dry-cleaned, so that the embroidery will not be flattened.

GAUZE: A loosely woven fabric that ranges in look and texture from lacy to sheer to nubbly opaque. Most suitable for flowing garments such as caftans, gauze can be plain woven or made with a patterned weave. It is available in cotton, silk, linen or in various combinations of yarns. Most gauzes have a somewhat wrinkled look that is considered part of their appeal. In addition, they are soft, and drape naturally and attractively. Cotton gauze, the most common, is usually a natural off-white, but it can also be found in many solid colors.

In transferring pattern markings to gauze, use light-colored tracing paper that will not show on the outside of the fabric. Seam allowances should be finished with zigzag machine stitches (Appendix). Machine stitch at 12 to 15 stitches to the inch, making more stitches on finer fabric. Hand wash, and press with a steam iron.

Synthetic gauzes: Blends are crisper than natural gauzes and hold their shape better.

KENTE CLOTH: A hand-woven cotton fabric composed of narrow strips of cloth—roughly 4 inches wide—that have been sewed together. Kente cloth, developed in West Africa, is characterized by bold, brightly colored designs that signify clan or social rank. In its native land and in the U.S. it is used most frequently for fashion accessories such as a sash or turban.

Since kente cloth ravels easily, cut wider-than-average seam allowances, and finish off the seam edges with a zigzag machine or overcast hand stitch. Sew with cotton thread and set the machine at 10 stitches to the inch. Press on the wrong side with a steam iron; dry-clean only. Exported in small quantities, kente cloth is expensive and is available only in stores specializing in African goods; there is no synthetic substitute.

MADRAS: Distinguished by its subtly colored plaids and stripes, authentic madras is woven from predyed cotton yarns. Because of the nature of the vegetable dyes that are traditionally used, the colors bleed, or change subtly, with every washing. Madras makes especially attractive sportswear; during the sewing process it can be handled in the same manner as other cottons.

Sew the fabric with the machine-stitch gauge set at 12 stitches to the inch, and finish the seams with pinking shears or a zigzag machine stitch.

Synthetic madras: Bright colors are often substituted for the natural tones of imported madras. Even if the quieter traditional colors are used, however, the synthetic will not bleed when washed.

TUSSAH: Tussah is the generic term for a range of silk fabrics woven from the filaments of the wild silkworm. (It is also the specific name for the coarsest of the tussahs.) Tussah fabrics share qualities of strength, crispness and relative coarseness, and all are irregularly slubbed. Most are resistant to dyeing unless the natural gum of the silkworm is removed from the yarn. The very coarse variation known specifically as tussah is characterized by a rich, natural brown tone; it makes handsome coats, jackets and skirts.

Since tussah can fray, cut out pattern pieces with slightly wider-than-average seam allowances. Use silk thread, and set the sewing machine for 12 stitches to the inch. Finish seams with a machine zigzag stitch, or an overcast hand stitch (Appendix). To avoid leaving an imprint on tussah when ironing, press with a steam iron on the wrong side with a pressing cloth, using a light touch. Dry-clean.

A light- to mediumweight variety of tussah called pongee retains some of the homespun quality of the heavier fabric, and is recommended for summer suits and coats, dresses, shirts and blouses. Pongee is most frequently available in a natural ecru color, but it can also be found bleached, in solid colors and even printed. When sewing pongee, use silk pins and silk thread, and set the machine at 12 to 14 stitches to the inch. Finish seams with a zigzag stitch or overcast by hand (Appendix). Press lightly with a pressing cloth on the wrong side, with a steam iron set for silk. Dry-clean only.

Shantung falls between heavy tussah and pongee in weight, and is most effective when used for tailored skirts, pants and dressmaker suits. Although shantung is at its classic best in its natural cream or pale beige tones, it is also available in a wide range of solid colors. Shantung should be handled in the same way as pongee.

Synthetic tussahs: In contrast to most of the natural tussahs—which tend to take dyes unevenly—the colors in the synthetic are uniform. However, synthetic tussahs blended with acetate or natural silk should be dry-cleaned.

VOILE: A lightweight, sheer fabric with a crisp feel and look, especially suitable for soft, airy blouses and dresses. It is made from hard twisted yarns—usually cotton—that give it great durability in spite of its delicate appearance.

Since voile tends to fray, cut wider-than-average seam allowances, and finish off the seam edges with an overcast stitch. Mark with tailor tacks—which will show more clearly on the sheer fabric than will tracing-wheel carbon markings. Sew with cotton thread, with the machine set at 12 to 15 stitches to the inch. Hand launder.

Synthetic voile: The synthetic counterpart tends to hold a firmer shape, and can therefore be used for tailored garments, such as shirts.

3
EXUBERANT EASTERN LOOKS

When you saw Dorothy Lamour in a sarong, you knew what was going on," says avant-garde designer Edith Head. "You certainly knew that she wasn't a housewife out shopping." Nor could anyone mistake that sarong for anything but what it was—an exotic fashion. Strictly speaking, it was not then a dressmaker design, nor is it one now. Except for a few stitches to hold it up, the sarong is a

STAR-QUALITY FASHIONS FROM THE EAST

garment that depends on proper draping —and, of course, the contours of the wearer. Yet the sarong is one of those landmark designs that helped to energize the current fancy for exotic clothing.

In the case of the sarong, public awareness began in 1936 when Miss Head, a noted designer of costumes for film stars, was called on to whip up an appropriately glamorous item for Dorothy Lamour to wear in the title role of *The Jungle Princess.* After settling on the sarong, Miss Head studied photographs of Balinese maidens to determine how the traditional, topless garment was draped. In deference to Hollywood's rigid self-censorship code of those days, she added an upper part to the garment, and worked in a few stitches to keep it from falling off. The rest is history.

After *Jungle Princess'* première, the sarong quickly became a conversation stopper at prewar dances across the country. Subsequent years saw the American debuts of other exotic fashions: the Chinese slit skirt, the mandarin collar, the South Pacific halter neckline and even the T-shirt that bares one shoulder. The latter, according to legend, came down from the Amazons, who cut off one breast in order to aim their arrows more accurately, and then draped their robes to cover the scar. Today these modes have been adapted to modern styling, so any home seamstress can become an instant seductress, as shown on pages 40-63. (No directions are given for the sarong, which needs only a quick wrap and a few stitches.)

The medium of drama also brought the slit skirt, which had been voguish 50 years earlier, back to public attention and acclaim in 1958. On October 14 of that year, the opening night of a play called *The World of Suzy Wong,* the curtain went up at New York's Broadhurst Theatre to show Nancy Kwan as a sexy Chinese strumpet in a low Hong Kong bar. When she moved, her tight skirt parted, flashing a wicked glimpse of thigh—and setting off an electric response in the audience. Broadway cheered. A few canny New York women phoned their dressmakers. After the film version was released, Nancy Kwan and her slinky slit skirt became universally celebrated.

The mandarin collar, another traditional detail of Chinese dress, paradoxically was popularized by India's late Prime Minister Jawaharlal Nehru. It is part of a simple, spare tunic that is commonplace in India. Nehru's enormous international appeal, together with the very simplicity and dignity of this stylistic detail, made the collar an overnight hit with American couturiers. Today it appears as the crowning touch of a wide variety of clothes, from pajamas to linen sheaths. Besides being flattering to a woman with a long, graceful neck—and artful concealment for a stocky neck—the mandarin can be enhanced by a deeply slit neckline that suggests asceticism while revealing just the opposite.

Asia's diaphanous sari arrived in the West on the back of Jacqueline Kennedy: she brought several of them home from a trip to India and had them translated into dresses—and a fashion trend. In like manner the Moorish caftan, the Japanese kimono and other Eastern designs were caught in the jet stream of wide-ranging travelers and adapted by U.S. designers.

The reopening of diplomatic, sport and social contact with Red China gave yet another boost to America's fascination with the Orient, accelerating still further the need for exotic fashion. As soon as American diplomats made their historic trip to Peking, says the designer Oscar de la Renta, "I knew China was in."

Stand-up collar with a seductive air

The round neckline on this simple dress stands transformed by a collar borrowed from the Chinese mandarins. Like the Chinese dignitaries, the Western-designed one- and two-piece mandarin collars and the standing bias collar hold themselves erect in decorous fashion.

The one-piece mandarin collar shown here wraps around the neck with a single slit in the front. Such a collar belongs on clothes that open at least partway down the front—like this provocatively plunging dress.

There is also a two-piece mandarin collar, which has a decorative slit in front and a functional slit in the back to provide an opening for a zipper. A third type, the standing bias collar, is slit only in back.

On all three, the finished ends must be matched carefully to ensure that the collar is the same height on both sides of each slit. All of them also require interfacing to achieve the stiffness they need; where patterns do not include a separate interfacing piece the collar pattern can serve as a cutting guide.

THE ONE-PIECE MANDARIN COLLAR

A. PREPARING THE GARMENT

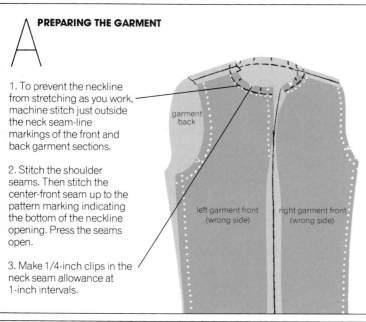

1. To prevent the neckline from stretching as you work, machine stitch just outside the neck seam-line markings of the front and back garment sections.

2. Stitch the shoulder seams. Then stitch the center-front seam up to the pattern marking indicating the bottom of the neckline opening. Press the seams open.

3. Make 1/4-inch clips in the neck seam allowance at 1-inch intervals.

B. ATTACHING THE INTERFACING TO THE COLLAR

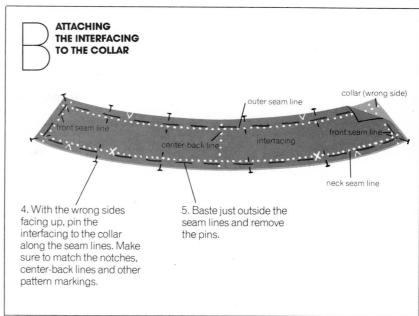

4. With the wrong sides facing up, pin the interfacing to the collar along the seam lines. Make sure to match the notches, center-back lines and other pattern markings.

5. Baste just outside the seam lines and remove the pins.

C. ATTACHING THE FACING TO THE COLLAR

6. Lay the collar with the interfaced side down on a flat surface and place the facing, wrong side up, on top of the collar, matching the seam lines, notches and other pattern markings. Pin the two pieces together along the two short front seam lines and the long outer seam line at the top edge of the collar.

7. Baste just outside the front and outer seam lines. Remove the pins.

8. Machine stitch along the front and outer seam lines, beginning and ending at the neck edge. Remove all bastings except for the basting securing the interfacing to the collar along the neck seam line.

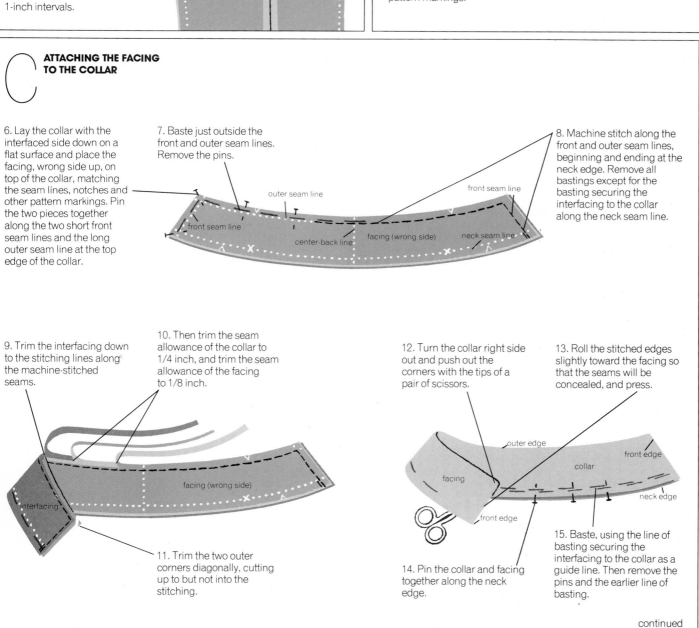

9. Trim the interfacing down to the stitching lines along the machine-stitched seams.

10. Then trim the seam allowance of the collar to 1/4 inch, and trim the seam allowance of the facing to 1/8 inch.

11. Trim the two outer corners diagonally, cutting up to but not into the stitching.

12. Turn the collar right side out and push out the corners with the tips of a pair of scissors.

13. Roll the stitched edges slightly toward the facing so that the seams will be concealed, and press.

14. Pin the collar and facing together along the neck edge.

15. Baste, using the line of basting securing the interfacing to the collar as a guide line. Then remove the pins and the earlier line of basting.

continued

D | ATTACHING THE COLLAR TO THE GARMENT

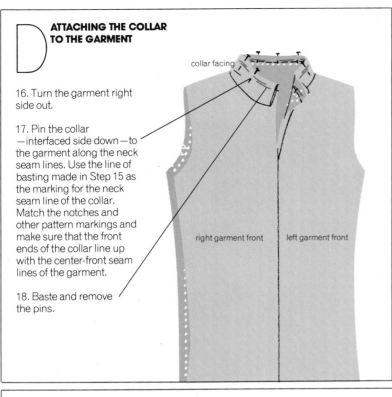

16. Turn the garment right side out.

17. Pin the collar —interfaced side down— to the garment along the neck seam lines. Use the line of basting made in Step 15 as the marking for the neck seam line of the collar. Match the notches and other pattern markings and make sure that the front ends of the collar line up with the center-front seam lines of the garment.

18. Baste and remove the pins.

E | PREPARING THE FACING

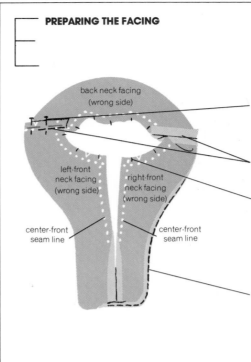

19. With the wrong sides out, pin the back neck and front neck facing sections together along the shoulder seam lines. Then pin the front neck sections together along the center-front seam line up to the pattern marking for the bottom of the neckline opening. Baste and remove the pins.

20. Machine stitch and remove the bastings. Press the seams open.

21. Make 1/4-inch clips in the neck seam allowance at 1-inch intervals.

22. To finish the outer edge of the facing when using a lightweight fabric, turn the edge under 1/4 inch, press flat and machine stitch 1/8 inch from the fold. For heavier fabrics, finish the outer edge with a machine zigzag stitch.

F | ATTACHING THE NECKLINE FACING TO THE GARMENT

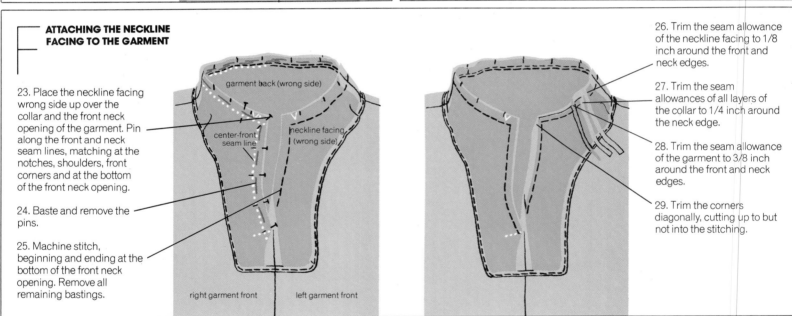

23. Place the neckline facing wrong side up over the collar and the front neck opening of the garment. Pin along the front and neck seam lines, matching at the notches, shoulders, front corners and at the bottom of the front neck opening.

24. Baste and remove the pins.

25. Machine stitch, beginning and ending at the bottom of the front neck opening. Remove all remaining bastings.

26. Trim the seam allowance of the neckline facing to 1/8 inch around the front and neck edges.

27. Trim the seam allowances of all layers of the collar to 1/4 inch around the neck edge.

28. Trim the seam allowance of the garment to 3/8 inch around the front and neck edges.

29. Trim the corners diagonally, cutting up to but not into the stitching.

G | FINISHING THE NECKLINE FACING

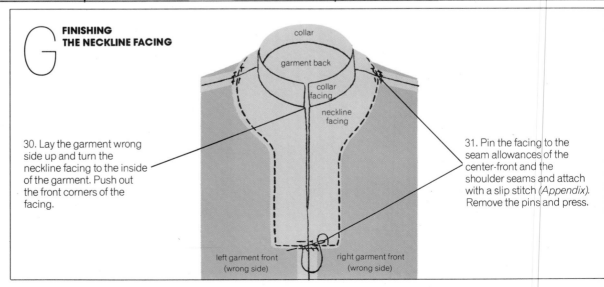

30. Lay the garment wrong side up and turn the neckline facing to the inside of the garment. Push out the front corners of the facing.

31. Pin the facing to the seam allowances of the center-front and the shoulder seams and attach with a slip stitch (Appendix). Remove the pins and press.

THE TWO-PIECE MANDARIN COLLAR

A PREPARING THE GARMENT

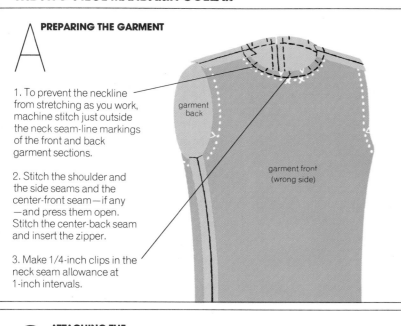

1. To prevent the neckline from stretching as you work, machine stitch just outside the neck seam-line markings of the front and back garment sections.

2. Stitch the shoulder and the side seams and the center-front seam—if any—and press them open. Stitch the center-back seam and insert the zipper.

3. Make 1/4-inch clips in the neck seam allowance at 1-inch intervals.

B ATTACHING THE INTERFACING TO THE COLLAR SECTIONS

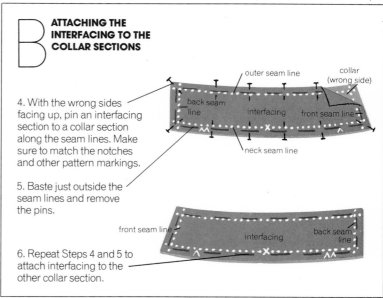

4. With the wrong sides facing up, pin an interfacing section to a collar section along the seam lines. Make sure to match the notches and other pattern markings.

5. Baste just outside the seam lines and remove the pins.

6. Repeat Steps 4 and 5 to attach interfacing to the other collar section.

C ATTACHING THE FACING TO THE COLLAR SECTIONS

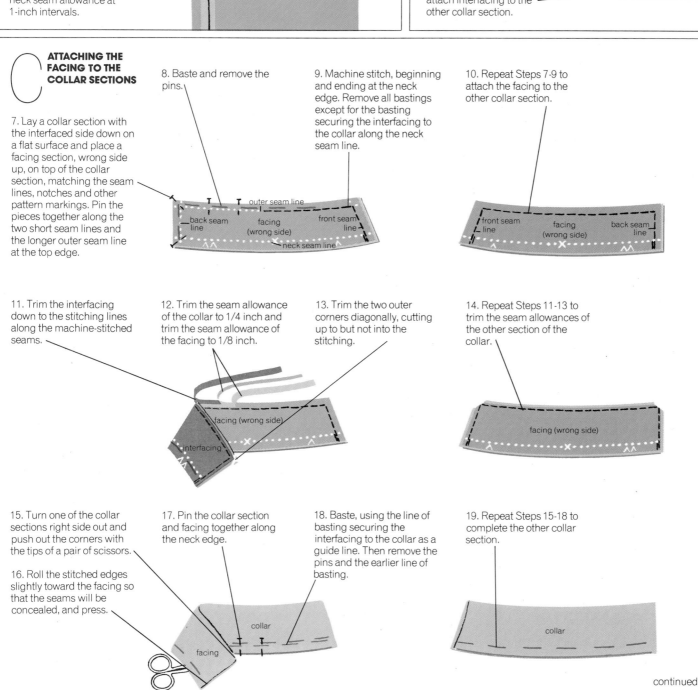

7. Lay a collar section with the interfaced side down on a flat surface and place a facing section, wrong side up, on top of the collar section, matching the seam lines, notches and other pattern markings. Pin the pieces together along the two short seam lines and the longer outer seam line at the top edge.

8. Baste and remove the pins.

9. Machine stitch, beginning and ending at the neck edge. Remove all bastings except for the basting securing the interfacing to the collar along the neck seam line.

10. Repeat Steps 7-9 to attach the facing to the other collar section.

11. Trim the interfacing down to the stitching lines along the machine-stitched seams.

12. Trim the seam allowance of the collar to 1/4 inch and trim the seam allowance of the facing to 1/8 inch.

13. Trim the two outer corners diagonally, cutting up to but not into the stitching.

14. Repeat Steps 11-13 to trim the seam allowances of the other section of the collar.

15. Turn one of the collar sections right side out and push out the corners with the tips of a pair of scissors.

16. Roll the stitched edges slightly toward the facing so that the seams will be concealed, and press.

17. Pin the collar section and facing together along the neck edge.

18. Baste, using the line of basting securing the interfacing to the collar as a guide line. Then remove the pins and the earlier line of basting.

19. Repeat Steps 15-18 to complete the other collar section.

continued

D ATTACHING THE COLLAR SECTIONS TO THE GARMENT

20. Turn the garment right side out.

21. With the interfaced side down, pin one collar section to the garment along the neck seam lines. Use the line of basting made in Step 18 as the marking for the neck seam line of the collar. Match the notches, shoulder seams and back edges. Also make sure that the front edges of the collar section line up with the marking or markings on the neckline of the garment front.

22. Baste the collar section to the garment neckline just outside the seam-line markings. At the center front, anchor the collar securely with a backstitch (*Appendix*). Remove the pins.

23. Repeat Steps 21 and 22 to pin and baste the other collar section to the garment.

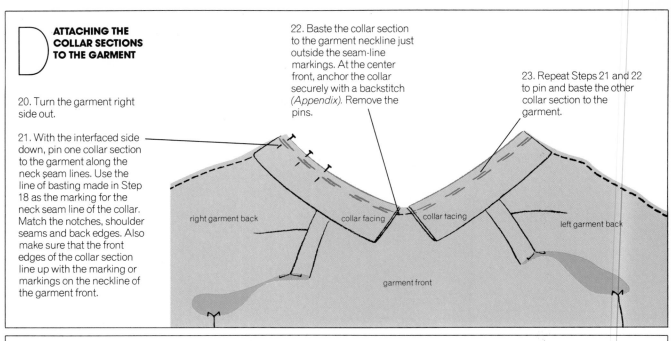

E PREPARING AND ATTACHING THE NECKLINE FACING

24. With the wrong sides out, pin the back neck and front neck facing sections together along the shoulder seam lines. Then baste and remove the pins.

25. Machine stitch and remove the bastings. Press the seams open.

26. Make 1/4-inch clips straight into the neck seam allowance at 1-inch intervals.

27. To finish the outer edge of the neckline facing when using lightweight fabrics, turn the edge under 1/4 inch, press flat and machine stitch 1/8 inch from the fold. For heavier fabrics, finish the outer edge with a machine zigzag stitch.

28. Place the neckline facing, wrong side up, over the collar and pin along the neck seam line. Match at the shoulders and at the notches and make sure that the center-back seam lines of the neckline facing align with the center-back edges of the garment.

29. Baste and remove the pins.

30. Machine stitch and remove all the bastings.

31. Trim the seam allowance of the neckline facing to 1/8 inch.

32. Trim the seam allowances of all layers of the collar to 1/4 inch.

33. Trim the seam allowance of the garment to 3/8 inch.

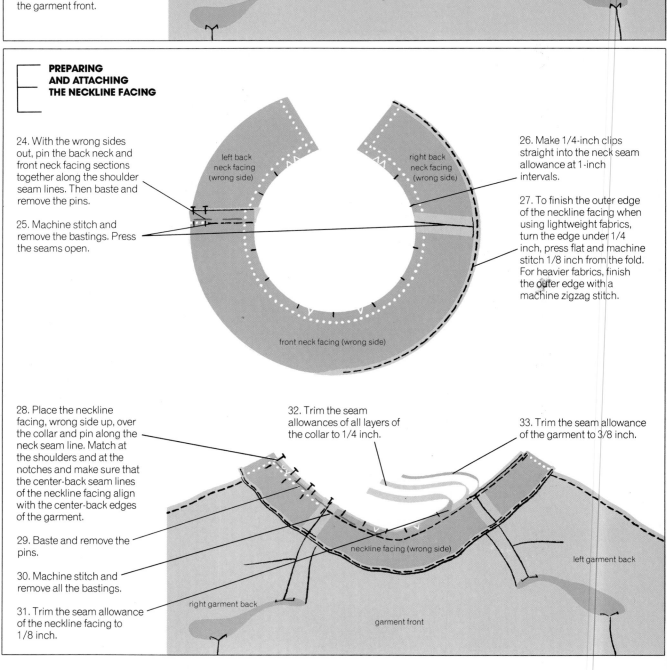

FINISHING THE NECKLINE FACING

34. Place the garment wrong side up and turn the neckline facing to the inside of the garment. Press.

35. Fold under the center-back edges of the facing so that they clear the zipper teeth. Pin and attach with a slip stitch (*Appendix*).

36. Pin the facing to the seam allowances of the garment shoulder seams and attach with a slip stitch. Remove all pins and press.

37. At the back neck opening, attach a hook and eye at the upper and lower edges of the collar.

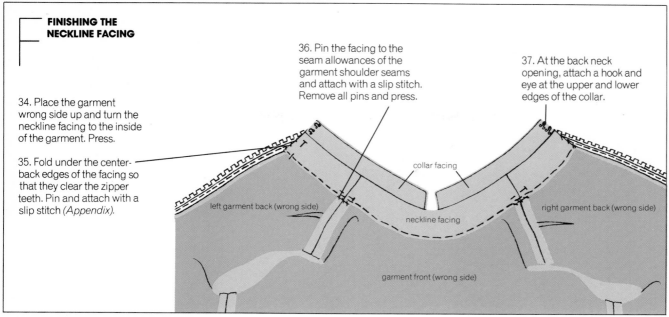

left garment back (wrong side)

collar facing

neckline facing

right garment back (wrong side)

garment front (wrong side)

THE STANDING BIAS COLLAR

A PREPARING THE GARMENT

1. To prevent the neckline from stretching as you work, machine stitch just outside the neck seam-line markings of the front and back garment sections.

2. Stitch the shoulder and side seams and press them open. Stitch the center-back seam and insert the zipper.

3. Make 1/4-inch clips straight into the neck seam allowance at 1-inch intervals.

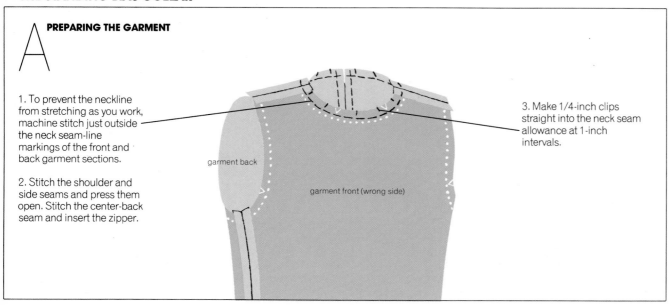

garment back

garment front (wrong side)

B PREPARING THE INTERFACING

4. Using the notched portion, fold the collar pattern piece 1/2 inch beyond the pattern fold line.

5. Pin the pattern to the interfacing on the bias as shown. Then cut out the interfacing and transfer all pattern markings.

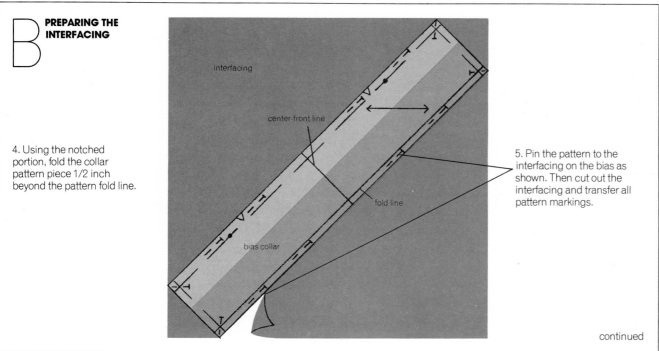

interfacing

center-front line

fold line

bias collar

continued

C ATTACHING THE INTERFACING TO THE COLLAR

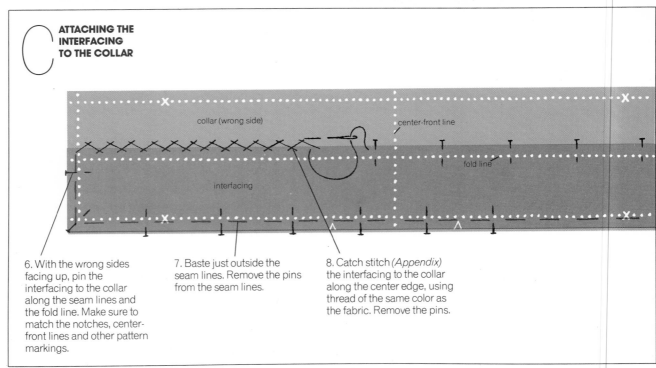

collar (wrong side)

center-front line

fold line

interfacing

6. With the wrong sides facing up, pin the interfacing to the collar along the seam lines and the fold line. Make sure to match the notches, center-front lines and other pattern markings.

7. Baste just outside the seam lines. Remove the pins from the seam lines.

8. Catch stitch (*Appendix*) the interfacing to the collar along the center edge, using thread of the same color as the fabric. Remove the pins.

D COMPLETING THE COLLAR

9. Fold the interfaced collar in half along the fold line, wrong sides out, and pin each of the short ends together along the seam lines.

10. Machine stitch the end seams. Begin at the fold and end at the neck seam line. Remove the pins.

11. Remove the bastings along the machine-stitched edges; leave the basting securing the interfacing to the collar along the neck line.

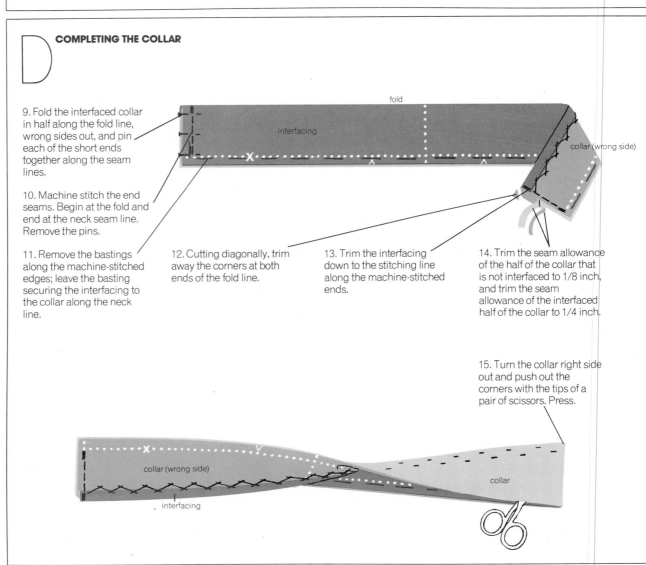

fold

interfacing

collar (wrong side)

12. Cutting diagonally, trim away the corners at both ends of the fold line.

13. Trim the interfacing down to the stitching line along the machine-stitched ends.

14. Trim the seam allowance of the half of the collar that is not interfaced to 1/8 inch, and trim the seam allowance of the interfaced half of the collar to 1/4 inch.

15. Turn the collar right side out and push out the corners with the tips of a pair of scissors. Press.

collar (wrong side)

interfacing

collar

ATTACHING THE COLLAR TO THE GARMENT

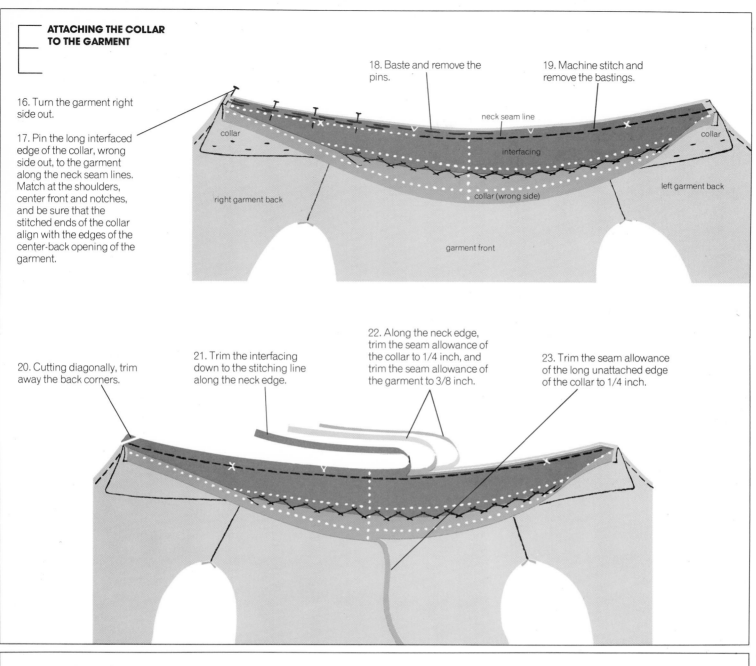

16. Turn the garment right side out.

17. Pin the long interfaced edge of the collar, wrong side out, to the garment along the neck seam lines. Match at the shoulders, center front and notches, and be sure that the stitched ends of the collar align with the edges of the center-back opening of the garment.

18. Baste and remove the pins.

19. Machine stitch and remove the bastings.

20. Cutting diagonally, trim away the back corners.

21. Trim the interfacing down to the stitching line along the neck edge.

22. Along the neck edge, trim the seam allowance of the collar to 1/4 inch, and trim the seam allowance of the garment to 3/8 inch.

23. Trim the seam allowance of the long unattached edge of the collar to 1/4 inch.

FINISHING THE COLLAR

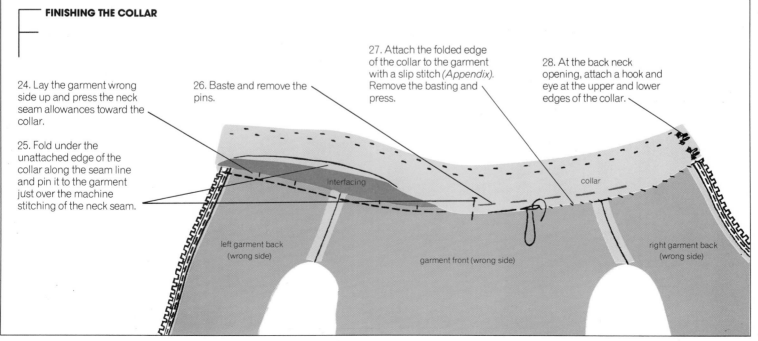

24. Lay the garment wrong side up and press the neck seam allowances toward the collar.

25. Fold under the unattached edge of the collar along the seam line and pin it to the garment just over the machine stitching of the neck seam.

26. Baste and remove the pins.

27. Attach the folded edge of the collar to the garment with a slip stitch (Appendix). Remove the basting and press.

28. At the back neck opening, attach a hook and eye at the upper and lower edges of the collar.

Necklines that entice

The diagonal neckline shown here is deceptively simple looking. When used on the Indian sari—from which it is borrowed—the neckline holds its shape by being tightly draped. On a dress it must achieve the same effect by the way it is sewed.

To sew the neckline, make a row of machine stitching all around the edge of the facing as well as the garment neckline before you start to assemble the dress; this will prevent the fabric from stretching as you work. Then add a layer of interfacing between the gown and the inside facing—as shown in the instructions that follow—even if the pattern does not provide for it. This will give the finished neckline the extra firmness needed to hold it in place.

Another Eastern look—this one conjuring up flowing Arab robes—is provided by the deep slit necklines (*pages 50-53*). Directions are provided for two versions: the center-front slit with an inside facing and an alternate version using the facing on the outside as a decorative effect.

THE ONE-SHOULDER NECKLINE

A PREPARING THE GARMENT

1. To prevent the neckline from stretching as you work, machine stitch just outside the neck seam-line markings of the front and back garment sections.

2. Pin the interfacing to the wrong side of the front and back garment sections along the neck seam lines.

3. Baste just outside the seam lines and remove the pins.

4. Trim away 3/8 inch from the lower edges of the front and back interfacing. Then trim away the seam allowances of the interfacing along the side seam-line markings.

5. Stitch and press any darts. Then stitch the side seams and press them open. Insert the zipper in the side opening.

6. Pin together the front and back garment sections along the shoulder seam markings. Then baste and remove the pins.

7. Machine stitch the shoulder seam and remove the basting along the shoulder. Do not remove the basting securing the interfacing to the garment.

8. Trim the interfacing close to the stitching line along the shoulder seam. Press the seam open.

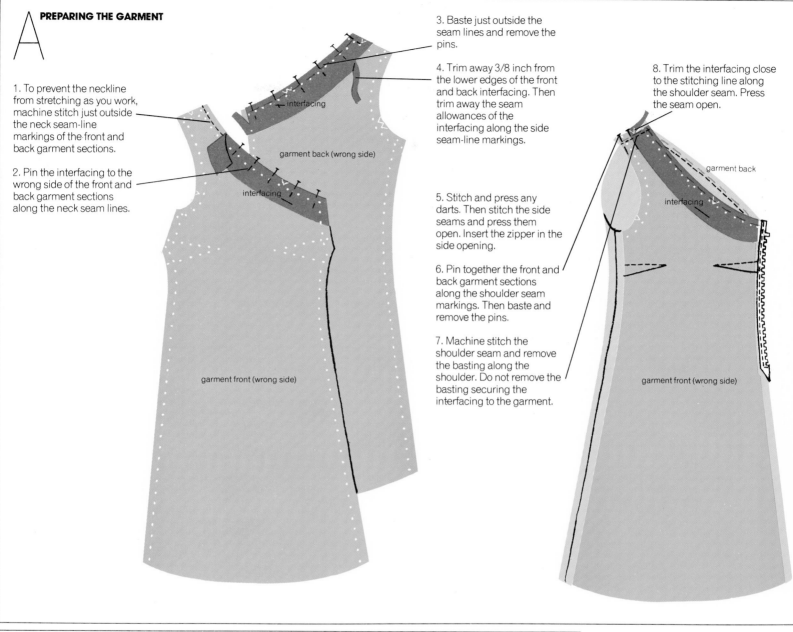

B PREPARING THE FACING

9. To prevent the neckline from stretching as you work, machine stitch just outside the neck seam-line markings of the front and back neckline facing sections.

10. With the wrong sides out, pin together the back and front neckline facing sections along the shoulder seam-line markings. Then baste and remove the pins.

11. Machine stitch and remove the bastings. Press the seam open.

12. To finish the outer edge of the neckline facing when using lightweight fabrics, turn the edge under 1/4 inch, press flat and machine stitch 1/8 inch from the fold. For heavier fabrics, finish the outer edge with a machine zigzag stitch.

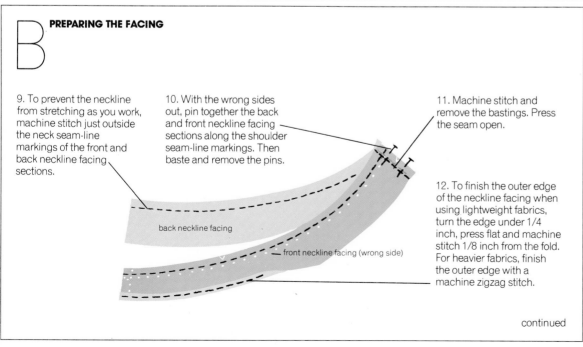

continued

ATTACHING THE FACING TO THE GARMENT

13. Turn the garment right side out.

14. Place the neckline facing, wrong side up, over the garment and pin along the neck seam line. Match the shoulder seams and the notches and make sure that the side seam lines of the neckline facing align with the side edges of the garment.

15. Baste and remove the pins.

16. Machine stitch and remove all the bastings.

17. Trim the facing seam allowance to 1/8 inch and the garment seam allowance to 1/4 inch. Trim the interfacing close to the stitching.

18. Clip the neck seam allowances at 1-inch intervals, cutting up to but not into the stitching.

19. Extend the facing away from the garment and press.

20. To prevent the facing from rolling out and showing on the finished garment, run a line of machine stitching—called understitching—around the facing and through the seam allowances beneath. Stitch as close to the neckline seam as possible.

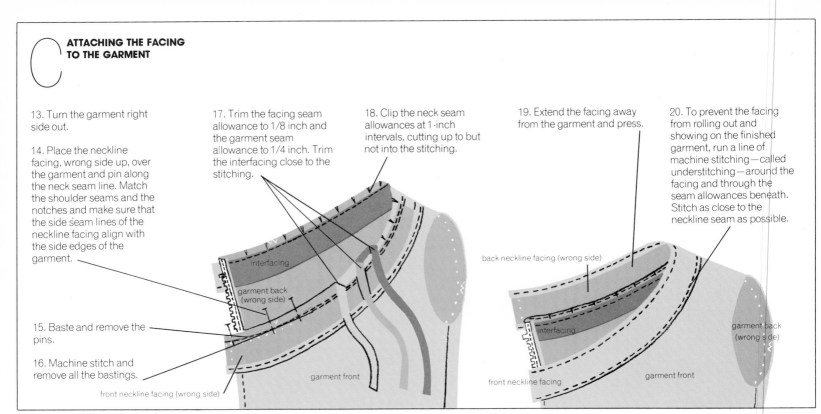

interfacing
garment back (wrong side)
front neckline facing (wrong side)
garment front
back neckline facing (wrong side)
interfacing
front neckline facing
garment back (wrong side)
garment front

D FINISHING THE NECKLINE

21. Turn the garment wrong side out. Turn the neckline facing to the inside of the garment. Press.

22. Pin the facing to the seam allowances of the garment shoulder seam and attach with a slip stitch (Appendix).

23. Fold under the side edges of the facing so that they clear the zipper teeth. Pin and attach the edges with a slip stitch. Remove all the pins and press.

24. At the side opening, attach a hook and eye above the zipper.

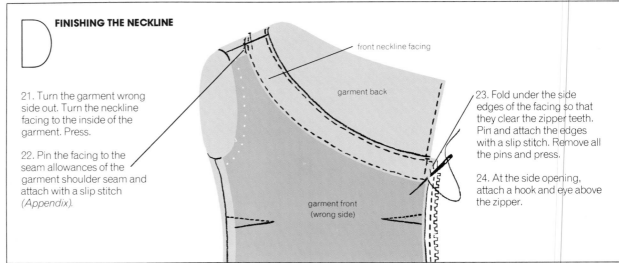

front neckline facing
garment back
garment front (wrong side)

THE FACED SLIT NECKLINE

A PREPARING THE NECKLINE INTERFACING

1. Cut out and mark the interfacing pieces for the front and back neckline. (If your pattern does not include interfacing, use the pattern pieces provided for the facings.)

2. Trim away 3/8 inch from the outer edges of the interfacing pieces.

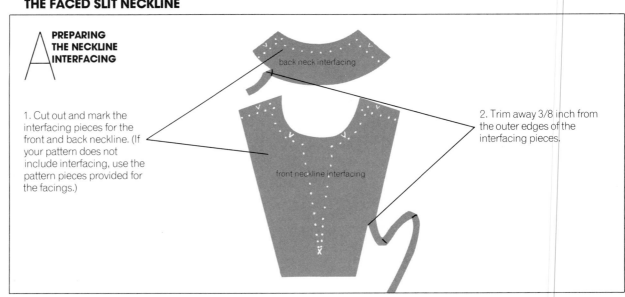

back neck interfacing
front neckline interfacing

B PREPARING THE GARMENT

3. To prevent the neckline from stretching as you work, machine stitch just outside the neck seam-line markings of the front and back garment sections.

4. Pin the interfacing to the wrong side of the front and back garment sections along the neck seam lines. On the front section also pin along the seam lines for the center slit.

5. Baste just outside the seam lines and remove the pins.

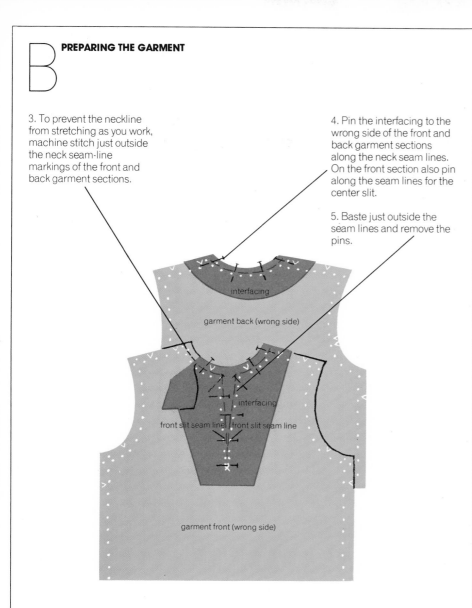

6. With the wrong sides out, pin together the front and back garment sections along the shoulder seam lines. Then baste and remove the pins.

8. Trim the interfacing close to the stitching along the shoulder seams.

9. Press the seams open.

7. Machine stitch the shoulder seams and remove the bastings along the shoulders. Do not remove the basting securing the interfacing to the garment.

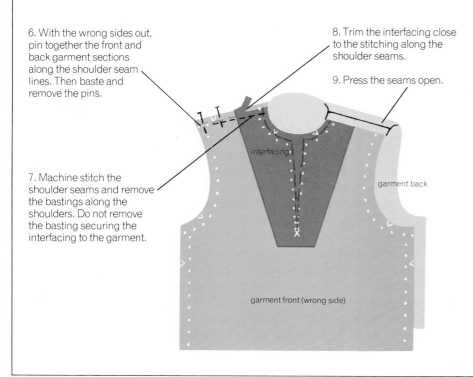

C PREPARING THE FACING

10. With the wrong sides out, pin together the back and front neckline facing sections along the shoulder seam lines. Then baste and remove the pins.

11. Machine stitch and remove the bastings. Press the seams open.

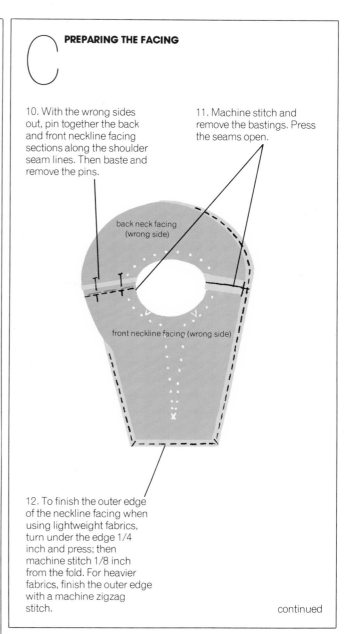

12. To finish the outer edge of the neckline facing when using lightweight fabrics, turn under the edge 1/4 inch and press; then machine stitch 1/8 inch from the fold. For heavier fabrics, finish the outer edge with a machine zigzag stitch.

continued

D ATTACHING THE FACING TO THE GARMENT

13. Lay the garment wrong side down.

14. Place the neckline facing, wrong side up, on the garment and pin along the neck seam line and the seam lines for the center-front slit. Match the shoulder seams, notches, front corners and the markings for the bottom point of the front slit.

15. Baste and remove the pins.

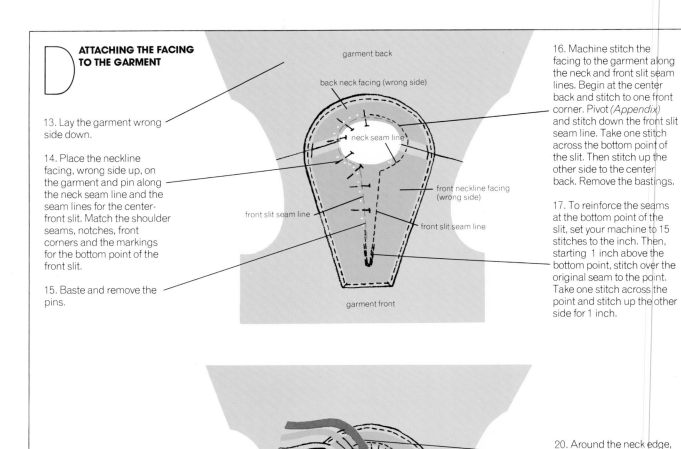

garment back

back neck facing (wrong side)

neck seam line

front neckline facing (wrong side)

front slit seam line

front slit seam line

garment front

16. Machine stitch the facing to the garment along the neck and front slit seam lines. Begin at the center back and stitch to one front corner. Pivot (Appendix) and stitch down the front slit seam line. Take one stitch across the bottom point of the slit. Then stitch up the other side to the center back. Remove the bastings.

17. To reinforce the seams at the bottom point of the slit, set your machine to 15 stitches to the inch. Then, starting 1 inch above the bottom point, stitch over the original seam to the point. Take one stitch across the point and stitch up the other side for 1 inch.

18. Slash the center front between the front slit seam lines, cutting up to but not into the stitches at the point.

19. Trim all the seam allowances along the slit opening to 1/8 inch.

20. Around the neck edge, trim the seam allowance of the facing to 1/8 inch and the seam allowance of the garment to 1/4 inch. Then trim the interfacing close to the stitching.

21. Trim the front corners diagonally, cutting up to but not into the stitching. Clip the neck seam allowances at 1/2-inch intervals.

E FINISHING THE FACING

22. Extend the facing away from the garment around the neck, and press.

23. To prevent the facing from rolling out and showing on the finished garment, run a line of machine stitching—called understitching—around the neckline of the facing, catching the seam allowances beneath. Begin and end 1 inch from the front corners and stitch as close as possible to the neckline seam.

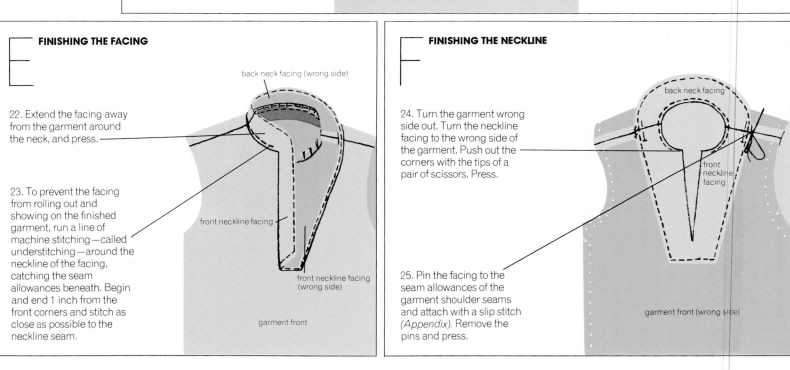

back neck facing (wrong side)

front neckline facing

front neckline facing (wrong side)

garment front

F FINISHING THE NECKLINE

24. Turn the garment wrong side out. Turn the neckline facing to the wrong side of the garment. Push out the corners with the tips of a pair of scissors. Press.

25. Pin the facing to the seam allowances of the garment shoulder seams and attach with a slip stitch (Appendix). Remove the pins and press.

back neck facing

front neckline facing

garment front (wrong side)

THE SLIT NECKLINE WITH AN OUTSIDE FACING

A PREPARING THE GARMENT

1. To prevent the neckline from stretching as you work, machine stitch just outside the neck seam-line markings of the front and back garment sections.

2. Stitch the shoulder seams and press them open.

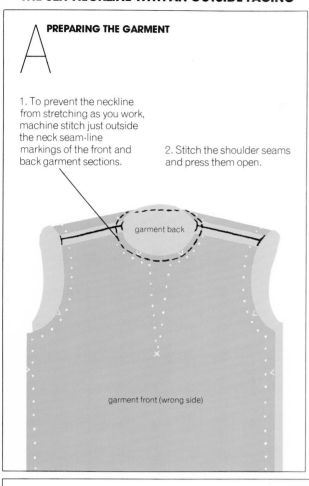

B PREPARING THE FACING

3. Cut and mark the interfacing for the front neckline only; then trim away 3/8 inch from the outer edges, as shown in the faced slit neckline (page 50, Box A).

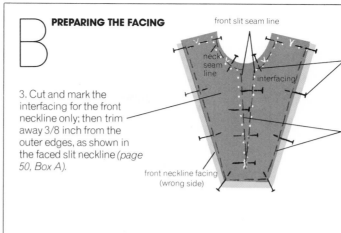

front slit seam line

neck seam line

interfacing

front neckline facing (wrong side)

4. Pin the interfacing to the wrong side of the front neckline facing along the neck seam line, and along the seam lines for the center-front slit. Then pin along the outer edges.

5. Baste just outside the seam lines. Then baste along the outer edge of the interfacing. Remove the pins.

6. With the wrong sides out, pin together the back and front neckline facing sections along the shoulder seam-line markings. Then baste and remove the pins.

7. Machine stitch and remove the bastings from the shoulder seams. Do not remove the bastings securing the interfacing to the front neckline facing.

back neck facing (wrong side)

interfacing

front slit seam line

8. Trim the interfacing close to the stitching along the shoulder seams. Press open the shoulder seams.

9. Turn under the outer edges of the facing 1/4 inch and baste. Remove the line of basting made along the outer edges in Step 5. Then press the edges.

C ATTACHING THE FACING TO THE GARMENT

10. To attach the facing to the garment, first lay the garment wrong side up and place the facing, also wrong side up, on the garment. Then follow the directions at left for the faced slit neckline (Box D, Steps 14-19).

11. Around the neck edge, trim the interfacing close to the stitching. Then trim the facing seam allowance to 1/4 inch and the garment seam allowance to 1/8 inch.

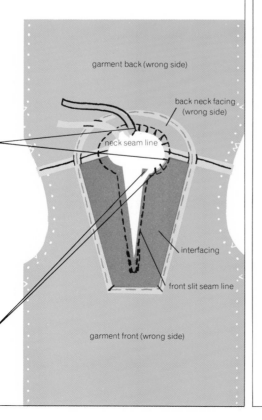

garment back (wrong side)

back neck facing (wrong side)

neck seam line

interfacing

front slit seam line

garment front (wrong side)

12. Trim the front corners diagonally, cutting up to but not into the stitching. Clip the neck seam allowances at 1/2-inch intervals.

D FINISHING THE NECKLINE

13. Turn the garment right side out. Turn the facing to the outside of the garment. Push out the front corners with a scissors.

14. Roll the neck and front slit seams slightly toward the inside of the garment to conceal the seams. As you roll, baste 1/4 inch from the edges to hold the seams in place. Press.

15. Pin the facing to the garment around the outer edge. Then baste and remove the pins.

16. To finish attaching the facing to the garment, run a line of machine stitching —called edge stitching —very close to the neck and the slit edges. Begin and end at the center back, and stitch from the finished side of the garment.

garment back

neckline facing

garment front

17. Edge stitch along the outer edge of the facing in the same manner. Remove all the bastings, and press.

Brief top, long on charm

Made with as little fabric as modesty and beauty allow, the halter top is a glamorous legacy of the South Seas sarongs first popularized in motion pictures of the '30s and '40s. Now, when the weather is fair, it goes everywhere—to the beach, the street, the patio and even the ballroom.

Making a halter top requires no fancy sewing, no fussy fitting—and not even fasteners, since the garment is usually tied on with straps or tie ends. The wraparound version shown here is seamed behind the neck and ties around the midriff, either in back or in front. The so-called tieback halter *(page 58)* ties both at the neck and at the midriff; or in a longer version, it ties at the waist.

A tieback halter can be made up in any fabric you like, but a wraparound that drapes from the neck requires a soft, pliable fabric. Your choice may be a polished cotton or polyester blend for a bathing-suit top, a knit to wear with shorts or slacks, and silk or even lace to team with a long skirt for evening wear.

With a full lining, attached as described on the following pages, a halter top will hold its shape through repeated tyings. But if your fabric is especially heavy, you can leave a wraparound halter unlined and finish the outside seams with bias tape.

THE WRAPAROUND HALTER

A PREPARING THE HALTER

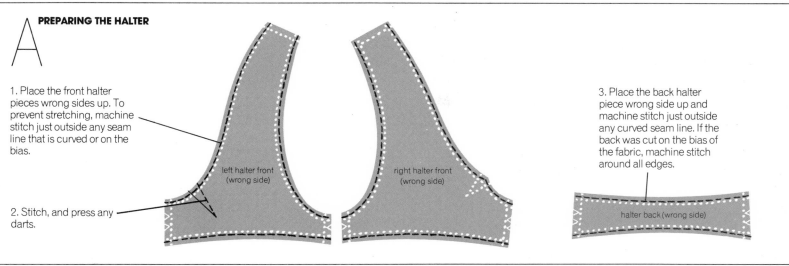

1. Place the front halter pieces wrong sides up. To prevent stretching, machine stitch just outside any seam line that is curved or on the bias.

2. Stitch, and press any darts.

left halter front (wrong side)

right halter front (wrong side)

3. Place the back halter piece wrong side up and machine stitch just outside any curved seam line. If the back was cut on the bias of the fabric, machine stitch around all edges.

halter back (wrong side)

B ATTACHING THE HALTER FRONT AND BACK

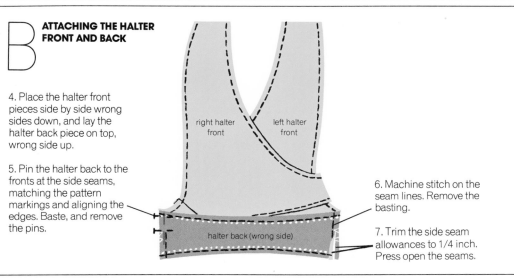

4. Place the halter front pieces side by side wrong sides down, and lay the halter back piece on top, wrong side up.

5. Pin the halter back to the fronts at the side seams, matching the pattern markings and aligning the edges. Baste, and remove the pins.

right halter front

left halter front

6. Machine stitch on the seam lines. Remove the basting.

7. Trim the side seam allowances to 1/4 inch. Press open the seams.

halter back (wrong side)

C MAKING THE TIES

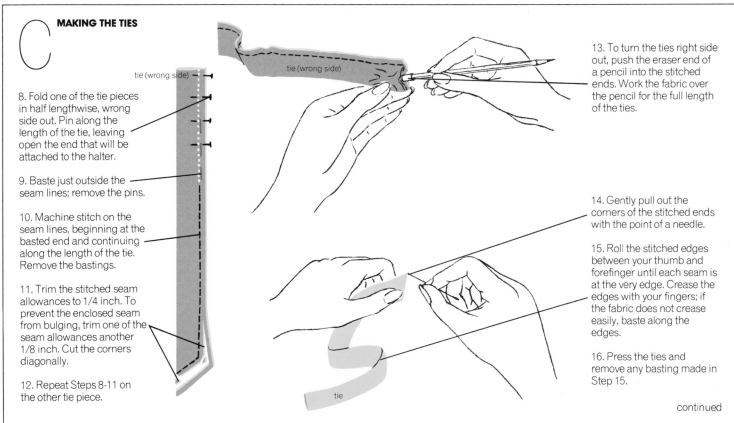

tie (wrong side)

tie (wrong side)

8. Fold one of the tie pieces in half lengthwise, wrong side out. Pin along the length of the tie, leaving open the end that will be attached to the halter.

9. Baste just outside the seam lines; remove the pins.

10. Machine stitch on the seam lines, beginning at the basted end and continuing along the length of the tie. Remove the bastings.

11. Trim the stitched seam allowances to 1/4 inch. To prevent the enclosed seam from bulging, trim one of the seam allowances another 1/8 inch. Cut the corners diagonally.

12. Repeat Steps 8-11 on the other tie piece.

13. To turn the ties right side out, push the eraser end of a pencil into the stitched ends. Work the fabric over the pencil for the full length of the ties.

14. Gently pull out the corners of the stitched ends with the point of a needle.

15. Roll the stitched edges between your thumb and forefinger until each seam is at the very edge. Crease the edges with your fingers; if the fabric does not crease easily, baste along the edges.

16. Press the ties and remove any basting made in Step 15.

tie

continued

D ATTACHING THE TIES TO THE HALTER

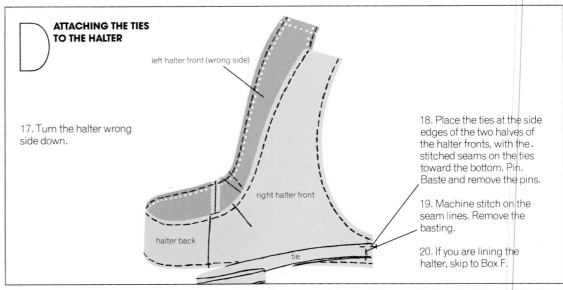

17. Turn the halter wrong side down.

18. Place the ties at the side edges of the two halves of the halter fronts, with the stitched seams on the ties toward the bottom. Pin. Baste and remove the pins.

19. Machine stitch on the seam lines. Remove the basting.

20. If you are lining the halter, skip to Box F.

E FINISHING AN UNLINED HALTER

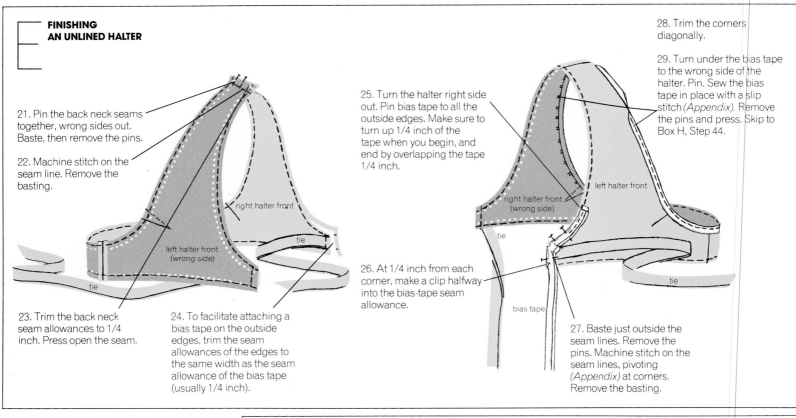

21. Pin the back neck seams together, wrong sides out. Baste, then remove the pins.

22. Machine stitch on the seam line. Remove the basting.

23. Trim the back neck seam allowances to 1/4 inch. Press open the seam.

24. To facilitate attaching a bias tape on the outside edges, trim the seam allowances of the edges to the same width as the seam allowance of the bias tape (usually 1/4 inch).

25. Turn the halter right side out. Pin bias tape to all the outside edges. Make sure to turn up 1/4 inch of the tape when you begin, and end by overlapping the tape 1/4 inch.

26. At 1/4 inch from each corner, make a clip halfway into the bias-tape seam allowance.

27. Baste just outside the seam lines. Remove the pins. Machine stitch on the seam lines, pivoting (Appendix) at corners. Remove the basting.

28. Trim the corners diagonally.

29. Turn under the bias tape to the wrong side of the halter. Pin. Sew the bias tape in place with a slip stitch (Appendix). Remove the pins and press. Skip to Box H, Step 44.

F LINING THE HALTER

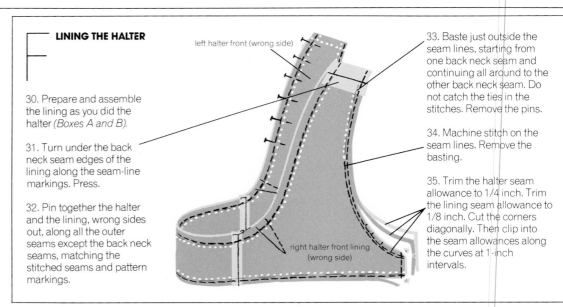

30. Prepare and assemble the lining as you did the halter (Boxes A and B).

31. Turn under the back neck seam edges of the lining along the seam-line markings. Press.

32. Pin together the halter and the lining, wrong sides out, along all the outer seams except the back neck seams, matching the stitched seams and pattern markings.

33. Baste just outside the seam lines, starting from one back neck seam and continuing all around to the other back neck seam. Do not catch the ties in the stitches. Remove the pins.

34. Machine stitch on the seam lines. Remove the basting.

35. Trim the halter seam allowance to 1/4 inch. Trim the lining seam allowance to 1/8 inch. Cut the corners diagonally. Then clip into the seam allowances along the curves at 1-inch intervals.

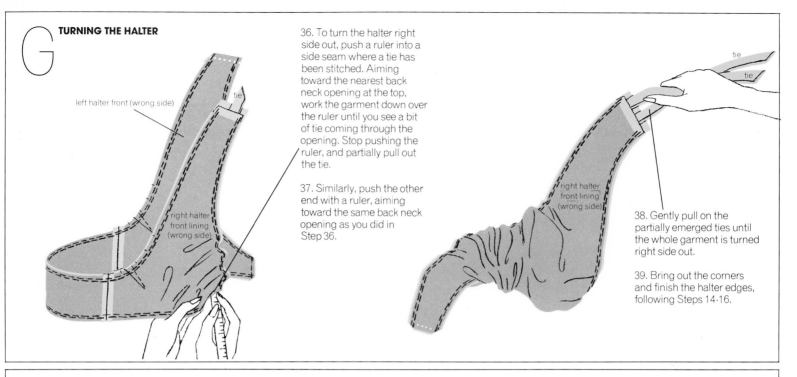

G TURNING THE HALTER

36. To turn the halter right side out, push a ruler into a side seam where a tie has been stitched. Aiming toward the nearest back neck opening at the top, work the garment down over the ruler until you see a bit of tie coming through the opening. Stop pushing the ruler, and partially pull out the tie.

37. Similarly, push the other end with a ruler, aiming toward the same back neck opening as you did in Step 36.

38. Gently pull on the partially emerged ties until the whole garment is turned right side out.

39. Bring out the corners and finish the halter edges, following Steps 14-16.

left halter front (wrong side)

right halter front lining (wrong side)

tie

tie

tie

right halter front lining (wrong side)

H ATTACHING THE BACK NECK SEAMS

40. Align the edges of the back neck seam of the halter, lining sides out. Baste.

41. Machine stitch on the seam line, taking care not to catch the folded seams of the lining in the stitches. Remove the basting.

42. Trim the back neck seam to 1/4 inch. Cut the corners diagonally. Open the seam and crease it with your fingers or press open the seam.

43. Close the back neck lining opening with a hemming stitch (Appendix).

lining

left halter front lining

44. If the back neck section of the halter is too long for your neck, make one or two small pleats in the fabric. Fold a 1/8- to 1/4-inch pleat toward the front of the halter. Pin. If you wish two pleats, space them evenly within the narrow back area. Baste and remove the pins.

45. Machine stitch on the center seam over the pleats. Remove the basting and press.

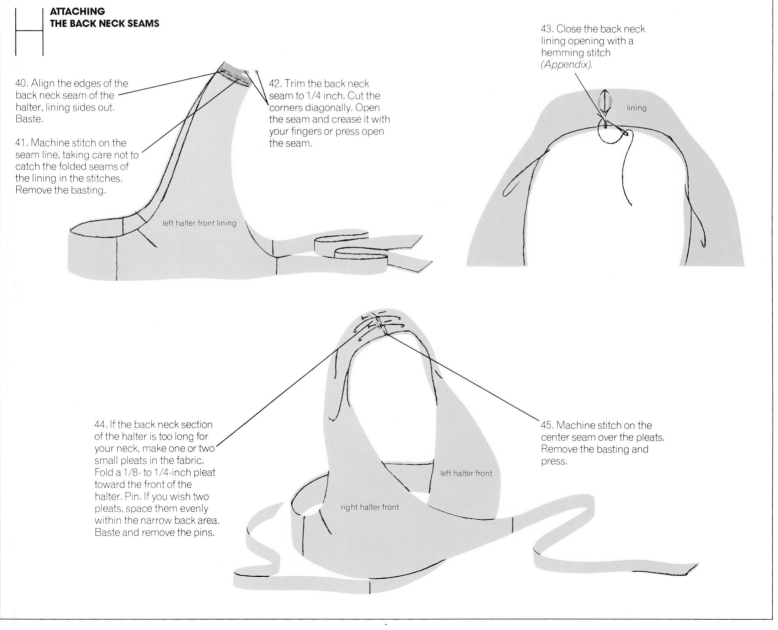

left halter front

right halter front

THE TIEBACK HALTER

A PREPARING THE HALTER

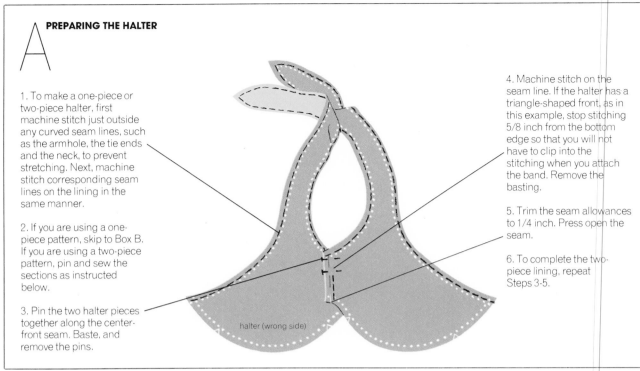

1. To make a one-piece or two-piece halter, first machine stitch just outside any curved seam lines, such as the armhole, the tie ends and the neck, to prevent stretching. Next, machine stitch corresponding seam lines on the lining in the same manner.

2. If you are using a one-piece pattern, skip to Box B. If you are using a two-piece pattern, pin and sew the sections as instructed below.

3. Pin the two halter pieces together along the center-front seam. Baste, and remove the pins.

4. Machine stitch on the seam line. If the halter has a triangle-shaped front, as in this example, stop stitching 5/8 inch from the bottom edge so that you will not have to clip into the stitching when you attach the band. Remove the basting.

5. Trim the seam allowances to 1/4 inch. Press open the seam.

6. To complete the two-piece lining, repeat Steps 3-5.

halter (wrong side)

B LINING THE HALTER

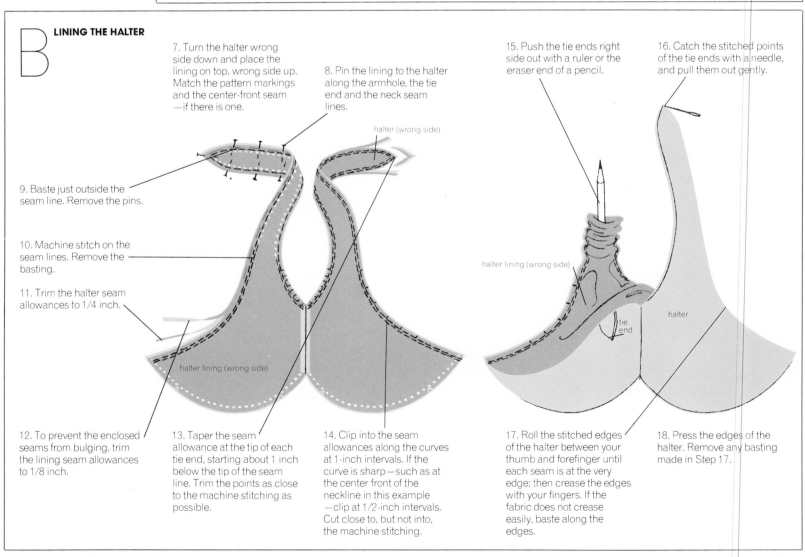

7. Turn the halter wrong side down and place the lining on top, wrong side up. Match the pattern markings and the center-front seam —if there is one.

8. Pin the lining to the halter along the armhole, the tie end and the neck seam lines.

9. Baste just outside the seam line. Remove the pins.

10. Machine stitch on the seam lines. Remove the basting.

11. Trim the halter seam allowances to 1/4 inch.

12. To prevent the enclosed seams from bulging, trim the lining seam allowances to 1/8 inch.

13. Taper the seam allowance at the tip of each tie end, starting about 1 inch below the tip of the seam line. Trim the points as close to the machine stitching as possible.

14. Clip into the seam allowances along the curves at 1-inch intervals. If the curve is sharp—such as at the center front of the neckline in this example —clip at 1/2-inch intervals. Cut close to, but not into, the machine stitching.

15. Push the tie ends right side out with a ruler or the eraser end of a pencil.

16. Catch the stitched points of the tie ends with a needle, and pull them out gently.

17. Roll the stitched edges of the halter between your thumb and forefinger until each seam is at the very edge; then crease the edges with your fingers. If the fabric does not crease easily, baste along the edges.

18. Press the edges of the halter. Remove any basting made in Step 17.

halter (wrong side)

halter lining (wrong side)

halter lining (wrong side)

halter lining (wrong side)

tie end

halter

C ATTACHING THE BAND TO THE HALTER

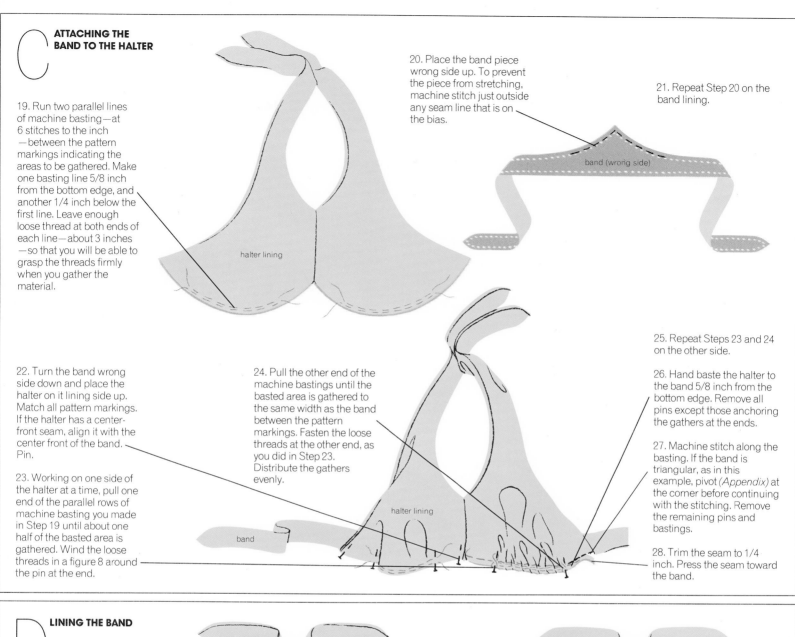

19. Run two parallel lines of machine basting—at 6 stitches to the inch—between the pattern markings indicating the areas to be gathered. Make one basting line 5/8 inch from the bottom edge, and another 1/4 inch below the first line. Leave enough loose thread at both ends of each line—about 3 inches—so that you will be able to grasp the threads firmly when you gather the material.

20. Place the band piece wrong side up. To prevent the piece from stretching, machine stitch just outside any seam line that is on the bias.

21. Repeat Step 20 on the band lining.

22. Turn the band wrong side down and place the halter on it lining side up. Match all pattern markings. If the halter has a center-front seam, align it with the center front of the band. Pin.

23. Working on one side of the halter at a time, pull one end of the parallel rows of machine basting you made in Step 19 until about one half of the basted area is gathered. Wind the loose threads in a figure 8 around the pin at the end.

24. Pull the other end of the machine bastings until the basted area is gathered to the same width as the band between the pattern markings. Fasten the loose threads at the other end, as you did in Step 23. Distribute the gathers evenly.

25. Repeat Steps 23 and 24 on the other side.

26. Hand baste the halter to the band 5/8 inch from the bottom edge. Remove all pins except those anchoring the gathers at the ends.

27. Machine stitch along the basting. If the band is triangular, as in this example, pivot (Appendix) at the corner before continuing with the stitching. Remove the remaining pins and bastings.

28. Trim the seam to 1/4 inch. Press the seam toward the band.

D LINING THE BAND

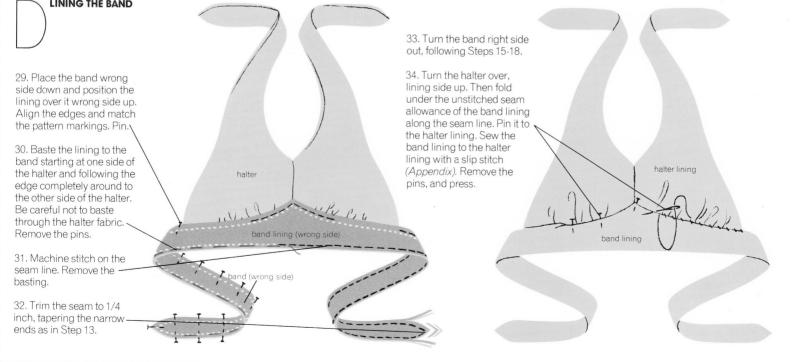

29. Place the band wrong side down and position the lining over it wrong side up. Align the edges and match the pattern markings. Pin.

30. Baste the lining to the band starting at one side of the halter and following the edge completely around to the other side of the halter. Be careful not to baste through the halter fabric. Remove the pins.

31. Machine stitch on the seam line. Remove the basting.

32. Trim the seam to 1/4 inch, tapering the narrow ends as in Step 13.

33. Turn the band right side out, following Steps 15-18.

34. Turn the halter over, lining side up. Then fold under the unstitched seam allowance of the band lining along the seam line. Pin it to the halter lining. Sew the band lining to the halter lining with a slip stitch (Appendix). Remove the pins, and press.

Slit skirts, sexy and sensible

An artful slit dividing the front and back panels of a sheath skirt is that real rarity in fashion engineering: a sexy touch that is also practical. While revealing a graceful curve or flash of leg, the slit preserves all of the flattery that is inherent in a straight-lined dress without curtailing freedom of movement.

A slit characteristically opens up from the hem and rises to the knee or even the hip on one or both sides of the garment; the length varies according to the design of the skirt and the courage of the wearer. Two methods of constructing the slit are demonstrated on the following pages. The one illustrated in the finished dress at right uses the seams and hems of the dress to form an inside facing with mitered corners. This method is especially recommended for heavy fabrics. A second, more showy method frames the outsides of the slit with narrow borders of a contrasting fabric—but one of the same weight as the garment fabric, to ensure a smooth finish.

THE FACED SLIT WITH MITERED CORNERS

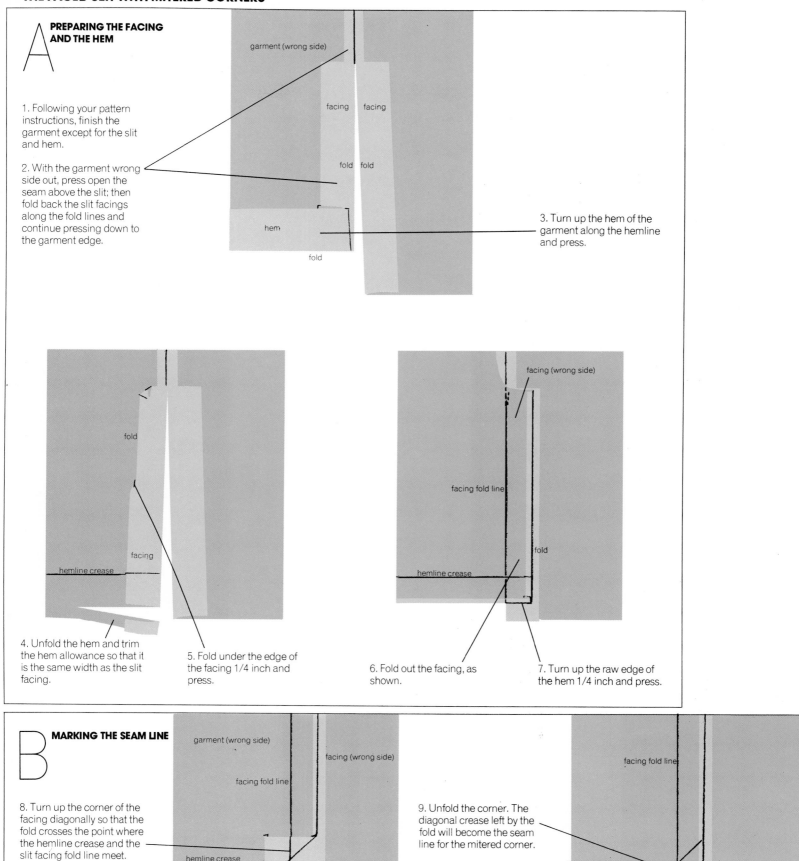

A PREPARING THE FACING AND THE HEM

1. Following your pattern instructions, finish the garment except for the slit and hem.

2. With the garment wrong side out, press open the seam above the slit; then fold back the slit facings along the fold lines and continue pressing down to the garment edge.

garment (wrong side)

facing   facing

fold   fold

hem

fold

3. Turn up the hem of the garment along the hemline and press.

fold

facing

hemline crease

facing (wrong side)

facing fold line

fold

hemline crease

4. Unfold the hem and trim the hem allowance so that it is the same width as the slit facing.

5. Fold under the edge of the facing 1/4 inch and press.

6. Fold out the facing, as shown.

7. Turn up the raw edge of the hem 1/4 inch and press.

B MARKING THE SEAM LINE

garment (wrong side)

facing (wrong side)

facing fold line

hemline crease

fold

facing fold line

hemline crease

seam line crease

8. Turn up the corner of the facing diagonally so that the fold crosses the point where the hemline crease and the slit facing fold line meet. Match the creases on the folded-up corner with those on the garment underneath.

9. Unfold the corner. The diagonal crease left by the fold will become the seam line for the mitered corner.

continued

C CLOSING THE SEAM

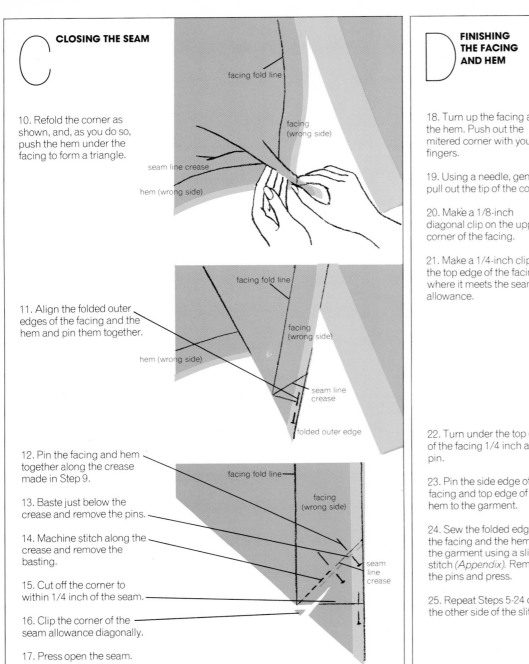

facing fold line

facing
(wrong side)

seam line crease

hem (wrong side)

10. Refold the corner as shown, and, as you do so, push the hem under the facing to form a triangle.

facing fold line

facing
(wrong side)

hem (wrong side)

seam line crease

folded outer edge

11. Align the folded outer edges of the facing and the hem and pin them together.

facing fold line

facing
(wrong side)

seam line crease

12. Pin the facing and hem together along the crease made in Step 9.

13. Baste just below the crease and remove the pins.

14. Machine stitch along the crease and remove the basting.

15. Cut off the corner to within 1/4 inch of the seam.

16. Clip the corner of the seam allowance diagonally.

17. Press open the seam.

D FINISHING THE FACING AND HEM

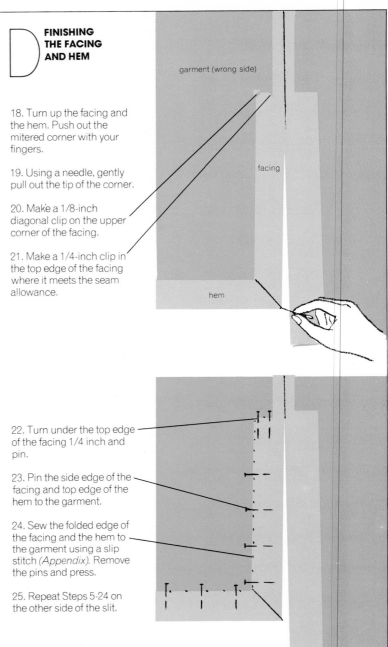

garment (wrong side)

facing

hem

18. Turn up the facing and the hem. Push out the mitered corner with your fingers.

19. Using a needle, gently pull out the tip of the corner.

20. Make a 1/8-inch diagonal clip on the upper corner of the facing.

21. Make a 1/4-inch clip in the top edge of the facing where it meets the seam allowance.

22. Turn under the top edge of the facing 1/4 inch and pin.

23. Pin the side edge of the facing and top edge of the hem to the garment.

24. Sew the folded edge of the facing and the hem to the garment using a slip stitch (Appendix). Remove the pins and press.

25. Repeat Steps 5-24 on the other side of the slit.

THE SLIT WITH A DECORATIVE BORDER

A PREPARING THE GARMENT

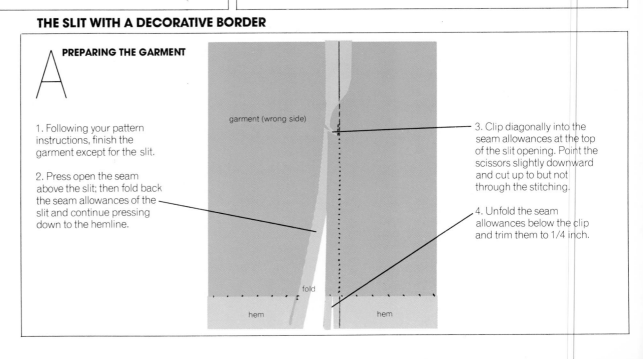

garment (wrong side)

fold

hem   hem

1. Following your pattern instructions, finish the garment except for the slit.

2. Press open the seam above the slit; then fold back the seam allowances of the slit and continue pressing down to the hemline.

3. Clip diagonally into the seam allowances at the top of the slit opening. Point the scissors slightly downward and cut up to but not through the stitching.

4. Unfold the seam allowances below the clip and trim them to 1/4 inch.

B PREPARING THE BORDER

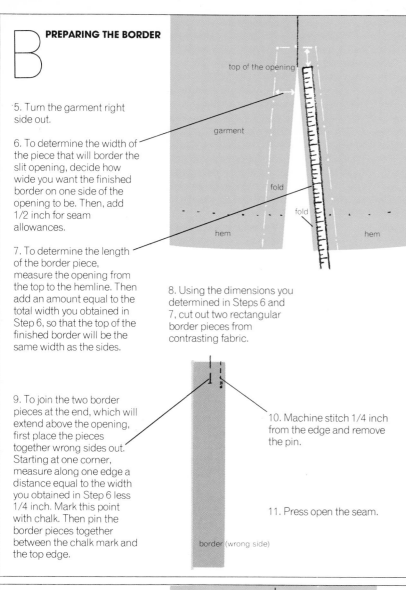

5. Turn the garment right side out.

6. To determine the width of the piece that will border the slit opening, decide how wide you want the finished border on one side of the opening to be. Then, add 1/2 inch for seam allowances.

7. To determine the length of the border piece, measure the opening from the top to the hemline. Then add an amount equal to the total width you obtained in Step 6, so that the top of the finished border will be the same width as the sides.

8. Using the dimensions you determined in Steps 6 and 7, cut out two rectangular border pieces from contrasting fabric.

9. To join the two border pieces at the end, which will extend above the opening, first place the pieces together wrong sides out. Starting at one corner, measure along one edge a distance equal to the width you obtained in Step 6 less 1/4 inch. Mark this point with chalk. Then pin the border pieces together between the chalk mark and the top edge.

10. Machine stitch 1/4 inch from the edge and remove the pin.

11. Press open the seam.

C ATTACHING THE BORDER TO THE GARMENT

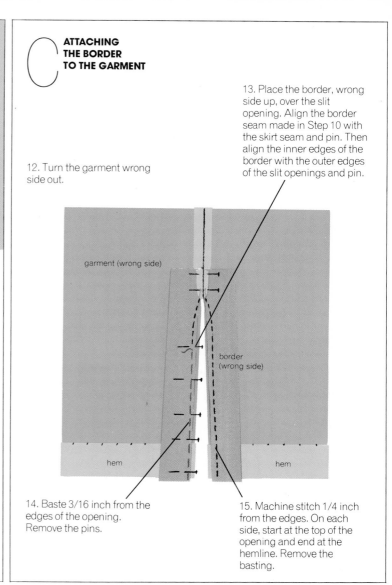

12. Turn the garment wrong side out.

13. Place the border, wrong side up, over the slit opening. Align the border seam made in Step 10 with the skirt seam and pin. Then align the inner edges of the border with the outer edges of the slit openings and pin.

14. Baste 3/16 inch from the edges of the opening. Remove the pins.

15. Machine stitch 1/4 inch from the edges. On each side, start at the top of the opening and end at the hemline. Remove the basting.

D FINISHING THE BORDER

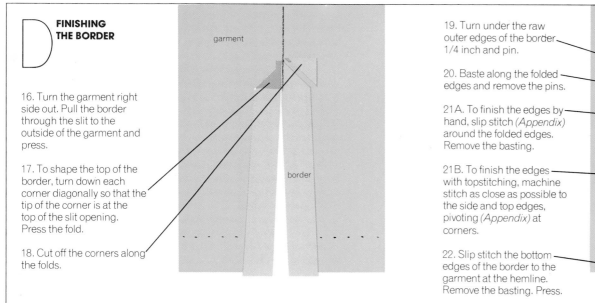

16. Turn the garment right side out. Pull the border through the slit to the outside of the garment and press.

17. To shape the top of the border, turn down each corner diagonally so that the tip of the corner is at the top of the slit opening. Press the fold.

18. Cut off the corners along the folds.

19. Turn under the raw outer edges of the border 1/4 inch and pin.

20. Baste along the folded edges and remove the pins.

21A. To finish the edges by hand, slip stitch (Appendix) around the folded edges. Remove the basting.

21B. To finish the edges with topstitching, machine stitch as close as possible to the side and top edges, pivoting (Appendix) at corners.

22. Slip stitch the bottom edges of the border to the garment at the hemline. Remove the basting. Press.

The intrigue of Oriental fripperies

King Francis I of France, a lover of fancy trim, once commanded his tailor to make a black velvet suit with 13,400 buttons sewed to it. And one of Francis' successors, Louis XIV, so delighted in jeweled buttons on his attire that "he sank beneath the weight of them," wrote the Duc de Saint-Simon, a dedicated dispenser of court gossip.

Clearly Their Majesties were overdoing it. Their addiction to fancy trimmings overwhelmed their clothes—not to mention Their Majesties. But in the proper proportion and place, trimmings can do for exotic fashions what whole cloves do for a baked ham: they heighten the flavor and enhance the appearance. And, like the cloves, they are integral to the result. From buttons and beads and braids to fringes and paillettes and pompons and tassels, trimmings are numerous and varied enough to italicize the elegant look of any costume. The proper use of each or any of these items depends, as the following pages explain in detail, on the shape of the garment, and the texture and pattern of the fabric.

Among top designers, sequins and their sisters, paillettes, are favorite trimmings. The distinction between sequins and paillettes is primarily one of size. The small, flat, shiny disks with holes in the center are known as sequins—unless they are slightly concave, in which case they are couvettes. But if the disk is larger and the hole is off center, then it is a paillette. Just to make things perfectly clear, some paillettes have a hole in the center. No matter to the home needlecrafter; they can all give marvelous sparkle to a dress.

Until the daring designer Norman Norell came along, neither the sequin nor the paillette enjoyed respectability in the 20th Century. They brought to mind dance-hall girls in gold or oil boomtowns and, a little later, the chorus girls of Broadway musical comedies. But Norell, who was to become the dean of American fashion designers, began his career contriving screen costumes for Theda Bara and other vamps in silent movies. In the 1930s, after he switched to fashion, he borrowed his own cinematic tricks and used masses of glittering disks hand stitched to costly fabrics. The result transformed his socially registered customers into a new and devastating genus of dryland mermaids, slinky, dazzling and exotic.

The dresses cost as much as $3,000, but they were impervious to the whims of style. Norell was still turning out similar fashions nearly four decades later. At a retrospective of his work held in New York's Metropolitan Museum of Art, shortly before he died in 1972, many *grande dames* paid tribute to the timelessness of his designs by proudly wearing the sequined gowns they had purchased from him decades before.

Norell's inventive influence survived him. Among current designers, James Galanos recently showed a floor-length black chiffon dress dotted with rhinestone disks. Oscar de la Renta put cyclamen scales on white crepe pajamas. Susy Perette imposed sequins on paisley prints in a collection that epitomized the mix of trimmings with exotic fabric. And R. Halston Frowick, better known as Halston, who is credited with first having made caftans fashionable outside of Islam, has taken to inlaying many of his creations with sequins. Fortunately for the home seamstress who fancies the baubles, they no longer have to be stitched to the fabric one by one. They are now available by the yard, machine stitched to backing materials, and can be applied to the garment in strips like any other trim.

Except perhaps for sequins and paillettes, whose origins are vaguely traceable only as far as late medieval times, trimmings are among humanity's most ancient heirlooms, some of them predating civilization. Beads were perhaps mankind's first indulgent luxury. Bead embroidery was practiced long before the last major ice age, with beads fashioned from sea shells, seeds, broken eggs—any colorful discard of nature.

Archeologists digging into Stone Age graves on Israel's Mount Carmel in 1937 unearthed human skeletons that had been buried with elaborately beaded headdresses, made from the thin, splintered bones of small gazelles and from white dentalium, a kind of shell that still washes up on the eastern Mediterranean's shores. Among many African tribes, whose basic social structure and mode of living are still relatively primitive, beads remain a primary source of adornment. The Ndebele, for example, produce fine beadwork, which is worn on aprons and other items of clothing. In Swaziland, the patterns of a nubile girl's embroidery are beadwork love letters that tell a wooer whether the maiden loves him or rejects him—but the messages can be so intricate that many a youth must ask a sister to decode them.

Fringes and tassels, which often adorn the creations of such modern designers as Arnold Scaasi and Stephen Burrows, are almost as ancient as beaded embroidery. A bas-relief surviving from 1900 B.C. depicts a Phoenician prince, his splendid raiment dripping with fringe and tassels, bestowing gifts on a pharaoh of Egypt's 18th Dynasty. And Moses, in the Old Testament, was commanded by God to instruct the children of Israel "that they make them fringes in the borders of their garments throughout their generation, and that they put upon the fringe a ribband of blue."

Fringes and tassels were originally the loose threads of warp on the edge of fabrics. They were tied, twisted and knotted to prevent unraveling. The ribband of blue served the same purpose. But all three quickly became decorative. Ancient sculptures from such places as Nineveh reveal that the Assyrians' fringes and tassels were not part of the original fabric, but had been stitched on for adornment.

The fashion never really died out. The wardrobe accounts of England's King Edward I (1272-1307) list "fringes of Venice gold at six shillings and four pence an ounce." In the first Queen Elizabeth's reign (1558-1603) petticoats had as many as six rows of fringe, one above the other. In the 19th Century, women in America, England and France wore tassels and fringes. At the height of the Victorian era, not only clothes but just about anything within a homemaker's field of vision was laden with fringes and tassels: pillows, upholstery, hangings, tablecloths, parasols—even the surrey with the fringe on top. This love of decoration, coupled with the celebrated Victorian prudery, finally dictated that piano legs must be covered with ornate fringed leggings. Otherwise, people would see the naked piano legs and might be reminded of the naked legs—limbs—of women.

Then during the 20th Century, in America at least, the tassel gradually acquired a rather naughty name for itself, associated with belly dancers, and with the stripper Blaze Starr and other ladies of the burlesque stage. Recently, however, tassels have emerged from their brief obloquy and taken on a new air of respectability.

Buttons, too, had their period of disgrace, much earlier and much longer than that of tassels. Though prehistoric man used buttons of bone, and the Egyptians and the Greeks were familiar with them, buttons were frowned on in most of Europe during what used to be called the Dark Ages. Clothes fastened with buttons and loops (the buttonhole was not invented until the 13th Century) were easy to undo, and the button was construed as proof of loose living. The only European country that had

Intent dressmakers hand sew beading, fringe, tassels and other elaborate decorations onto segments of dresses in the trimming room of a New York dress factory before World War I. The dressmakers' dummies (*left*

middle ground) are right out of the ornate Victorian and Edwardian eras. The fad lapsed in the 1920s, then came back with the advent of Norman Norell to the fashion industry in the 1930s.

no objection to buttons in those puritanical days was France.

Medieval noblemen tried to safeguard their opulent—or risqué—styles of dress by passing laws against the wearing of frills and trims by commoners. Apparently the laws were enthusiastically abused. In trying to fine a woman for wearing buttons on her dress, an exasperated administrator in Florence encountered arguments "such as are not to be found in any book of law." In her defense, the woman held that "these are not buttons but studs and if ye do not believe me, look . . . they have no loops and moreover there are no buttonholes."

Buttons, beads, braids—in fact virtually all of the trimmings that are the spice in the modern taste for the exotic—remained luxuries until the 19th Century's machine age brought them into mass production at prices within the reach of the home seamstress. In 1826, a Massachusetts storekeeper's wife named Emily Williston, having grown weary of the chore of covering buttons with fabric by hand, complained to a friend, Joseph Hayden. He responded by devising a machine to do the job. Soon Williston factories accounted for half the world's production. Similarly a modern braiding machine invented about 1870 produced the spectrum of low-cost braids still familiar and popular today. Among them are flat braid, which can be used to outline jacket fronts, necklines or pockets; soutache braid, which can be employed effectively with frog and button closings; and zigzag rickrack, which is perhaps the most popular of all modern braids.

What mass production came to mean to the home seamstress is reflected in the Sears, Roebuck catalogue for 1898. On a page devoted to trimmings, it offered under the heading Soutache and Tubular Braid:

25054: Mohair Soutache Braid, for trimming, black and staple colors. Per yard, 1 cent; 12 yards, 11 cents.

25056: Silk Soutache Braid, for trimming, black and colors. Per yard, 4 cents; 12 yards, 43 cents.

25058: Silk Tubular Braid, for dress trimmings. 1/4 inch wide, see illustration for size and pattern. Black and colors. Per yard, 9 cents.

Today an even wider choice of trims is available to the home needlecrafter. These choices include colorful bands of pre-strung beads, countless combinations of braids, dazzling buttons and fringes that can be easily attached to garments with sewing machines. However, many home seamstresses with the time and skill to devote to the minute details of sewing prefer to give their creations a personal look by fashioning their own trims.

An effective fringe for a shawl can be created by simply knotting yarn. Buttons can be made to sparkle by stitching them with metallic thread or by sewing on beads, and a Chinese frog fastening can be made at home by stitching together loops of soutache braid or corded tubing. Chinese ball buttons can be made according to the directions on page 75. But whether they are home-made or store-bought, the trimmings whose uses are described on the following pages permit any home sewer to achieve the exotic elegance to which the great modern designers are dedicated.

A medley of harmonious grace notes

"Unknown spices and savors" was the phrase that the innovative French couturier Paul Poiret gave to the plumage, veils, tassels and beads with which he began to decorate his customers in 1904. These dramatic grace notes heightened the sense of *exotica* in Poiret's dress collections. And they inspired his competitors to add similar fancies to their own lines of dresses.

Shown here are several examples of pioneering Parisian artistry, as displayed at the Costume Institute of New York's Metropolitan Museum. The ostrich-feathered turban on the figure shown at right is the crowning touch for a black velvet theater wrap designed in 1912 by Mme. Paquin, one of Poiret's more successful rivals. The gold net veil worn by the next figure, over a ruby red velvet evening gown by couturier Madeleine Vionnet, is embroidered in the so-called Art Deco motifs of the 1920s.

The figures at far right show off two of Poiret's own creations. The evening coat, salted and peppered in beads to match its white and black panels, appeared in 1912. The purple and emerald-green satin toga, trimmed with fringe and tassels, was offered in his 1917 collection.

Decorative trim and braid

Colorful slashes of braid, cording and corded tubing play cameo roles in fashion, giving distinctive touches to garments without stealing the show. An example of this deft play is shown on the dress at left, where braid bands accent a slim waist.

Braids, which are too complex to make at home, can be bought ready-made in an array of patterns and colors, and can be attached by either of the two methods shown opposite. Cording and corded tubing, on the other hand, can be custom made, and the narrow color choice in stores makes the effort worthwhile.

Both cording and corded tubing consist of a length of manufactured cotton cord, covered with bias-cut strips of fabric as described on the following pages. In cording, the cover is made right side out and the exposed seam allowance subsequently sewed into seams—such as those around the collar of a kimono. With corded tubing, the cover is sewed wrong side out and then inverted and drawn over the cord. Thus finished, it can be sewed on a garment or used to make loops and frogs.

FLAT BRAID

A ATTACHING THE BRAID

1. If you are not attaching the braid along a seam or an edge, draw a chalk line on the garment as a guide for positioning your braid.

2. Cut a length of braid equal to the length of the garment area to be trimmed (a neckline yoke in this example), plus 1 inch.

3. Turn under the raw edge of one end 1/8 inch and tack it with a hemming stitch (*Appendix*).

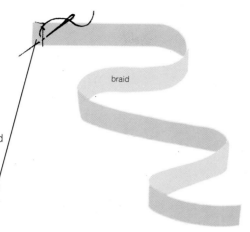

braid

4. Place the braid, wrong side down, along the seam, edge or chalk line, and pin it to the garment at 1-inch intervals. Insert the pins parallel to the edges.

5. At corners, ease the braid so that the corners are slightly rounded rather than sharp, and insert several pins at right angles to the edges to hold the braid flat.

6. When you reach the other end, trim the braid if necessary and turn under the other raw edge 1/8 inch. Tack the edge as you did in Step 3. Then pin the finished end to the garment.

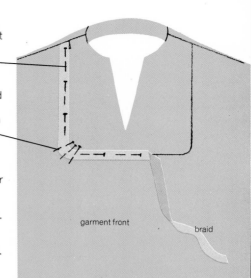

garment front

braid

B FINISHING THE BRAID

7A. Hand sew the braid to the garment, catching only the outer layer of fabric if the garment is faced or lined. Use prick stitches (*Appendix*) 1/2 inch apart. On narrow braids, sew down the center; on wider braids, sew along both edges. Remove the pins as you stitch. At corners, make your stitches closer together to take up the ease evenly.

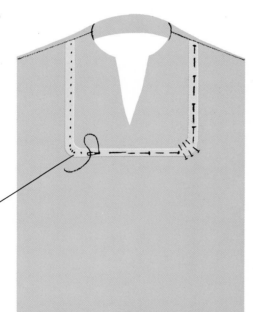

7B. Machine stitch the braid to the garment. On narrow braids, sew down the center; on wider braids, sew along both edges.

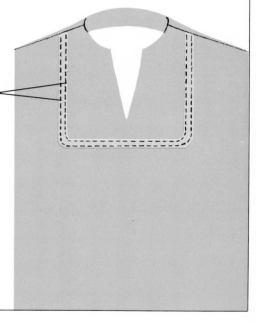

CORDING

A CUTTING THE FABRIC STRIPS FOR THE CASING

1. To determine the total length of the casing you will require for the cording, measure the seam that you will be sewing the cording into. Then, add 2 inches.

2. To prepare the fabric you are using to make the casing, first fold it diagonally so that a crosswise edge is aligned with a lengthwise (selvage) edge and the wrong sides are together. Pin the edges.

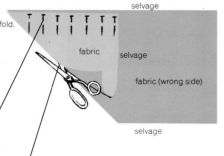

selvage

fold

fabric

selvage

fabric (wrong side)

selvage

3. Then cut the fabric along the folded edge. Remove the pins and set aside the top piece of fabric.

4. Determine the number of strips of fabric you will need to make the total length of casing required, making sure to add 1/2 inch for seam allowances on every strip.

5. To mark off the strips, draw a series of chalk lines parallel to the diagonal edge. Make each strip wide enough so that it will fit around the cord, plus 1 inch for seam allowances.

6. Trim off both of the selvages.

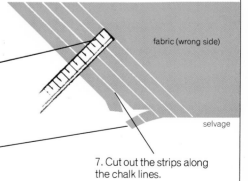

fabric (wrong side)

selvage

7. Cut out the strips along the chalk lines.

continued

B JOINING THE STRIPS

8. Mark a 1/4-inch seam allowance with chalk on the ends of each strip.

9. Place two strips together, wrong sides out, so that they form a V shape. Align the seam lines and pin.

10. Machine stitch and remove pins.

11. Repeat Steps 8-10 to make one long strip.

12. Press open the seams.

13. Cut off one end of the strip at right angles to the long edges.

14. Measure the length you determined in Step 1 and cut off the other end of the strip. Again make the cut at right angles to the long edge.

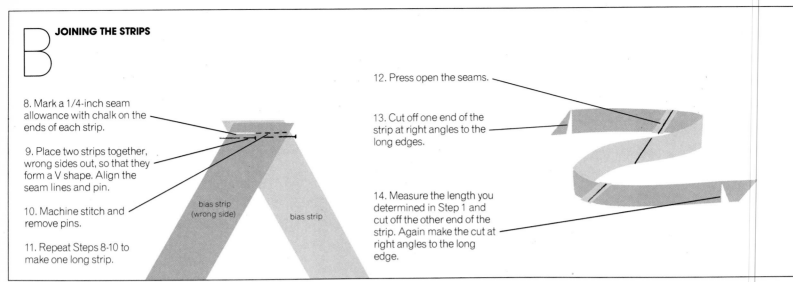

bias strip (wrong side)

bias strip

C MAKING THE CORDING

15. Cut a piece of cord the length of the strip plus 1 inch.

16. Fold the strip, wrong sides together, around the cord and align the edges.

17. Using a zipper foot, machine baste at 6 stitches to the inch close to the cord but not up against it. Hold the edges to keep them aligned as you stitch.

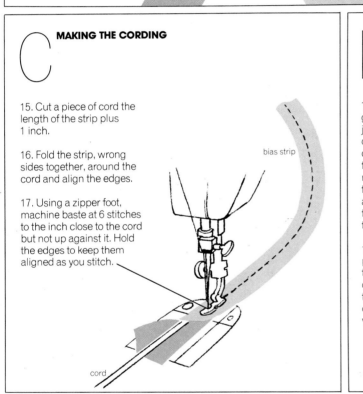

bias strip

cord

D ATTACHING THE CORDING

18. Lay one of the two garment pieces that will be joined together with the corded seam wrong side down. Pin the cording along the seam line so that the rounded cord edge is inside the seam line, as shown, and the machine basting on the cording is just outside the seam line.

19. After you pin along portions of the seam line that curve inward, notch the outer edge of the cording up to but not through the line of machine basting so that it will lie flat.

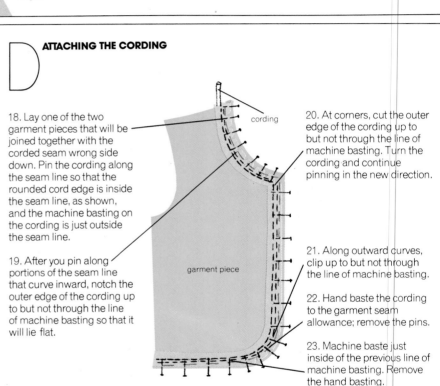

cording

garment piece

20. At corners, cut the outer edge of the cording up to but not through the line of machine basting. Turn the cording and continue pinning in the new direction.

21. Along outward curves, clip up to but not through the line of machine basting.

22. Hand baste the cording to the garment seam allowance; remove the pins.

23. Machine baste just inside of the previous line of machine basting. Remove the hand basting.

E CLOSING THE CORDED SEAM

24. Lay the other garment piece wrong side down. Place the garment piece to which you have attached the cording wrong side up over it, so that the cording is between the pieces.

25. Align the seam lines and pin.

26. Hand baste just outside the line of machine basting made in Step 23 and remove the pins.

27. With the zipper foot pressed up against the cording, run a line of machine stitching —resetting the machine to the normal 12 stitches to the inch—along the seam line.

28. Trim the cording seam allowances to 1/8 inch.

29. Trim the garment seam allowances to 1/4 inch.

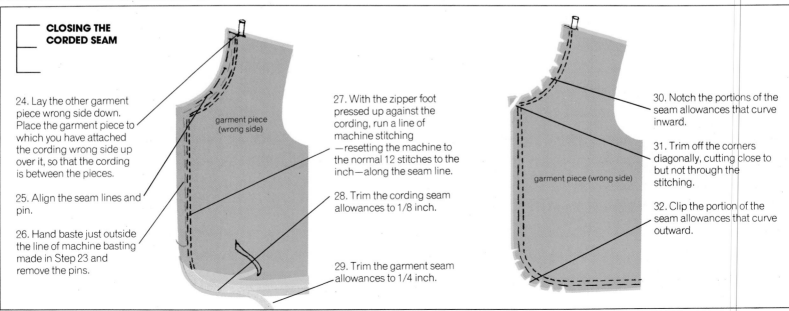

garment piece (wrong side)

garment piece (wrong side)

30. Notch the portions of the seam allowances that curve inward.

31. Trim off the corners diagonally, cutting close to but not through the stitching.

32. Clip the portion of the seam allowances that curve outward.

CORDED TUBING

A MAKING THE TUBING

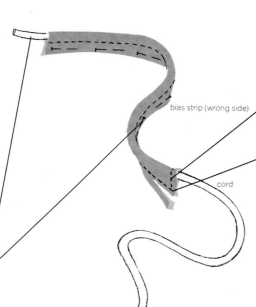

1. To determine the length of tubing you will need, add 4 inches to the total called for by your pattern or project.

2. To cut out and join the fabric strip that will form the tubing and encase the cord, follow the instructions for making plain cording *(Steps 2-14)*.

3. Cut a piece of cord that is twice the length of the strip.

4. Leaving 1/2 inch of cord free at one end, fold the fabric strip wrong side out around the cord and pin the edges together at 1-inch intervals. Leave half of the cord free at the other end.

bias strip (wrong side)

cord

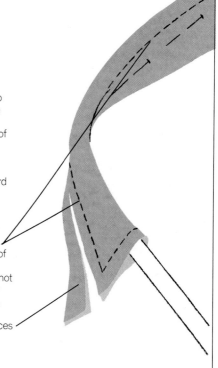

5. Using a zipper foot, machine stitch the strip to the cord, as shown. Make sure to stitch 1/16 inch beyond the bottom edge of the cord.

6. Pivot *(Appendix)* and stitch in at an angle toward the cord.

7. Stretching the strip slightly and removing the pins as you go, stitch straight down the length of the strip. Keep the zipper foot close to the cord but not right up against it. End by backstitching *(Appendix)*.

8. Trim the seam allowances to 1/8 inch.

B TURNING THE TUBING

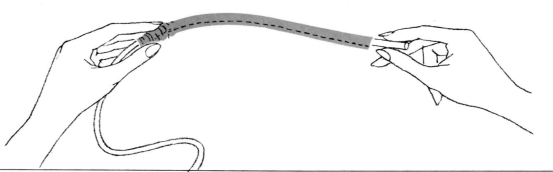

9. To turn the tubing right side out, grasp the loose 1/2 inch of cord left at one end of the tubing in Step 4, and pull the enclosed cord out of the tubing with one hand as you work the tubing over the free half of the cord with the other hand.

C FINISHING THE ENDS

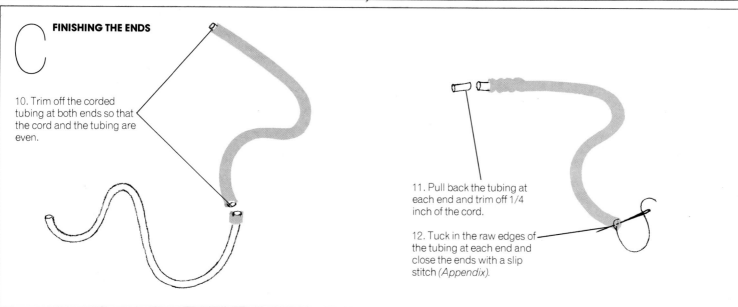

10. Trim off the corded tubing at both ends so that the cord and the tubing are even.

11. Pull back the tubing at each end and trim off 1/4 inch of the cord.

12. Tuck in the raw edges of the tubing at each end and close the ends with a slip stitch *(Appendix)*.

Fasteners with a flair

Fanciful fasteners from the Far East provide an exotic alternative to conventional closings like zippers. The braided frogs on the dress at right, for example, make decorative replacements for hooks and eyes. These particular frogs are doubly intriguing because each one fastens with a Chinese ball button—a special kind of rounded knot.

Frogs function in pairs, shaped separately. To make the first frog, tie a Chinese ball button at one end of a length of braid or corded tubing; then twist its long tail into a cloverleaf pattern. For the second frog, start with the cloverleaf and end with a loop for encircling the button.

Less showy, but just as ingenious, is a row of Chinese ball buttons tucked into continuous button loops. They are called continuous because they are formed by a single strip of braid or corded tubing caught in the seam at regular intervals (pages 78-79). When measuring for these loops, add on a few extra inches to avoid being left short.

CHINESE BALL BUTTONS

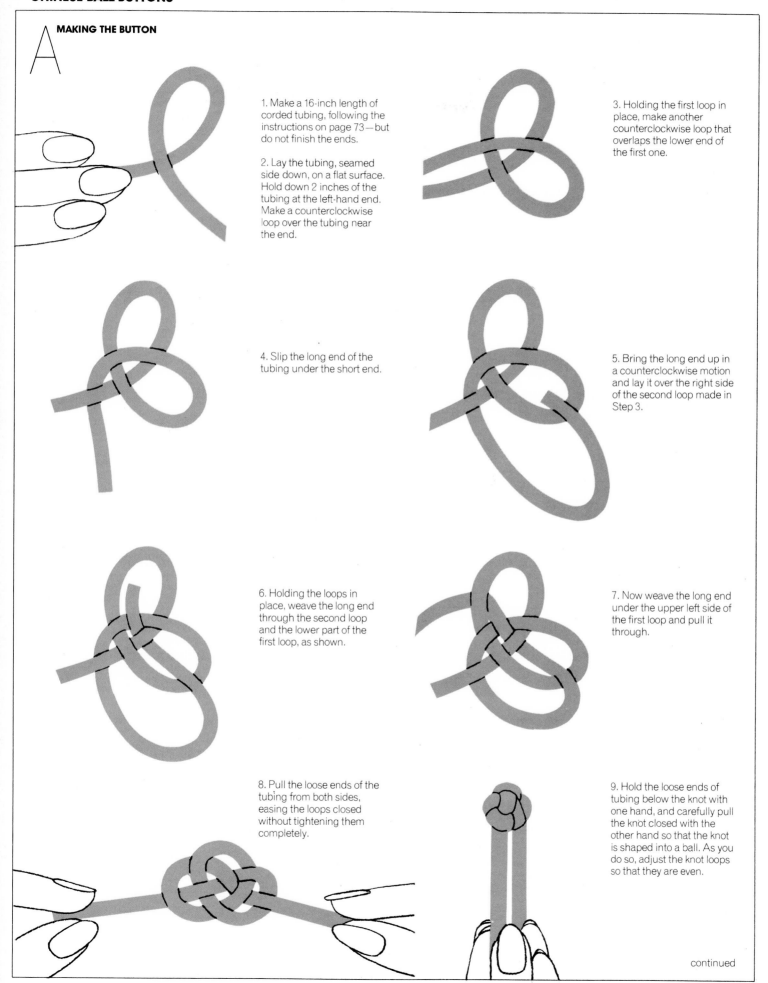

A MAKING THE BUTTON

1. Make a 16-inch length of corded tubing, following the instructions on page 73—but do not finish the ends.

2. Lay the tubing, seamed side down, on a flat surface. Hold down 2 inches of the tubing at the left-hand end. Make a counterclockwise loop over the tubing near the end.

3. Holding the first loop in place, make another counterclockwise loop that overlaps the lower end of the first one.

4. Slip the long end of the tubing under the short end.

5. Bring the long end up in a counterclockwise motion and lay it over the right side of the second loop made in Step 3.

6. Holding the loops in place, weave the long end through the second loop and the lower part of the first loop, as shown.

7. Now weave the long end under the upper left side of the first loop and pull it through.

8. Pull the loose ends of the tubing from both sides, easing the loops closed without tightening them completely.

9. Hold the loose ends of tubing below the knot with one hand, and carefully pull the knot closed with the other hand so that the knot is shaped into a ball. As you do so, adjust the knot loops so that they are even.

continued

FINISHING THE BUTTON

10. Clip the ends of the tubing to 1/4 inch.

11. Pull back the tubing on each end and trim off about 1/4 inch of the cord.

12. Sew one end of the tubing to the bottom of the button, using a hemming stitch (Appendix). On the other end, tuck the raw edges inside the tubing.

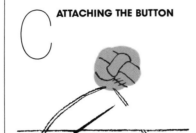

13. Sew the loose end of the tubing over the attached end, using a hemming stitch.

ATTACHING THE BUTTON

14. Using a double strand of knotted thread the same color as the garment fabric, take a small stitch in the fabric at the point where the center of the button is to fall. Then insert the needle through the bottom of the button at its center and pull the thread through.

15. Angle the button away from the fabric with your thumb, and make two or three small stitches joining the button and the fabric.

16. Wind the thread several times tightly around the stitches below the button to create a thread shank. Then end by making a fastening stitch (Appendix) in the thread shank.

THE FROG WITH A BALL BUTTON

MAKING THE BUTTON LOOP ON THE LEFT HALF OF THE FROG

1. Make a 2-yard length of corded tubing following the instructions on page 73 —but do not finish the ends.

2. For the left half of the frog, cut a 40-inch piece of the tubing.

3. Make a Chinese ball button with the tubing, following the instructions on page 75, Steps 2-9. Hold down about 3 inches of the tubing as you start so that the button will be formed near one end.

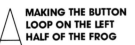

4. Along both fronts of the garment where the frog will be attached, run a line of basting to mark the center front line.

5. Pin the right garment front over the left front, matching the center front lines.

6. Place the tubing on the garment so that the Chinese ball button is positioned on the center front line of the right front, as shown, and the ends extend over the left front.

7. Lay the long end of the tubing over the short end so that they cross about 1/2 inch from the edge of the right front.

right garment front

left garment front

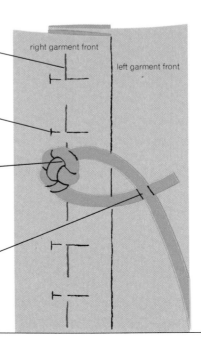
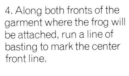

8. Holding the crossed ends in place, pick up the tubing and turn it over so that the seamed side is up. Hand stitch the short end of the tubing to the long end with a small fastening stitch (Appendix). Keep the needle threaded and do not cut the thread, so you can readily attach the other loops as they are formed.

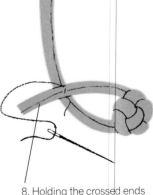

B COMPLETING THE LEFT HALF OF THE FROG

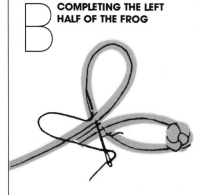

9. To form the top loop of the frog, make a clockwise loop of the desired size with the tubing. Bring the end of the loop over the tubing so that it is next to the attached end of the first loop. Secure the loop with a fastening stitch.

10. To form the side loop, make another clockwise loop of the desired size—not necessarily the same as the top loop. Bring the end of the loop under the tubing so that it is next to the left side of the top loop. Secure the loop with a fastening stitch.

11. To form the bottom loop, make a clockwise loop the same size as the top loop. Place the end of the tubing next to the attached end and secure it with a fastening stitch; then cut the thread.

12. Trim both ends of the tubing to 1/4 inch.

13. Pull back the tubing on both ends and trim off about 1/4 inch of cord. Then tuck in the ends of the tubing and close them with a hemming stitch (Appendix).

14. Turn the frog half over wrong side down, and stitch the loops together on the upper side with small fastening stitches.

C MAKING THE RIGHT HALF OF THE FROG

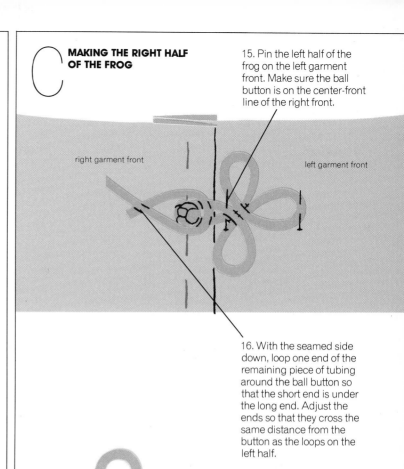

15. Pin the left half of the frog on the left garment front. Make sure the ball button is on the center-front line of the right front.

16. With the seamed side down, loop one end of the remaining piece of tubing around the ball button so that the short end is under the long end. Adjust the ends so that they cross the same distance from the button as the loops on the left half.

17. Make the right half of the frog following the instructions for the left half (Steps 8-14).

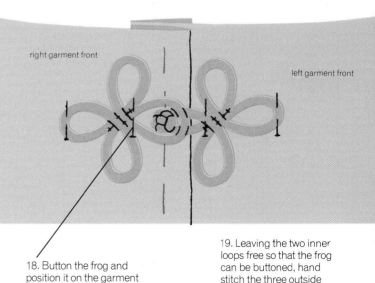

18. Button the frog and position it on the garment fronts with the button on the center-front line. Pin the frog in place.

19. Leaving the two inner loops free so that the frog can be buttoned, hand stitch the three outside loops to each garment front with the hemming stitch (Appendix).

CONTINUOUS BUTTON LOOPS

A MARKING THE POSITION FOR THE LOOPS

1. Run a line of basting to mark the center-front seam line on the right garment front.

2. Place the garment front wrong side down on a flat surface.

3. Measure the length of the portion of the seam line along which the loops will be made.

4. Make a length of corded tubing *(page 73)* equal to at least four times the length measured in Step 3. Do not finish the ends of the tubing.

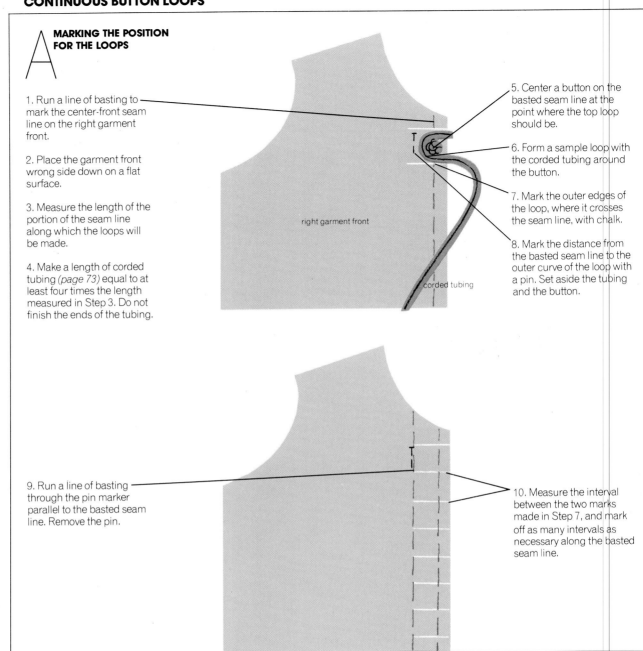

right garment front

corded tubing

5. Center a button on the basted seam line at the point where the top loop should be.

6. Form a sample loop with the corded tubing around the button.

7. Mark the outer edges of the loop, where it crosses the seam line, with chalk.

8. Mark the distance from the basted seam line to the outer curve of the loop with a pin. Set aside the tubing and the button.

9. Run a line of basting through the pin marker parallel to the basted seam line. Remove the pin.

10. Measure the interval between the two marks made in Step 7, and mark off as many intervals as necessary along the basted seam line.

B ATTACHING THE LOOPS

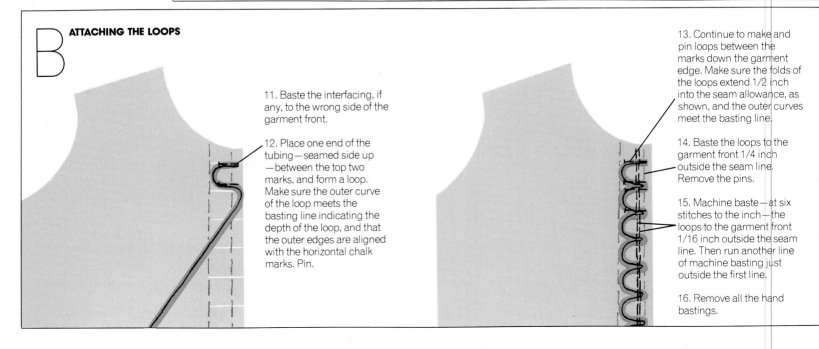

11. Baste the interfacing, if any, to the wrong side of the garment front.

12. Place one end of the tubing—seamed side up —between the top two marks, and form a loop. Make sure the outer curve of the loop meets the basting line indicating the depth of the loop, and that the outer edges are aligned with the horizontal chalk marks. Pin.

13. Continue to make and pin loops between the marks down the garment edge. Make sure the folds of the loops extend 1/2 inch into the seam allowance, as shown, and the outer curves meet the basting line.

14. Baste the loops to the garment front 1/4 inch outside the seam line. Remove the pins.

15. Machine baste—at six stitches to the inch—the loops to the garment front 1/16 inch outside the seam line. Then run another line of machine basting just outside the first line.

16. Remove all the hand bastings.

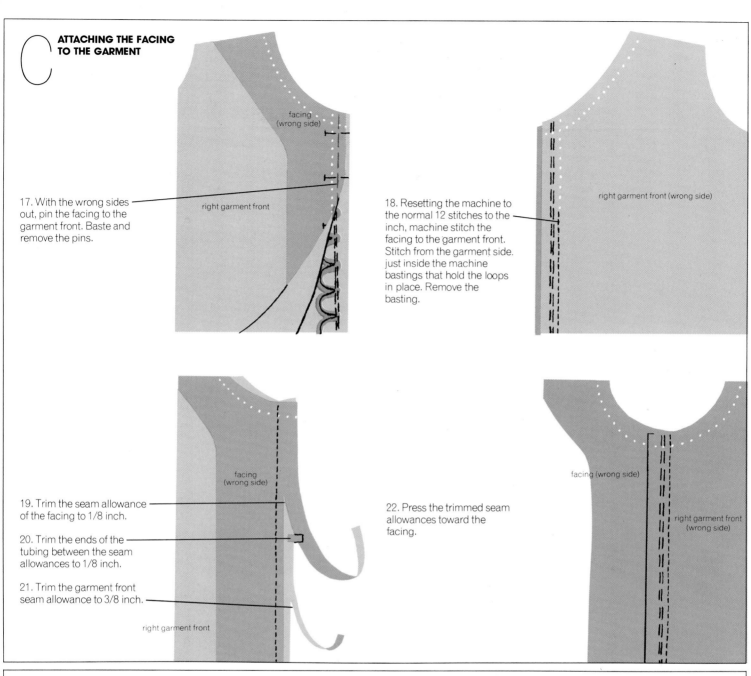

C ATTACHING THE FACING TO THE GARMENT

17. With the wrong sides out, pin the facing to the garment front. Baste and remove the pins.

facing (wrong side)

right garment front

18. Resetting the machine to the normal 12 stitches to the inch, machine stitch the facing to the garment front. Stitch from the garment side, just inside the machine bastings that hold the loops in place. Remove the basting.

right garment front (wrong side)

19. Trim the seam allowance of the facing to 1/8 inch.

20. Trim the ends of the tubing between the seam allowances to 1/8 inch.

21. Trim the garment front seam allowance to 3/8 inch.

facing (wrong side)

right garment front

22. Press the trimmed seam allowances toward the facing.

facing (wrong side)

right garment front (wrong side)

D FINISHING THE LOOPS

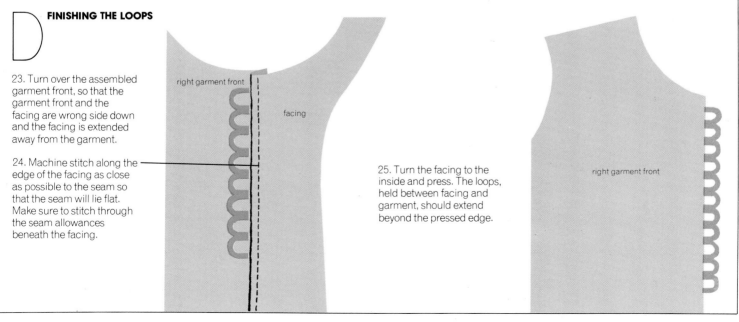

23. Turn over the assembled garment front, so that the garment front and the facing are wrong side down and the facing is extended away from the garment.

24. Machine stitch along the edge of the facing as close as possible to the seam so that the seam will lie flat. Make sure to stitch through the seam allowances beneath the facing.

right garment front

facing

25. Turn the facing to the inside and press. The loops, held between facing and garment, should extend beyond the pressed edge.

right garment front

Highlights for gala evenings

Pearls and rhinestones and other tinsel-pretty trimmings are the sartorial equivalent of champagne—their mere presence suggests a festive occasion. One glittering example is the blouse at left, sprinkled above with tiny pearls and splashed at the hip with star-bursts of oversized sequins called paillettes.

Trimmings like these can be used for all manner of party wear, sewed on in clusters, in rows, in traceries that delineate the designs of patterned fabrics—or in any random manner the needlecrafter chooses. Except for rhinestones, which are applied with a prong device, trimmings can be sewed in place with a regular needle and thread that is reinforced with beeswax.

Any kind of trimming, however, must be chosen to suit the fabric: gossamer-weight paillettes for any sheer, flowing material; rhinestones for heavier weights such as jerseys or wools, which are substantial enough to hold its pronged settings. Depending on their size, beads can be sewed on everything from chiffon to heavy wools.

APPLYING A SINGLE PAILLETTE

fabric (wrong side)

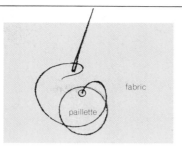

fabric

paillette

1. Lay the fabric wrong side up on a flat surface and mark it with tiny chalk dots to indicate where the paillettes will be applied.

2. Turn the fabric wrong side down.

3. Using a knotted strand of thread that is the same color as the paillette and coated with beeswax, bring the needle up from the wrong side of the fabric at one of the chalk dots. Then insert the needle through the hole in the paillette and pull the thread through.

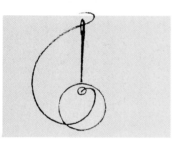

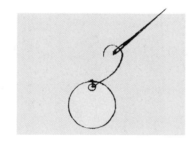

4. Insert the needle back into the fabric at the edge of the paillette close to the hole. Pull the thread through.

5. Bring the needle up from the wrong side of the fabric through the hole in the paillette.

6. Insert the needle back into the fabric at the edge of the paillette close to the hole. Pull the thread through.

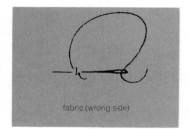

fabric (wrong side)

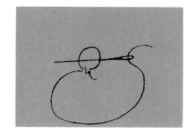

7. Turn the fabric wrong side up.

8. To secure the paillette, insert the needle under —and at right angles to —the stitch holding the paillette to the fabric. Pick up a few threads of the fabric with the needle and pull the thread partially through, leaving a loop.

9. Insert the needle through the loop made in Step 8. Draw the thread through and pull it tight to close the loop. Cut the thread.

10. To apply the remaining paillettes, repeat Steps 2-9.

APPLYING A SINGLE BEAD

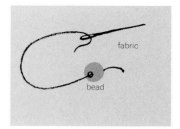

fabric (wrong side)

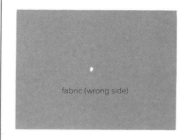

fabric

bead

1. Lay the fabric wrong side up on a flat surface, and mark the fabric with tiny chalk dots to indicate where the beads will be applied.

2. Turn the fabric wrong side down.

3. Using a knotted single thread that is the same color as the fabric and coated with beeswax, bring the needle up from the wrong side of the fabric at one of the chalk dots. Then thread a bead onto the needle and pull the thread through.

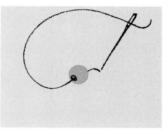

4. Insert the needle back into the fabric close to the place where the thread first emerged. Pull the thread through so that it is taut enough for the bead to lie flat against the fabric—with its hole parallel to the fabric —but not so taut that the fabric puckers.

5. Bring the needle up from the wrong side of the fabric close to the point from which it emerged in Step 3.

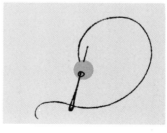

6. Pass the needle through the bead and pull the thread through.

7. Insert the needle back into the fabric at the point that it entered in Step 4.

8. Pull the thread through so that it is reasonably taut but does not cause the fabric to pucker. End off the thread as shown at left for applying a single paillette (Steps 7-9), repeating these steps twice.

9. To apply additional beads, repeat Steps 2-8.

APPLYING A PAILLETTE WITH A BEAD

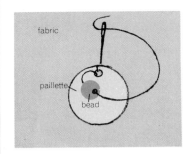

1. Attach the first paillette following the instructions for applying the single paillette (page 81, Steps 1-5). Then thread a bead onto the needle and let it drop down to the paillette.

2. Insert the needle back into the fabric at the edge of the paillette close to the hole.

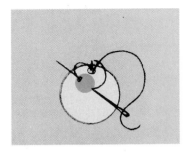

3. Pull the thread through. Then bring the needle up from the wrong side of the fabric through the hole in the paillette. Insert the needle in the hole in the bead and pull the thread through.

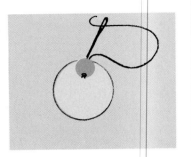

4. Reinsert the needle into the fabric, as in Step 2. End off the thread as shown for applying a single paillette, (Steps 7-9), repeating these steps twice.

5. To apply the rest of the paillettes and beads, repeat Steps 1-4.

CREATING A SIMPLE CLUSTER OF PAILLETTES AND BEADS

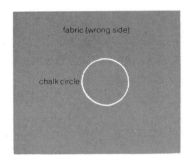

1. Place the fabric wrong side up on a flat surface. Using one paillette as a guide, trace a circle with chalk to mark the desired center of the first cluster. Set aside the paillette.

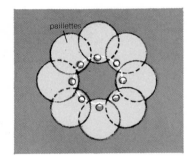

2. Arrange paillettes around the edge of the chalk circle, with their holes lined up along the chalk marking.

3. Make a pencil mark through the hole of each paillette; then set them aside.

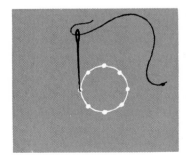

4. Using a knotted single thread that is the same color as the paillettes and coated with beeswax, insert the needle through any one of the pencil marks made in Step 3. Pull the thread through.

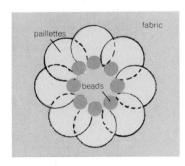

5. Turn the fabric wrong side down. Apply the first paillette and bead, following the instructions above for applying the paillette and bead (Steps 1-4). Then add paillettes and beads at the marked points to complete the circle.

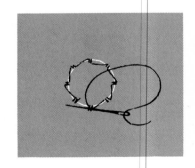

6. Turn the fabric wrong side up. End off the thread, as shown for applying a single paillette (page 81, Steps 7-9), repeating these steps twice. This completes a single cluster.

CREATING AN ORNATE CLUSTER OF PAILLETTES AND BEADS

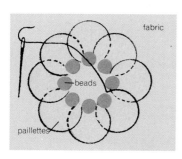

1. First make a simple cluster (opposite). Then, using a knotted single thread that has been coated with beeswax, bring the needle up from the wrong side of the fabric at a point between two beads, as shown.

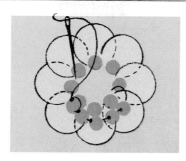

2. Thread onto the needle enough beads to stretch across the center circle; then add one bead and draw them all down the thread to the fabric.

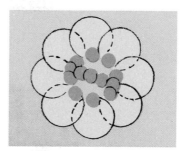

3. Insert the needle between two beads opposite the place it last emerged. Pull the thread through. Turn the fabric wrong side up. End off the thread, as shown for applying a single paillette (page 81, Steps 7 and 9), repeating these steps twice.

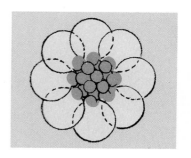

4. Make additional rows of beads, parallel to the one made in Steps 2 and 3 until the open center is completely filled.

APPLYING PRONGED RHINESTONES

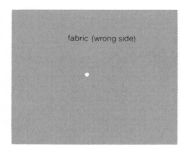

1. Lay the fabric wrong side up on a flat surface and mark it with tiny chalk dots to indicate the position for the rhinestones.

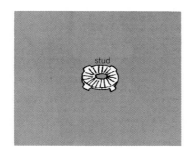

2. Position a pronged stud, with the prongs downward, over one of the chalk dots.

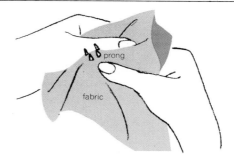

3. Hold the fabric taut and push the prongs through to the right side of the fabric, that is, the side that will show when the garment is completed. Do not pucker the fabric, but make sure to push the prongs completely through.

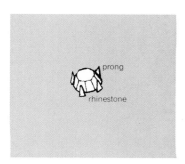

4. Turn the fabric wrong side down, taking care not to dislodge the stud. Place a rhinestone, faceted side up, in the center of the protruding prongs.

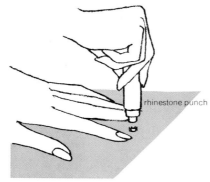

5. Grasp the handle of the rhinestone punch. Use your other hand to keep the fabric flat and taut around the rhinestone. Position the punch so that it is perpendicular to your work surface, with the concave tip centered over the rhinestone and prongs.

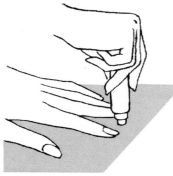

6. Lower the tool gently until the concave tip covers, but barely touches, the rhinestone and prongs. Then press down the punch firmly to close the prongs over the stone. Be sure to keep the tool in a perpendicular position and to use even pressure.

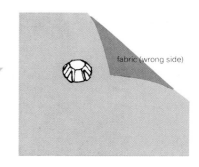

7. To apply the rest of the rhinestones, repeat Steps 1-6.

Tassels, fringes and pompons

Knotted fringes, fluffy pompons and slinky tassels are the icing on exotic clothing: festive toppings and trimmings to enhance any garment. And all these touches are easy to prepare and attach, using the instructions at right and on the following pages.

A fringe border like the one on this shawl can be made in two ways. On sturdy fabrics, such as cotton or wool, strands of wool or silk are drawn with a crochet hook through holes poked in the edge of the garment. Then the strands are knotted. For delicate fabrics, the border is crocheted first and the fringes attached with the hook afterward.

A tassel (*page 87*) is little more than a gather of fringe knotted at one end. Pompons are strands of wool tied in the middle with the loose ends fluffed off to form balls.

For wool or cotton fabrics, wool yarns produce the thick tassels and fringes or the plump pompons generally preferred. Silk buttonhole twist creates fragile tassels and fringe for silks and lightweight synthetics. And it is tricky to work with, so be sure to experiment first on scrap fabric.

MAKING A SINGLE-KNOTTED FRINGE

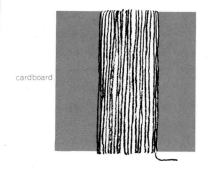

1. Cut out a rectangular piece of cardboard on which to wind your thread (or yarn). Make the cardboard wide enough to hold the entire fringe and long enough to equal twice the desired length of the fringe, plus 1 inch.

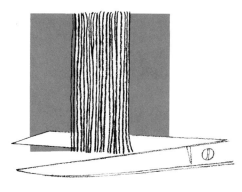

2. Wind the thread around the cardboard as many times as needed for the edge you are fringing. Cut off the excess thread about 1/2 inch below one edge of the cardboard.

3. At one edge, insert the top blade of a pair of sharp scissors between the cardboard and the wound thread. Cut along the edge.

4. Then, holding the thread so that it will not slip off the cardboard, cut along the other edge.

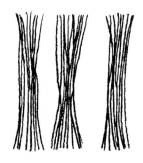

5. Divide the strands equally into groups of the desired size. Then straighten and align the strands in each group.

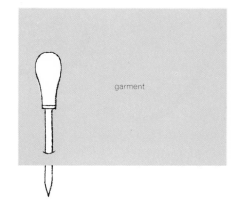

6. Starting near one end of the edge of the garment, use a dressmaker's awl or a sharp-pointed knitting needle to make a hole for the first group of strands. If the fabric is tightly woven, make the hole 1/4 inch from the edge; if loosely woven, 1/2 inch from the edge.

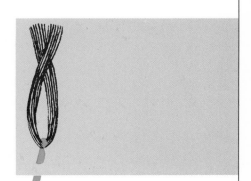

7. Insert a crochet hook through the hole from the wrong side of the garment. Then center one group of strands on the tip of the hook.

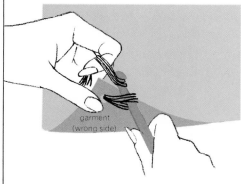

8. Pull the hook through the hole, bringing a small loop of strands to the wrong side. Then catch the loose strands on the other side of the fabric on the hook.

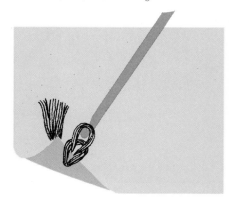

9. Pull the strands completely through the loop to make a knot.

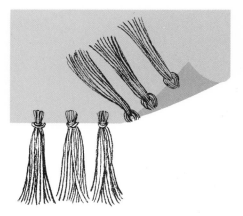

10. Make another hole the desired distance from the first, and repeat Steps 7-9. Continue the process until the edge is completely fringed.

MAKING A DOUBLE-KNOTTED FRINGE

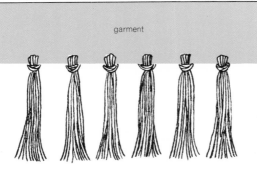

1. Cut out a piece of cardboard on which to wind your thread (or yarn). Make the cardboard wide enough to hold the entire fringe and long enough to equal twice the desired length of the fringe, plus 2 inches.

2. Make a fringe consisting of an even number of units, following the instructions for the single-knotted fringe *(page 85)*.

3. Tie the first two units together with a conventional knot the desired distance below the edge of the garment. Then continue knotting the units in pairs until the entire fringe is knotted.

MAKING A POMPON

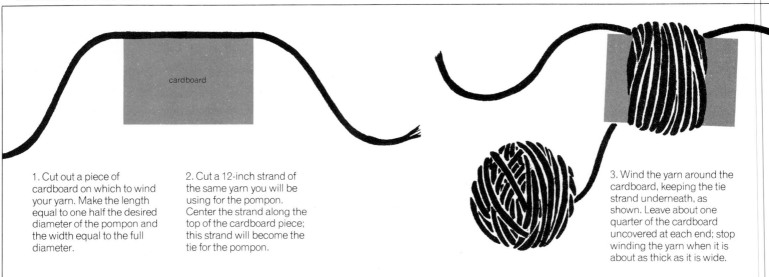

1. Cut out a piece of cardboard on which to wind your yarn. Make the length equal to one half the desired diameter of the pompon and the width equal to the full diameter.

2. Cut a 12-inch strand of the same yarn you will be using for the pompon. Center the strand along the top of the cardboard piece; this strand will become the tie for the pompon.

3. Wind the yarn around the cardboard, keeping the tie strand underneath, as shown. Leave about one quarter of the cardboard uncovered at each end; stop winding the yarn when it is about as thick as it is wide.

4. Knot the strand tightly over the wound yarn.

5. Cut off the excess yarn about 1/2 inch below the cardboard.

6. At the untied edge, insert the top blade of a pair of sharp scissors between the cardboard and the yarn. Cut along the edge and remove the cardboard.

7. To shape the yarn into a pompon, shake and fluff it out with your fingers. Trim off any overlong strands to create a smooth rounded shape.

8. Use the two ends of the strand to tie, sew or crochet the pompon to a garment.

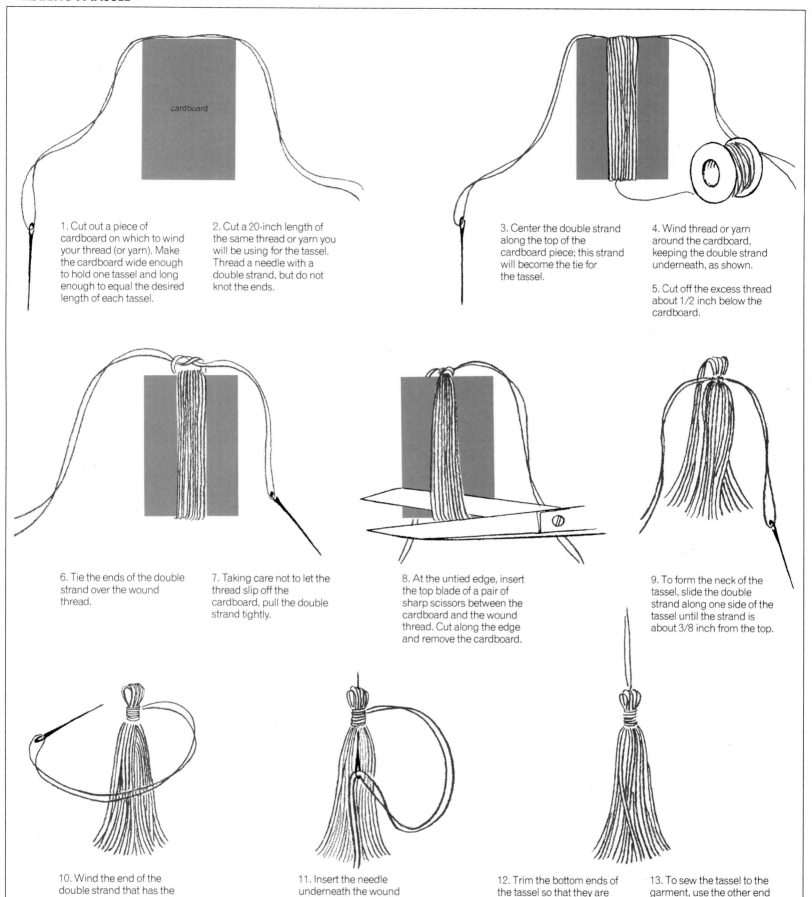

1. Cut out a piece of cardboard on which to wind your thread (or yarn). Make the cardboard wide enough to hold one tassel and long enough to equal the desired length of each tassel.

2. Cut a 20-inch length of the same thread or yarn you will be using for the tassel. Thread a needle with a double strand, but do not knot the ends.

3. Center the double strand along the top of the cardboard piece; this strand will become the tie for the tassel.

4. Wind thread or yarn around the cardboard, keeping the double strand underneath, as shown.

5. Cut off the excess thread about 1/2 inch below the cardboard.

6. Tie the ends of the double strand over the wound thread.

7. Taking care not to let the thread slip off the cardboard, pull the double strand tightly.

8. At the untied edge, insert the top blade of a pair of sharp scissors between the cardboard and the wound thread. Cut along the edge and remove the cardboard.

9. To form the neck of the tassel, slide the double strand along one side of the tassel until the strand is about 3/8 inch from the top.

10. Wind the end of the double strand that has the needle on it around the thread about five or six times.

11. Insert the needle underneath the wound strand, as shown. Then bring the needle up and out at the center top of the tassel. Pull the strand taut.

12. Trim the bottom ends of the tassel so that they are even. Make sure to cut the unwound ends of the double strand so that it becomes a part of the tassel.

13. To sew the tassel to the garment, use the other end of the double strand, with the needle still attached.

4
VARIATIONS ON AN EXOTIC SILHOUETTE

Extra triangles of fabric, to be added where indicated in this montage, lend flare to the basic T shape of Eastern garments.

More than a century ago Commodore Matthew Perry of the U.S. Navy sailed into Edo Bay, Japan, demanding to be warmly welcomed ashore by the isolationist rulers of the island empire. He succeeded in landing, and in the process got a glimpse of the kimonoed ladies of a city called Edo (present-day Tokyo). The blunt Perry sputtered his Victorian sense of distaste. Japanese kimonos, he said, were "an ungraceful

TRANSLATIONS OF THE BASIC T-SHAPE

drapery—with much of the undress look of dressing gowns."

How Perry could possibly call the kimono look "undressed" is baffling. A Japanese woman clad in a formal kimono is not only sheathed from neck to ankles in multiple layers of wrappings, but also is quite literally tied up in knots.

Just getting into a traditional kimono was an accomplishment. First a woman had to put on a white cotton vest and an underskirt that reached below the knees. Then she slipped into an ankle-length underkimono and tied it around her waist with a cord and sash. Next came the colorful outer kimono, which she wrapped left side over right side so tightly that she was hobbled at the knees.

Two additional cords were tied around the outer kimono—one below the waist and one above. An undersash concealed the cords and this in turn was hidden by the final outer sash, or obi. The obi—often of thick brocade, and always stiff—measured at least a foot in width and four to five yards in length. Taking a deep breath, the woman wound the obi around and around her waist before tying it in a fancy bow behind. For good measure she put a decorative cord, the *obijime,* over the obi.

No one lashed up in such an outfit could possibly be indecorous—as Perry's Japanese critics were quick to point out. They went on to suggest that Perry must have seen the kimonos he deplored in the dockside bordellos of Edo, where more casual styles seem to have prevailed.

Having served as the formal national costume for almost a thousand years, the kimono today has become a ceremonial costume even in Japan. The elaborate old style is prohibitively expensive (a Tokyo businessman recently paid $20,000 for his daughter's bridal kimono). And liberated young Japanese women refuse to wear such formal garb except for festivals, parties or weddings. On those occasions, though, almost everyone can still dress as regally as she pleases—in finery hired from Japan's thriving kimono rental shops.

While the traditional kimono has thus fallen into limited use, other versions of it have proliferated around the globe. Freed from its ties and sashes, the simplified kimono has become a smashingly attractive robe made primarily of two square-cut, T-shaped pieces of cloth. These are sewed together across the top and bottom of the cross-T's, except at the center, and down the outside edges of the stem. The center front is slit from top to bottom.

Perhaps because of its simplicity, this T shape on which the kimono was conceived is also the backbone of other exotic garments. Even before the kimono, a similar T-shaped garment, the caftan, appeared in Persia some 4,800 miles away.

The earliest version of the caftan originated in the Sixth Century B.C., during the reign of Cyrus the Great. Unlike the straight-cut kimono, the Persian T shape flared out at the hem to become a sort of floor-length A-line robe. Both men and women wore the robe open down the front, tying it around the waist with a soft cloth sash. This comfortable garment was standard dress for all the subject peoples of Cyrus' empire—a colossus that stretched west across Turkey, south to Egypt and eastward to India.

By the 18th Century wealthy Turkish women had turned the simple flowing caftan into a garment almost as cumbersome and formal as the obi-tied kimono. Those who could afford the richest raiment wore caftans of heavy brocaded silk, satin and velvet, bordered with furs and lavishly decorated with gold and silver embroidery. A French savant of the day with the grandiose appellation of Venture de Paradis was intrigued to discover Turkish women dragging themselves to parties weighted down by three or four golden caftans worn one on top of the other. According to his reports, these chic ladies were struggling under 60 pounds or more of extravagant attire.

Affluent Turkish, Lebanese and Egyptian women of today still wear caftans, usually as evening gowns. Unlike their predecessors, they commonsensically wear only one at a time, and these modern caftans are often made of fabrics light as air. The caftan is no longer popular as day wear in the Arab nations except in peasant villages and, curiously, among café waiters.

As with the kimono, the caftan's decline in popularity in the modern East has been matched by a surge of interest in the salons and boutiques of the West. Such designers as Halston, Victor Costa, Mollie Parnis and Oscar de la Renta have given the caftan some artful, dress-up touches such as sequins, starting a vogue for Middle Eastern wear of all kinds. De la Renta, and his wife Françoise, according to fashion reporters, not only clothe themselves in caftans but dress company in them too. ("All our guests will need for a visit is a toothbrush.")

In much the same stylish way, California's James Galanos has exploited the kimono look with wide-sleeved dresses of brilliant brocade. Couturier Hanae Mori, who designs in Tokyo for markets like Dallas' Neiman Marcus and Manhattan's Bergdorf Goodman, turns the kimono shape into floating chiffon evening gowns made up of layers in different colors, or of prints that depict Japanese landscapes. In such deft

hands both the kimono and the caftan are proving to be as graceful, comfortable and sexy as they are practical—just exotic enough to be fun.

Surprisingly, not everything labeled a caftan in a Western boutique springs from the Persian prototype. Over the centuries, as the caftan was adopted by the various cultures of the Arab world, changes occurred in both its names and its styling details. In the mountain regions in northwest Africa —where temperatures can plunge from 104° F. to −4° F. overnight—the robes are sewed from wool instead of cotton. (Wool insulates against the sun as well as keeping out the bone-chilling night air.) To suit this "cold country with a hot sun," as the Arabs call it, caftans are buttoned and often hooded; the resulting garment is called a djellaba, and adaptations of it have appeared at evening galas in the U.S.

When even the days grow cold, North Africans put another hooded garment over their robes—this one a long voluminous cape with hand slits instead of sleeves. Called a burnoose, the cape doubles as a blanket on the Bedouins' lonely treks. By contrast, the fashion world's adaptation is frequently cut from a loose-weave terry cloth and worn in summer as a beach robe.

Within this spectrum of styles, the one item of Arabian clothing that most designers pick to imitate for the boutique trade is the tobe. In North Africa, a tobe is an ankle-length, long-sleeved, T-shaped undergarment. Unlike a caftan, it opens only partway down the front, pulls over the head like a chemise and buttons like a shirt.

Designers from New York and Los Angeles, however, are neither the only nor the first non-Arabs to admire the tobe. A century ahead of the Americans, the West Africans of the Yoruba nation borrowed the tobe's upper half for their shirtlike, T-shaped dashiki. During the last decade the dashiki has ventured from West Africa to the U.S. and has become a fashionable symbol of cultural identity among black Americans. Curiously, it was U.S. Peace Corps volunteers who took the garment to East Africa in the 1960s. East Africans adopted it immediately and gave the dashiki a local twist by making it out of native fabrics.

In similar fashion, Western home seamstresses can turn dashikis and all their T-shaped relatives into clothes that are as intriguing and appropriate in Tucson as in Timbuktu. Within the basic outline itself, moreover, the individual elements lend themselves to an elegant range of variations. The caftan on pages 108-109, for example, flaunts the romantic trailing sleeves of its traditional Persian prototype, rather than the conveniently straight-cut ones worn today. And Western-style godets inserted from sleeve to hem add flourishes of extra fabric to the already enveloping skirts. With adaptions such as these—and others —the T shape holds fast to its fundamental simplicity, at the same time exuding an air of mystery that makes it exotic.

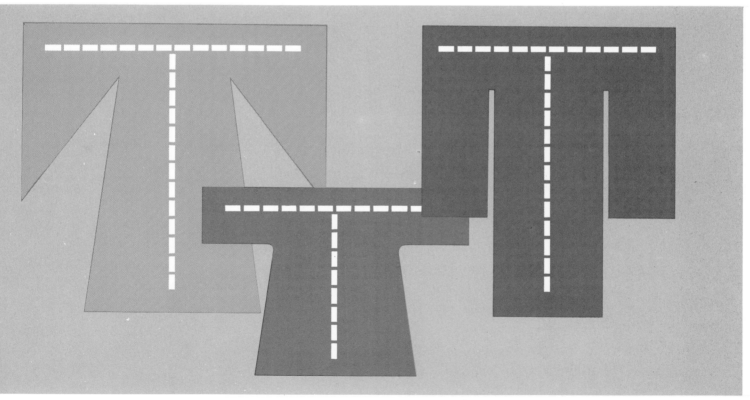

The ultrasimple T-shaped outline is the common denominator for the three most popular styles of exotic dress: the Arabian caftan, the African dashiki and the Japanese kimono. The caftan, at left above, is a floor-length robe—worn open or loosely tied—with long sleeves. The dashiki (center) is hip length with short sleeves. The classic kimono (right) has rectangular sleeves, and is worn tightly wrapped around the waist.

Adjusting a pattern to fit to a T

Few women's figures exactly match the dimensions on standard, printed patterns. So even with exotic styles such as the free-flowing kimonos, caftans and dashikis shown on the following pages the pattern must be carefully adjusted before any fabric is cut or a stitch sewed.

The first step is to trim all the pattern pieces on the cutting lines and press them flat with a warm iron. Then take your own measurements and compare them with those on the pattern envelope. Add or subtract the difference on the pattern pieces; do not try to estimate by holding the pattern up to your body.

To shorten or lengthen the vertical pattern pieces, first cut along the adjustment lines, as shown at right. Alterations in horizontal measurements, such as bustline and hips, are made next, on the side seam lines. These simple steps will ensure that the finished garment flows with proper liquid elegance.

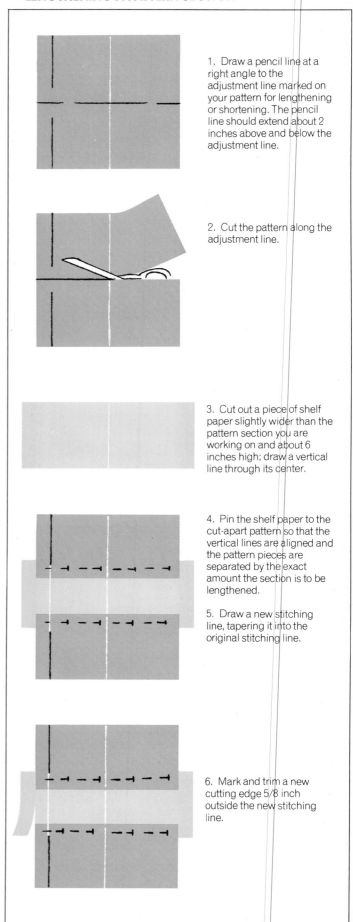

1. Draw a pencil line at a right angle to the adjustment line marked on your pattern for lengthening or shortening. The pencil line should extend about 2 inches above and below the adjustment line.

2. Cut the pattern along the adjustment line.

3. Cut out a piece of shelf paper slightly wider than the pattern section you are working on and about 6 inches high; draw a vertical line through its center.

4. Pin the shelf paper to the cut-apart pattern so that the vertical lines are aligned and the pattern pieces are separated by the exact amount the section is to be lengthened.

5. Draw a new stitching line, tapering it into the original stitching line.

6. Mark and trim a new cutting edge 5/8 inch outside the new stitching line.

SHORTENING A PATTERN SECTION

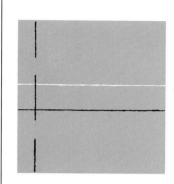

1. Draw a line above the adjustment line marked on your pattern for lengthening or shortening. The distance should be exactly equal to the amount the pattern section is to be shortened.

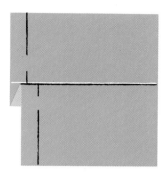

2. Fold the pattern so that the adjustment line meets the new line.

3. Press the fold flat with a warm iron.

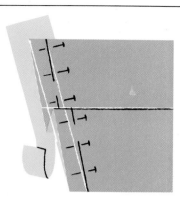

4. Pin a paper extension to your pattern.

5. Draw a new stitching line, tapering it into the original stitching line.

6. Mark and trim a new cutting edge 5/8 inch outside the new stitching line.

REDUCING A PATTERN SECTION

1. Divide the total amount to be reduced by the number of side seams on your garment. At the point where your pattern piece needs to be reduced, measure in from each stitching line and mark a distance equal to the resulting figure.

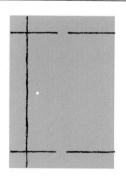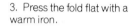

2. Draw a new stitching line, making a graduated curve from the point of reduction to the original stitching line.

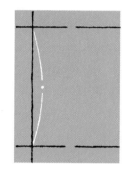

3. Mark and trim a new cutting edge 5/8 inch outside the new stitching line.

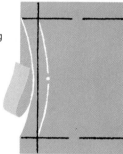

ENLARGING A PATTERN SECTION

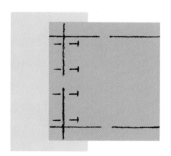

1. Lay your pattern piece on a strip of shelf paper cut to extend about 2 inches underneath the pattern and about 2 inches beyond the edge. Pin the pattern to the shelf paper.

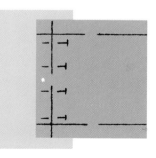

2. Divide the total amount to be enlarged by the number of side seams on your garment. At the point where your pattern piece needs to be enlarged, measure out from each stitching line and mark a distance equal to the resulting figure.

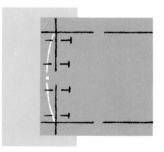

3. Draw a new tapered stitching line from the point of enlargement into the original stitching line.

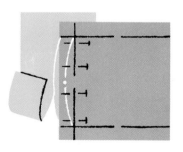

4. Mark and trim a new cutting edge 5/8 inch outside the new stitching line.

The doubly dazzling kimono

Japanese in name and tradition, the kimono is one of the ornaments of Oriental fashion. But in most Occidental wardrobes only its T-shaped outline survives in a not-so-elegant dressing gown of the same name.

The silken version shown at right and described overleaf is calculated to restore the kimono to its splendid potential. It is based on a standard Western kimono pattern (usually listed under "lingerie" in pattern catalogues), but has a number of deluxe features: added width for a luxurious flare, a contrasting contoured border, corded seams and a very long sash. Most notably, the garment is made reversible, creating two hostess gowns—one a brilliant print, the other a solid—for little more effort than making one would entail.

The printed and solid-colored sides will require 1/4 yard more fabric than called for in the base pattern; and the border and cording will take 2 yards of a third fabric. This version also requires nine yards of No. 12 size uncovered cording and 1/2 yard of interfacing fabric.

The Western-style kimono modeled here derives from the classic modes of Japan *(top)* and those of China *(lower left and far right).*

ADJUSTING THE PATTERN

A TAKING YOUR MEASUREMENTS

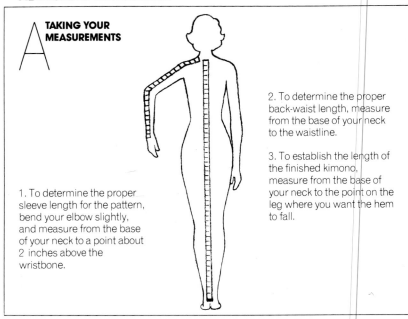

1. To determine the proper sleeve length for the pattern, bend your elbow slightly, and measure from the base of your neck to a point about 2 inches above the wristbone.

2. To determine the proper back-waist length, measure from the base of your neck to the waistline.

3. To establish the length of the finished kimono, measure from the base of your neck to the point on the leg where you want the hem to fall.

B MARKING THE HEMLINE

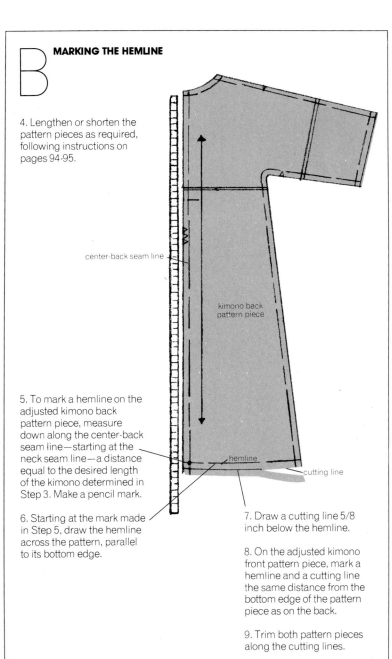

4. Lengthen or shorten the pattern pieces as required, following instructions on pages 94-95.

5. To mark a hemline on the adjusted kimono back pattern piece, measure down along the center-back seam line—starting at the neck seam line—a distance equal to the desired length of the kimono determined in Step 3. Make a pencil mark.

6. Starting at the mark made in Step 5, draw the hemline across the pattern, parallel to its bottom edge.

7. Draw a cutting line 5/8 inch below the hemline.

8. On the adjusted kimono front pattern piece, mark a hemline and a cutting line the same distance from the bottom edge of the pattern piece as on the back.

9. Trim both pattern pieces along the cutting lines.

C ADDING FLARE TO THE SIDES

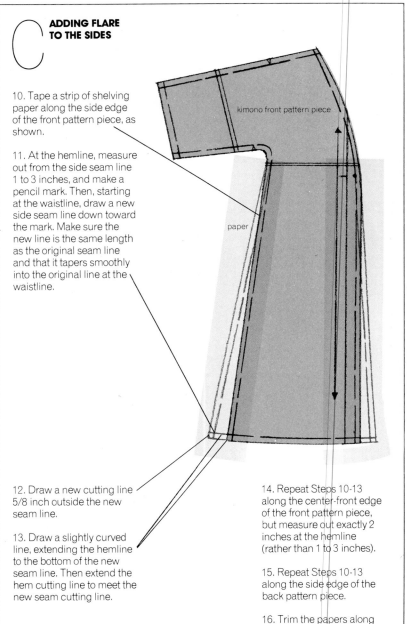

10. Tape a strip of shelving paper along the side edge of the front pattern piece, as shown.

11. At the hemline, measure out from the side seam line 1 to 3 inches, and make a pencil mark. Then, starting at the waistline, draw a new side seam line down toward the mark. Make sure the new line is the same length as the original seam line and that it tapers smoothly into the original line at the waistline.

12. Draw a new cutting line 5/8 inch outside the new seam line.

13. Draw a slightly curved line, extending the hemline to the bottom of the new seam line. Then extend the hem cutting line to meet the new seam cutting line.

14. Repeat Steps 10-13 along the center-front edge of the front pattern piece, but measure out exactly 2 inches at the hemline (rather than 1 to 3 inches).

15. Repeat Steps 10-13 along the side edge of the back pattern piece.

16. Trim the papers along the new cutting lines.

D ▸ MARKING THE BORDER LINES

17. Decide how wide you want the finished borders on the print-fabric side of the kimono to be—usually 1 1/2 to 2 inches.

18. On both the front and back pattern pieces, measure up from the hemline the desired width of the border, and draw a line parallel to the hemline. Then repeat along the sleeve hemlines. Use a colored pencil to distinguish the lines from other pencil lines.

19. On the front pattern piece, also draw a line the same distance from the front seam line. Then at the lower corner, draw a diagonal line between the intersection of the border lines and the intersection of the seam lines.

20. On the back pattern piece, also draw a line the same distance from the neck seam line, making sure to follow the neckline curve.

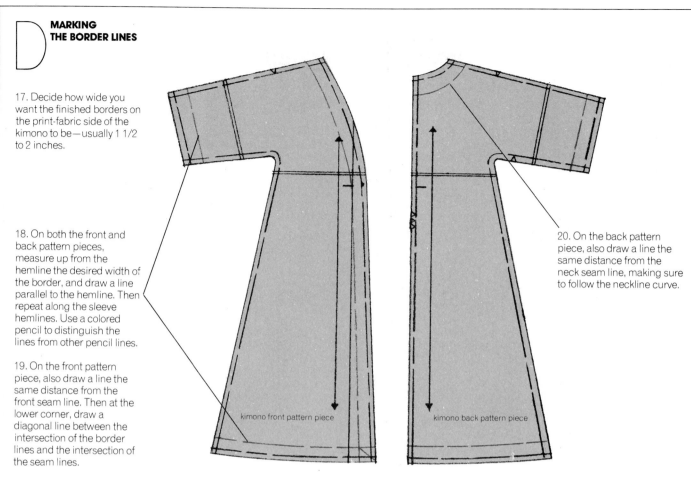

kimono front pattern piece

kimono back pattern piece

E ▸ RESTYLING THE FRONT BAND PATTERN INTO A COLLAR PATTERN

21. To determine the lower end of the collar on the long front band pattern piece, first measure the front garment pattern piece from the shoulder seam line to the waistline. Then on the band pattern piece, measure down from the shoulder marks (usually two dots) the same distance, and make a mark on one of the side seam lines.

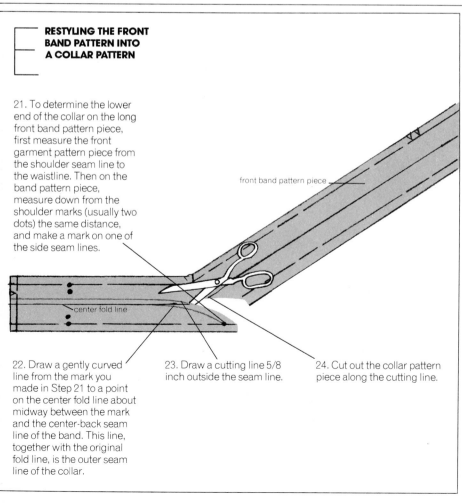

front band pattern piece

center fold line

22. Draw a gently curved line from the mark you made in Step 21 to a point on the center fold line about midway between the mark and the center-back seam line of the band. This line, together with the original fold line, is the outer seam line of the collar.

23. Draw a cutting line 5/8 inch outside the seam line.

24. Cut out the collar pattern piece along the cutting line.

CUTTING OUT AND MARKING THE REVERSIBLE KIMONO

A CUTTING OUT THE SOLID-COLORED FRONT, BACK AND COLLAR PIECES

45-INCH FABRIC WITH OR WITHOUT NAP

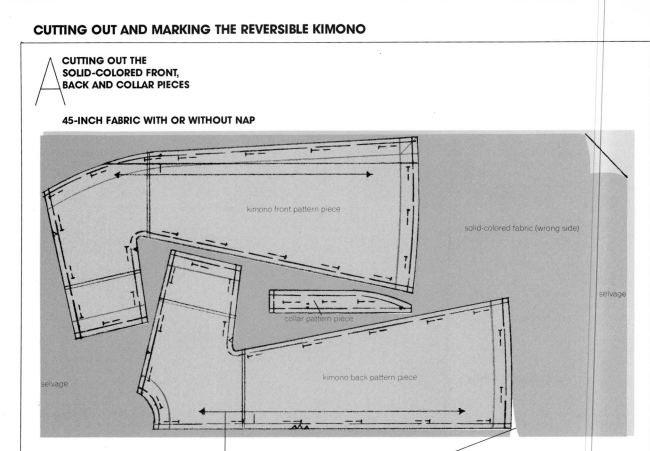

kimono front pattern piece

solid-colored fabric (wrong side)

selvage

collar pattern piece

selvage

kimono back pattern piece

1. Fold the fabric in half crosswise, so that the fold is at right angles to the selvages and the wrong sides are out.

2. If the fabric has nap, cut along the fold, and turn the top layer of fabric around so that its nap runs in the same direction as the bottom layer.

3. Arrange and pin the front, back and collar pattern pieces on the fabric, as shown. Make sure the grainline arrows on the front and back pieces—and the long straight edge on the collar piece—are parallel to the selvages. Leave as much space as possible at one end of the fabric for a sash to be cut out later.

4. Cut out the garment pieces.

5. Using dressmaker's carbon paper and a tracing wheel, transfer the pattern markings to the wrong side of both fabric thicknesses. On the collar pieces, make a 1/4-inch clip into the seam allowances at the shoulder mark.

6. Remove the patterns.

B MAKING THE PATTERN PIECES FOR THE BORDER AND THE PRINT-FABRIC FRONT AND BACK

7. Cut the front and back pattern pieces apart along the lines indicating the borders. This will give you separate pattern pieces for the borders and for the print-fabric fronts and back. Make sure to cut along the diagonal line, separating the front border from the front-hem border.

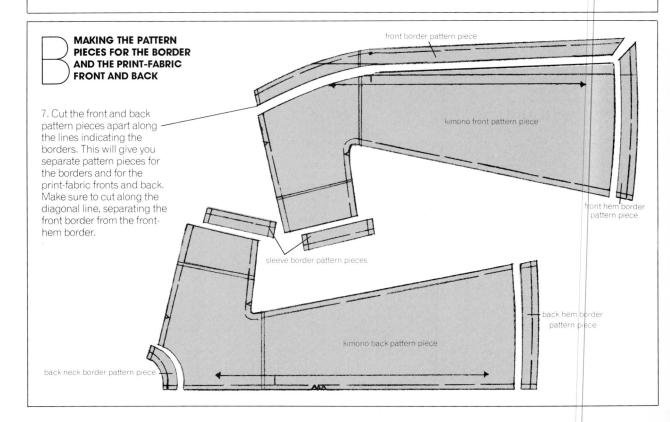

front border pattern piece

kimono front pattern piece

front hem border pattern piece

sleeve border pattern pieces

back hem border pattern piece

kimono back pattern piece

back neck border pattern piece

C CUTTING OUT THE PRINT FRONT, BACK AND COLLAR

ALL 45-INCH FABRICS

kimono front pattern piece

collar pattern piece

print fabric (wrong side)

selvage

selvage

kimono back pattern piece

8. Fold the fabric in half crosswise, so that the fold is at right angles to the selvages.

9. If you are working with a one-way design, cut along the fold, and turn the top layer of fabric around so that the design runs in the same direction as the bottom layer.

10. Arrange the front and back pattern pieces made in Box B as well as the original collar piece used in Box A on the fabric as shown.

11. Using chalk, mark new cutting lines 5/8 inch outside the edges of the front and back pieces—the edges from which the borders were cut.

12. Cut out the garment pieces along the cutting lines.

13. Transfer the pattern markings as you did on the solid-colored pieces in Step 5. To mark seam lines along the edges from which the borders were cut, trace directly on the cut edges.

14. Remove the patterns.

D CUTTING OUT THE BORDER PIECES

fabric (wrong side)

36- OR 45-INCH FABRIC WITH OR WITHOUT NAP

selvage

front border pattern piece

back hem border pattern piece

front hem border pattern piece

fabric (wrong side)

sleeve border pattern pieces

front hem border pattern piece

back neck border pattern piece

fold

fold

15. Fold the fabric in half lengthwise so that the selvages are together and the wrong side is out.

16. Place the front border pattern piece near the selvage, as shown, making sure the center-front line is parallel to the selvage. Pin the pattern piece in place.

17. Arrange the back neck border pattern piece near one end of the fabric, so that its center-back seam line is on the fold. Next to it, place the sleeve border pieces so that their upper seam lines are also on the fold. Pin the pattern pieces in place.

18. Place the back hem border pattern piece at the opposite end of the fabric so that its center-back seam line is on the fold of the fabric. Pin the pattern piece in place.

19. If the front hem border pattern piece will fit, arrange it next to the back hem border piece, with the center-front line parallel to the selvage. Pin. Otherwise, set it aside and cut it out separately, as shown at upper right.

20. Using chalk, mark new cutting lines 5/8 inch outside the edges along which the border pieces were cut.

21. Cut out the pieces along the cutting lines.

22. Transfer the pattern markings as you did on the print-fabric pieces in Step 13. To indicate the center back, make a mark on the upper edge of the back hem piece and make a small clip on the lower edge of the back neck piece.

ASSEMBLING THE REVERSIBLE KIMONO

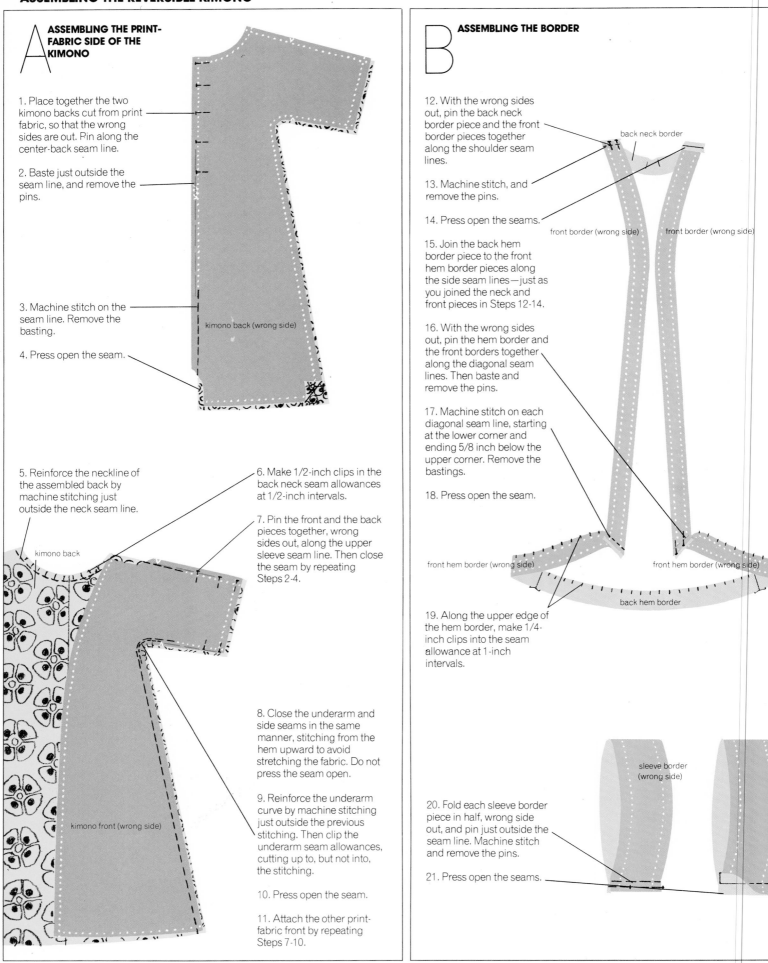

A ASSEMBLING THE PRINT-FABRIC SIDE OF THE KIMONO

1. Place together the two kimono backs cut from print fabric, so that the wrong sides are out. Pin along the center-back seam line.

2. Baste just outside the seam line, and remove the pins.

3. Machine stitch on the seam line. Remove the basting.

4. Press open the seam.

kimono back (wrong side)

5. Reinforce the neckline of the assembled back by machine stitching just outside the neck seam line.

kimono back

kimono front (wrong side)

6. Make 1/2-inch clips in the back neck seam allowances at 1/2-inch intervals.

7. Pin the front and the back pieces together, wrong sides out, along the upper sleeve seam line. Then close the seam by repeating Steps 2-4.

8. Close the underarm and side seams in the same manner, stitching from the hem upward to avoid stretching the fabric. Do not press the seam open.

9. Reinforce the underarm curve by machine stitching just outside the previous stitching. Then clip the underarm seam allowances, cutting up to, but not into, the stitching.

10. Press open the seam.

11. Attach the other print-fabric front by repeating Steps 7-10.

B ASSEMBLING THE BORDER

12. With the wrong sides out, pin the back neck border piece and the front border pieces together along the shoulder seam lines.

13. Machine stitch, and remove the pins.

14. Press open the seams.

back neck border

front border (wrong side)   front border (wrong side)

15. Join the back hem border piece to the front hem border pieces along the side seam lines—just as you joined the neck and front pieces in Steps 12-14.

16. With the wrong sides out, pin the hem border and the front borders together along the diagonal seam lines. Then baste and remove the pins.

17. Machine stitch on each diagonal seam line, starting at the lower corner and ending 5/8 inch below the upper corner. Remove the bastings.

18. Press open the seam.

front hem border (wrong side)   front hem border (wrong side)

back hem border

19. Along the upper edge of the hem border, make 1/4-inch clips into the seam allowance at 1-inch intervals.

sleeve border (wrong side)

20. Fold each sleeve border piece in half, wrong side out, and pin just outside the seam line. Machine stitch and remove the pins.

21. Press open the seams.

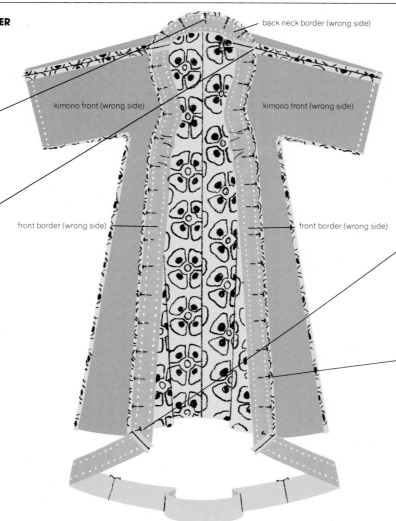

22. With the wrong sides out, pin the back neck border to the print-fabric kimono back along the neck seam line. Begin by matching the center-back mark on the border with the center-back seam on the kimono back.

23. Match the shoulder seams and pin. Then pin the rest of the back neckline at 1/2-inch intervals.

24. Next, pin at each lower front corner, matching the diagonal seam of the front border piece with the intersection of the front and hem seam lines on the kimono front.

25. Working up from the hem, pin the front borders to the kimono fronts along the seam lines. Be careful not to stretch the edges of the border as you pin.

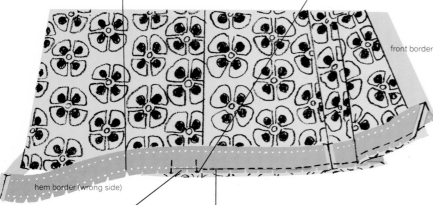

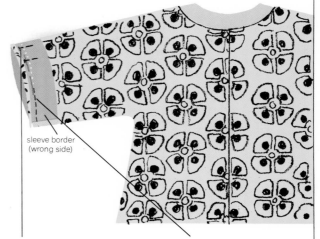

26. Turn the kimono right side out. Place the hem border wrong side up on the kimono, and align the seam lines.

27. Match the side seams and pin.

28. Match the center-back mark on the border with the center-back seam of the kimono and pin. Then pin along the seam line.

29. Baste just outside the seam line all around the border. Remove the pins.

30. Starting and ending at the center-back hem, machine stitch the border to the kimono on the seam lines. When you reach the front corner, pivot (*Appendix*), and turn up the border as shown, before you continue stitching. Remove the basting.

31. Press the seam toward the border—away from the kimono.

32. Pin the sleeve borders and the kimono sleeves together, wrong sides out, matching the seams on the borders with the underarm seams of the kimono. Then baste and remove the pins.

33. Machine stitch and remove the bastings. Turn the borders away from the sleeves. Press the seams toward the borders.

continued

ASSEMBLING THE SOLID-COLORED SIDE OF THE KIMONO

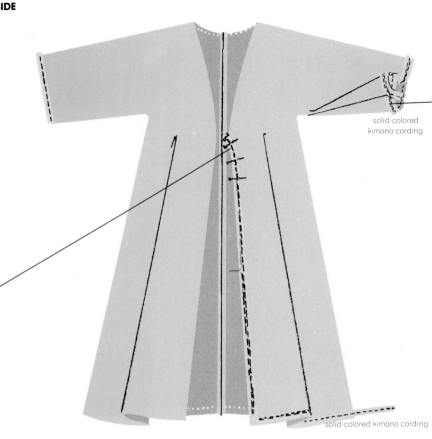

34. Join together the kimono fronts and backs cut from solid-colored fabric just as you did the print-fabric kimono *(Steps 1-13)*, but do not stitch or clip the back neckline.

35. Measure the neck, front, hem and sleeve edges of the assembled solid-colored kimono. Then, using the remaining border fabric, make a length of cording equal to the total measurement plus 7 inches, following the instructions on pages 71-72, Boxes A-C.

36. Attach cording along the front and hem edges of the solid-colored kimono, following instructions for attaching cording on page 72, Steps 18-32. Begin and end at the waistline marks on the front edges. Do not attach cording along the neckline.

37. Attach cording to each sleeve edge in the same manner, beginning and ending at the underarm seam. To finish the ends of the cording, cross them and turn them away from the garment, so that they will be concealed when the sleeve seam is closed.

solid-colored kimono cording

solid-colored kimono cording

ASSEMBLING THE COLLAR

38. Cut out two interfacing pieces for the collar, using the collar pattern piece. With dressmaker's carbon paper and a tracing wheel, transfer all pattern markings.

39. Pin an interfacing piece to the wrong side of a solid-colored collar piece, and align the edges.

40. Baste the pieces together just outside the seam lines, and remove the pins.

41. Baste interfacing to the other solid-colored collar piece by repeating Steps 39 and 40.

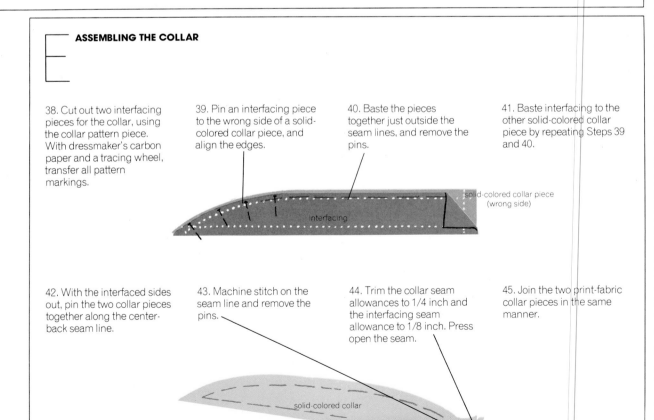

interfacing

solid-colored collar piece (wrong side)

42. With the interfaced sides out, pin the two collar pieces together along the center-back seam line.

43. Machine stitch on the seam line and remove the pins.

44. Trim the collar seam allowances to 1/4 inch and the interfacing seam allowance to 1/8 inch. Press open the seam.

45. Join the two print-fabric collar pieces in the same manner.

solid-colored collar

interfacing

F | FINISHING THE COLLAR

46. Attach cording along the curved outer edge of the solid-colored collar, and then attach the print-fabric collar, following the instructions on page 72, Steps 18-32.

47. Trim the interfacing very close to the stitching, and trim the collar seam allowances to 1/4 inch.

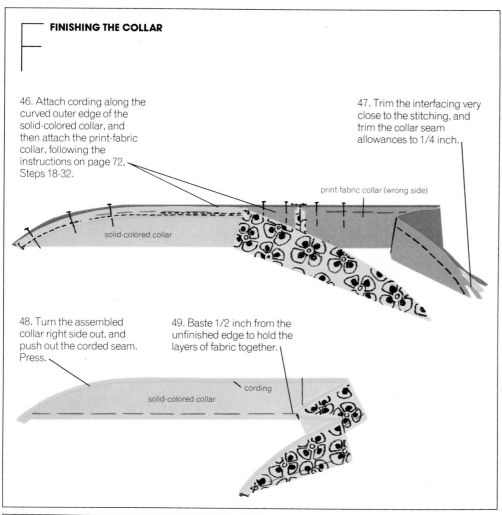

print-fabric collar (wrong side)

solid-colored collar

48. Turn the assembled collar right side out, and push out the corded seam. Press.

49. Baste 1/2 inch from the unfinished edge to hold the layers of fabric together.

solid-colored collar

cording

G | ATTACHING THE COLLAR TO THE SOLID-COLORED SIDE OF THE KIMONO

50. With the solid-colored kimono turned right side out, place the assembled collar, print side up, on it, and align the neck seam lines. Match the center-back seams, and pin.

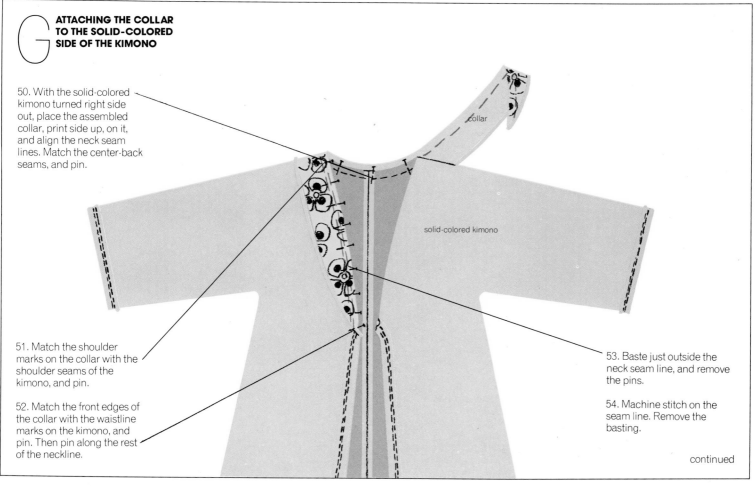

collar

solid-colored kimono

51. Match the shoulder marks on the collar with the shoulder seams of the kimono, and pin.

52. Match the front edges of the collar with the waistline marks on the kimono, and pin. Then pin along the rest of the neckline.

53. Baste just outside the neck seam line, and remove the pins.

54. Machine stitch on the seam line. Remove the basting.

continued

JOINING THE PRINT AND SOLID-COLORED SIDES

55. Turn the print-fabric kimono wrong side out, and insert the solid-colored kimono inside it.

56. Align the stitching lines on the neck, front and hem edges, and pin along them, matching the seams and any pattern markings.

57. Baste along the edges and remove the pins.

58. Using a zipper foot, machine stitch as close as possible to the cording. Begin at a point on the back hem and end about 10 inches from the starting point, leaving an opening that will be used to turn the garment right side out. Remove the basting.

59. Trim the seam allowances to 1/4 inch, and cut the corners diagonally.

60. Clip the neckline seam allowances at 1/2- to 1-inch intervals, cutting up to, but not into, the stitching.

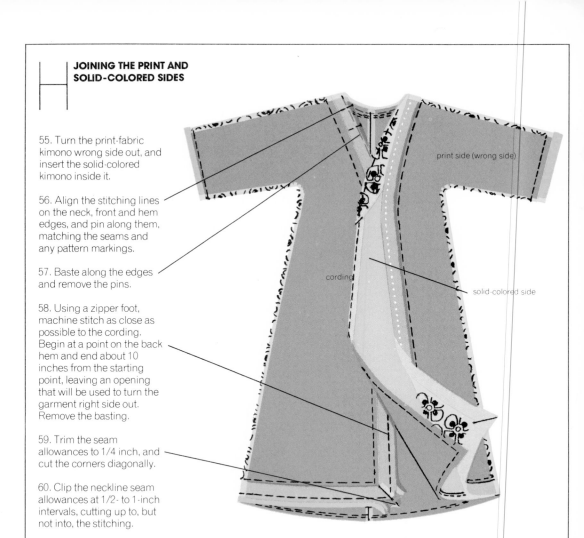

FINISHING THE REVERSIBLE KIMONO

61. Turn the kimono right side out through the back hem opening. Then lay it on a flat surface with the print-fabric side facing up.

62. Push out the corded front and hem edges. Press.

63. On the solid-colored sleeve hems—which are now inside the garment —fold over the corded seam allowances as shown, and press.

64. Turn under the hem allowance of the border strip that is attached to the print-fabric sleeve and align it with the corded edge of the solid-colored sleeve. Pin.

65. Slip stitch (Appendix) the folded border edge to the cording, and remove the pins. Press.

66. Close the opening in the hem in the same manner.

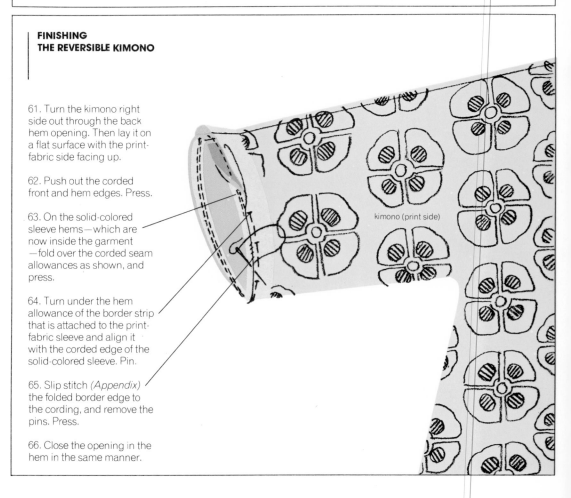

MAKING A SASH FOR THE KIMONO

A CUTTING OUT THE SASH

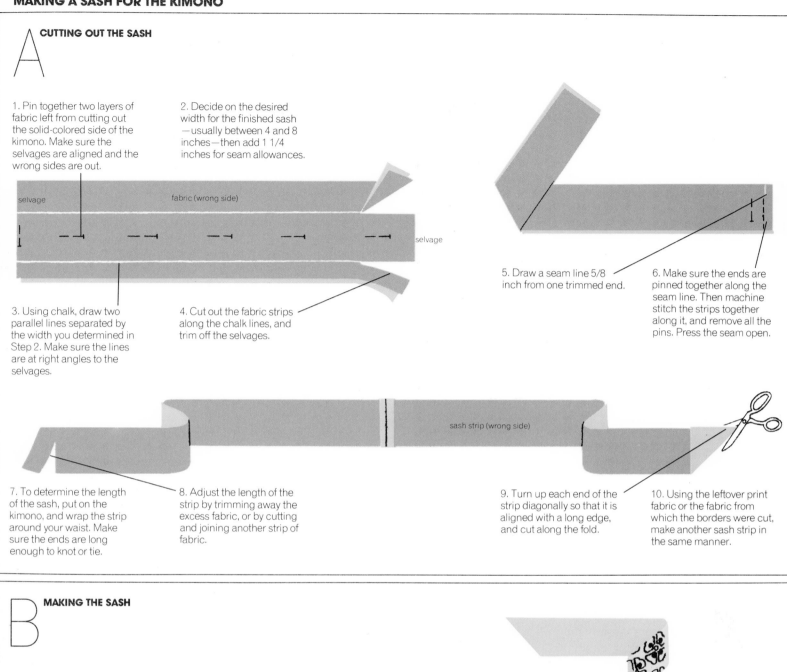

1. Pin together two layers of fabric left from cutting out the solid-colored side of the kimono. Make sure the selvages are aligned and the wrong sides are out.

2. Decide on the desired width for the finished sash —usually between 4 and 8 inches—then add 1 1/4 inches for seam allowances.

selvage

fabric (wrong side)

selvage

5. Draw a seam line 5/8 inch from one trimmed end.

6. Make sure the ends are pinned together along the seam line. Then machine stitch the strips together along it, and remove all the pins. Press the seam open.

3. Using chalk, draw two parallel lines separated by the width you determined in Step 2. Make sure the lines are at right angles to the selvages.

4. Cut out the fabric strips along the chalk lines, and trim off the selvages.

sash strip (wrong side)

7. To determine the length of the sash, put on the kimono, and wrap the strip around your waist. Make sure the ends are long enough to knot or tie.

8. Adjust the length of the strip by trimming away the excess fabric, or by cutting and joining another strip of fabric.

9. Turn up each end of the strip diagonally so that it is aligned with a long edge, and cut along the fold.

10. Using the leftover print fabric or the fabric from which the borders were cut, make another sash strip in the same manner.

B MAKING THE SASH

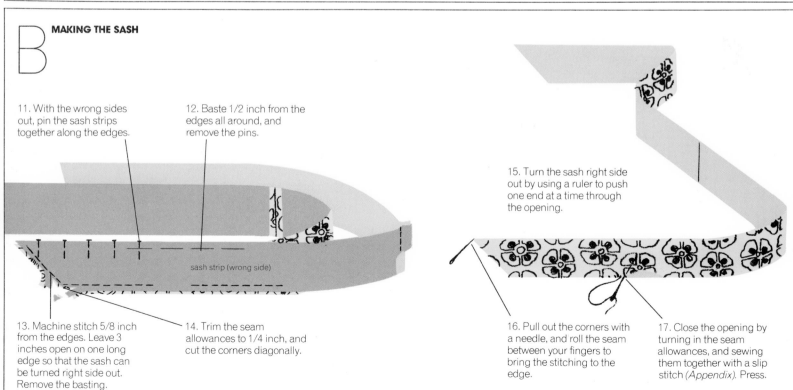

11. With the wrong sides out, pin the sash strips together along the edges.

12. Baste 1/2 inch from the edges all around, and remove the pins.

15. Turn the sash right side out by using a ruler to push one end at a time through the opening.

sash strip (wrong side)

13. Machine stitch 5/8 inch from the edges. Leave 3 inches open on one long edge so that the sash can be turned right side out. Remove the basting.

14. Trim the seam allowances to 1/4 inch, and cut the corners diagonally.

16. Pull out the corners with a needle, and roll the seam between your fingers to bring the stitching to the edge.

17. Close the opening by turning in the seam allowances, and sewing them together with a slip stitch (Appendix). Press.

The flowing elegance of the caftan

The caftan shown here is resplendent in three silks and, with its exotic details, conjures up visions of mysteriously veiled Bedouin charmers. Its distinguishing features—the contrasting side panels, the cord-trimmed yoke and the wide-winged sleeves—are not, however, those of any particular Arab people but a pleasing combination of several vigorous traditions.

This handsome garment begins with a simple commercial caftan pattern—one that is designed with the sleeves cut as one with the bodice. Even though the sleeves and body will ultimately be made separately and of different fabrics, this design provides certain interim guides needed to cut out the new version. In addition the pattern must include a neckline with a front slit.

If the base pattern has features not seen on the gown at right—such as a front zipper or sleeves of a different shape—these will not matter. Directions for eliminating such elements are included in the instructions that begin overleaf.

A modern version of the many-faceted caftan distills ideas from an array of traditional Middle Eastern garments *(background)*.

MAKING THE PATTERN

A TAKING BODY MEASUREMENTS

1. To determine the proper shoulder width for the pattern, measure from the base of your neck to the shoulder bone.

2. To determine the proper sleeve length, bend your elbow slightly, and measure along the outside of the arm from the shoulder bone to a point about 3 inches above the wristbone.

3. To establish the length of the finished caftan, measure from the top of your spine to the point on the leg where you want the hem to fall.

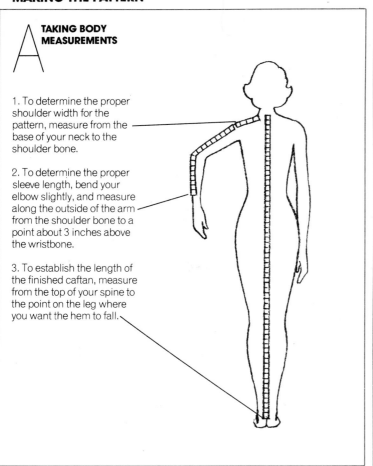

B TRACING THE BASIC PATTERN PIECE FOR THE CAFTAN FRONT

4. Lengthen or shorten the basic pattern piece for the caftan front as required, following the instructions on pages 94-95. Do not adjust the sleeve length.

5. Tape together two large sheets of brown wrapping paper and pin the caftan front pattern piece to the paper. Make sure that the center-front seam line of the pattern is parallel to one long edge of the paper.

6. Measure up from the bottom edge of the pattern piece a distance equal to the hem allowance provided by your pattern, and indicate the hemline with a series of pencil marks.

7. Using a tracing wheel and dressmaker's carbon paper, transfer the hemline and all seam lines onto the brown paper.

8. Transfer the large dot on the center front indicating the base of the neck slit.

9. Remove the pattern piece.

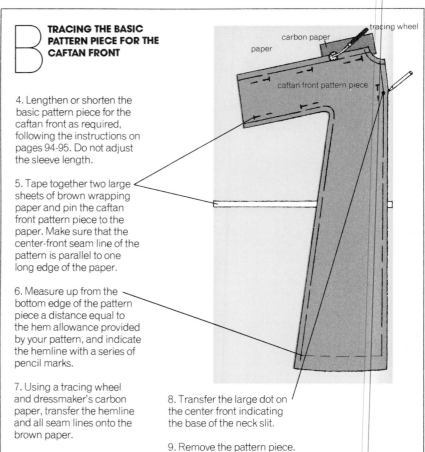

tracing wheel
carbon paper
paper
caftan front pattern piece

C RESHAPING THE SLEEVE

10. To mark the new shoulder seam line, start at the neck edge, and draw a straight line the length of your shoulder width, as measured in Step 1. Make the line perpendicular to the long edges of the paper, so that it will be perpendicular to the center-front fold line of the pattern; make a dot at the end of the line.

11. To mark the new upper sleeve seam line, extend the new shoulder line a distance equal to your sleeve length, as measured in Step 2.

12. To mark the new armhole seam line, connect the shoulder dot made in Step 10 with the side seam at a point just below the underarm curve.

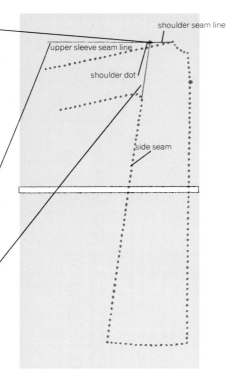

shoulder seam line
upper sleeve seam line
shoulder dot
side seam

13. To mark the new sleeve hemline, start at the outer end of the upper sleeve seam line and draw a line at a right angle to it. Make the line equal to one half of the body length measurement obtained in Step 3.

14. To mark the new lower sleeve seam line, connect the bottom of the new sleeve hemline with the new armhole seam line. Make sure that the new line passes through the center of the underarm curve, and mark the point where the new line intersects the armhole seam line with a large dot.

15. Mark the new armhole seam line, midway between the upper and lower sleeve seam lines; this mark will serve as a notch when you assemble the garment.

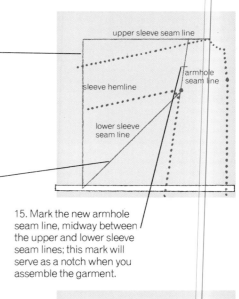

upper sleeve seam line
armhole seam line
sleeve hemline
lower sleeve seam line

16. To mark the new sleeve opening, make a dot on the sleeve hemline 10 inches below the upper sleeve line.

17. Draw a grain-line arrow on the sleeve section parallel to the sleeve hemline.

18. Label the sleeve front section.

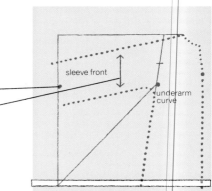

sleeve front
underarm curve

D ADDING A YOKE

19. To establish the outer edge of the yoke, make a mark on the new shoulder line 1 1/2 inches out from the neckline.

20. To determine the depth of the yoke, make a mark on the center-front line 2 inches below the dot made in Step 8, designating the bottom of the neckline slit.

21. Position an L square so that one edge is on the mark made in Step 19 and the other edge is on the mark made in Step 20. Make sure the vertical edge is parallel to the long edge of the paper.

22. Make a mark 1/2 inch in from the corner of the L square as shown.

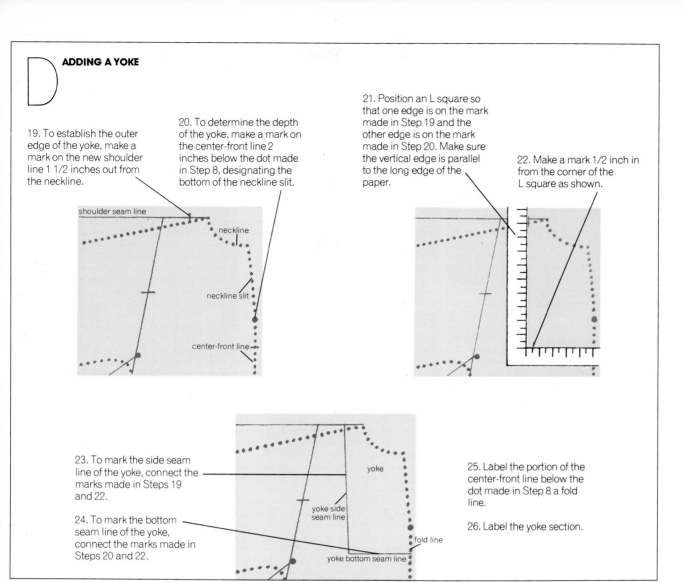

shoulder seam line
neckline
neckline slit
center-front line

23. To mark the side seam line of the yoke, connect the marks made in Steps 19 and 22.

24. To mark the bottom seam line of the yoke, connect the marks made in Steps 20 and 22.

yoke
yoke side seam line
yoke bottom seam line
fold line

25. Label the portion of the center-front line below the dot made in Step 8 a fold line.

26. Label the yoke section.

E ADDING A GODET

27. Measure the hemline from the center-front line to the side seam line, and divide by four.

28. Measure in from the side seam line a distance equal to that obtained in the preceding step, and make a mark on the hemline.

29. Then measure out from the side seam line the same distance, and make another mark.

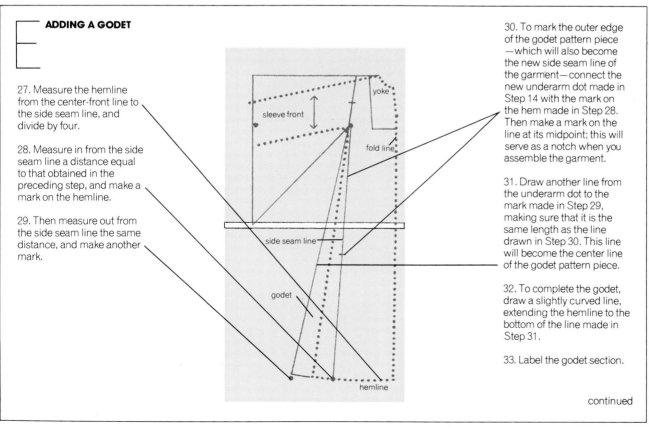

sleeve front
yoke
fold line
side seam line
godet
hemline

30. To mark the outer edge of the godet pattern piece —which will also become the new side seam line of the garment—connect the new underarm dot made in Step 14 with the mark on the hem made in Step 28. Then make a mark on the line at its midpoint; this will serve as a notch when you assemble the garment.

31. Draw another line from the underarm dot to the mark made in Step 29, making sure that it is the same length as the line drawn in Step 30. This line will become the center line of the godet pattern piece.

32. To complete the godet, draw a slightly curved line, extending the hemline to the bottom of the line made in Step 31.

33. Label the godet section.

continued

F CUTTING OUT THE PATTERN PIECES FOR THE CAFTAN FRONT

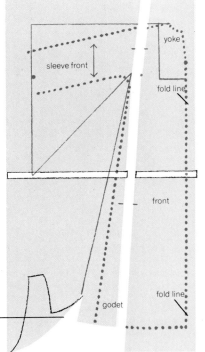

34. Label the front body piece and the center-front fold line.

35. Cut out the new pattern pieces—the front body piece, the sleeve and the godet. Do not separate the yoke section from the front body section.

G TRACING THE PATTERN PIECES FOR THE CAFTAN BACK

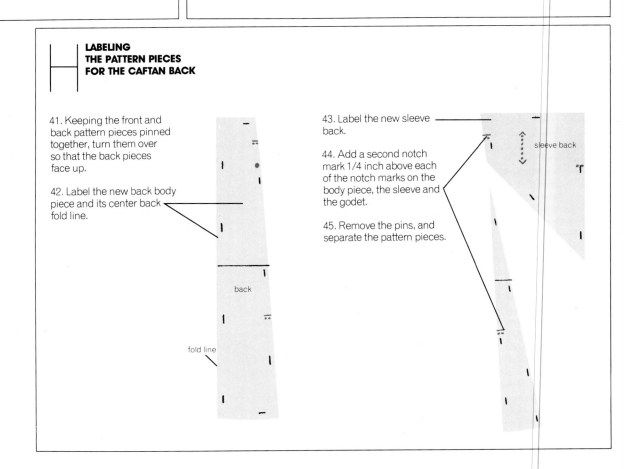

36. Tape together two large sheets of paper, as in Step 5.

37. Arrange the pattern pieces, cut out in Step 35 for the front half of the caftan, on the paper. Pin in place.

38. To square off the center back at the neckline edge, position an L square so that one edge is aligned with the center fold line below the dot indicating the front neckline slit—then align the other edge with the shoulder seam line. Trace along both edges to form new cutting lines.

39. Cut out all pattern pieces.

40. Using a tracing wheel and dressmaker's carbon paper, transfer the following markings from the pattern pieces for the caftan front to the newly cutout pattern pieces for the caftan back: the grain-line arrow, the dot indicating the sleeve opening, the underarm dot and all notches.

H LABELING THE PATTERN PIECES FOR THE CAFTAN BACK

41. Keeping the front and back pattern pieces pinned together, turn them over so that the back pieces face up.

42. Label the new back body piece and its center back fold line.

43. Label the new sleeve back.

44. Add a second notch mark 1/4 inch above each of the notch marks on the body piece, the sleeve and the godet.

45. Remove the pins, and separate the pattern pieces.

FINISHING THE PATTERN PIECE FOR THE CAFTAN BACK

46. Lay the new pattern piece for the back body section, marked side up, on a flat surface. Over it lay the back pattern piece that came with your purchased pattern. Align the center-back lines of both patterns. Make sure the intersection of the neck and shoulder seam lines on the commercial pattern aligns with the shoulder edge of the new pattern piece as shown. Pin.

47. Using a tracing wheel and dressmaker's carbon paper, transfer the neck seam-line marking from the commercial pattern to the new one.

48. Separate the patterns, and cut along the line made in the preceding step.

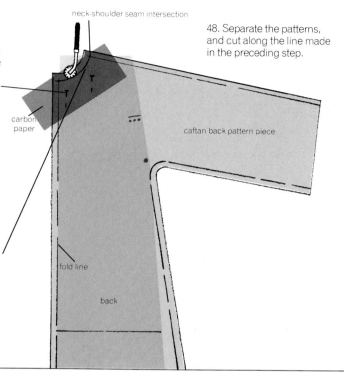

neck-shoulder seam intersection

carbon paper

caftan back pattern piece

fold line

back

FINISHING THE PATTERN FOR THE YOKE

49. Cut out the yoke from the front body piece, following the markings made in Steps 19-24.

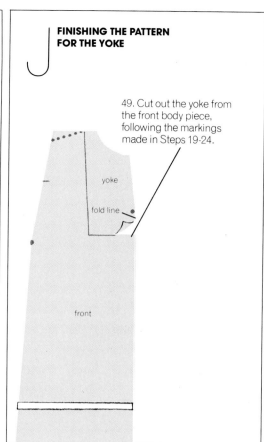

yoke

fold line

front

FINISHING THE PATTERN FOR THE GODETS

50. Tape the godet pieces together along their center lines made in Step 31.

51. Draw a grain-line arrow parallel to the center line.

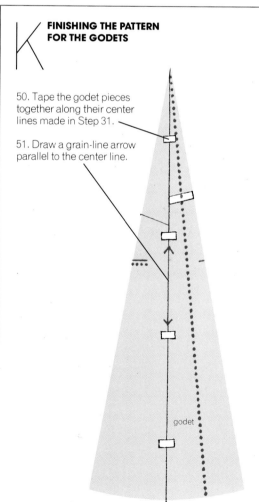

godet

MAKING THE PATTERN FOR THE NECK FACING

52. Pin a piece of tracing paper over the neck area of the new back pattern piece.

53. Trace the neckline edge.

54. Trace the center-back fold line from the neck to a point 1 1/2 inches below it.

55. Trace the shoulder line from the neckline edge to a point 1 1/2 inches outside of it.

56. Connect the lower ends of the lines drawn in Steps 54 and 55 with a curved line parallel to the neck edge.

57. Remove the pins, and cut out the back neck facing pattern piece.

58. Label the fold line.

59. Label the back neck facing pattern piece.

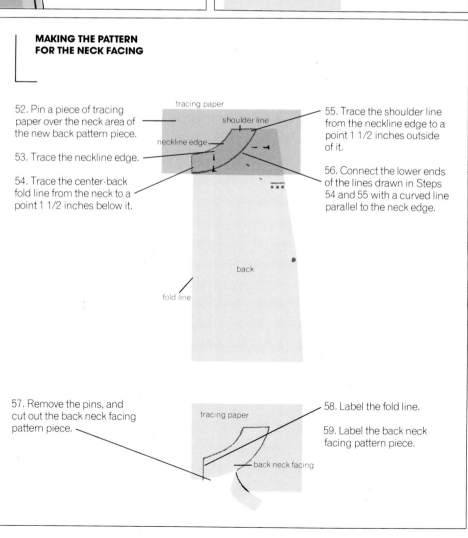

tracing paper

shoulder line

neckline edge

back

fold line

tracing paper

back neck facing

DETERMINING FABRIC REQUIREMENTS

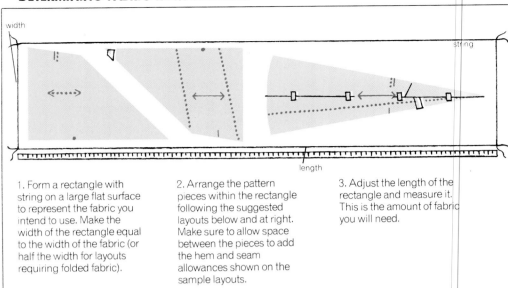

1. Form a rectangle with string on a large flat surface to represent the fabric you intend to use. Make the width of the rectangle equal to the width of the fabric (or half the width for layouts requiring folded fabric).

2. Arrange the pattern pieces within the rectangle following the suggested layouts below and at right. Make sure to allow space between the pieces to add the hem and seam allowances shown on the sample layouts.

3. Adjust the length of the rectangle and measure it. This is the amount of fabric you will need.

CUTTING OUT AND MARKING THE CAFTAN

A | THE CAFTAN FRONT AND BACK

36- OR 45-INCH FABRIC WITH OR WITHOUT A ONE-WAY DESIGN

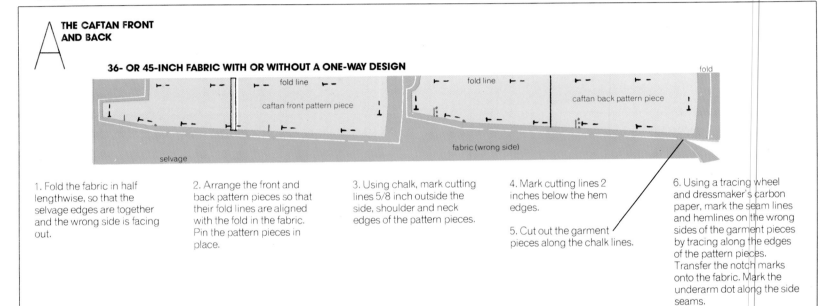

1. Fold the fabric in half lengthwise, so that the selvage edges are together and the wrong side is facing out.

2. Arrange the front and back pattern pieces so that their fold lines are aligned with the fold in the fabric. Pin the pattern pieces in place.

3. Using chalk, mark cutting lines 5/8 inch outside the side, shoulder and neck edges of the pattern pieces.

4. Mark cutting lines 2 inches below the hem edges.

5. Cut out the garment pieces along the chalk lines.

6. Using a tracing wheel and dressmaker's carbon paper, mark the seam lines and hemlines on the wrong sides of the garment pieces by tracing along the edges of the pattern pieces. Transfer the notch marks onto the fabric. Mark the underarm dot along the side seams.

B | THE YOKE AND BACK NECK FACING

36- OR 45-INCH FABRIC WITH OR WITHOUT A ONE-WAY DESIGN

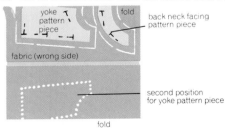

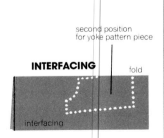

7. Lay the fabric wrong side down on a flat surface. Fold up both selvage edges, so that they meet in the center, forming a double layer of fabric.

8. Arrange the yoke and back neck facing pattern pieces so that their fold lines are on one of the folds in the fabric. Pin in place.

9. Using chalk, mark cutting lines 5/8 inch outside all edges of the pattern pieces except the center-front slit.

10. Cut out the pieces along the chalk lines.

11. Mark the seam lines as you did in Step 6. Make sure to transfer the seam lines for the front slit.

12. Remove the pins. Turn the yoke pattern piece over and reposition it along the other fold, as indicated by the dotted lines. Then mark and cut the facing for the yoke as you did the yoke in Steps 9-11.

13. To make the interfacing for the yoke, fold a piece of interfacing fabric in half and use the yoke pattern piece to mark and cut the interfacing piece as you did the yoke in Steps 8-11.

45-INCH FABRIC WITHOUT A ONE-WAY DESIGN

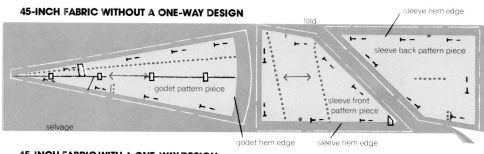

45-INCH FABRIC WITH A ONE-WAY DESIGN

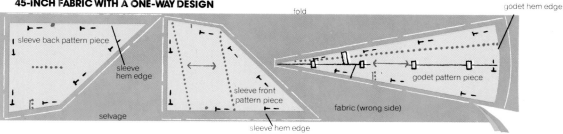

14A. Fold the fabric in half lengthwise so that the selvage edges are together and the wrong side is out.

15A. Arrange the sleeve and godet pattern pieces on the fabric, as shown. Make sure the grain-line arrows are parallel to the selvages. Pin the pattern pieces in place.

16A. Using chalk, mark a cutting line 2 inches below the hem edge of the godet pattern piece.

17A. Mark 1 1/4 inches outside the hem edges of the sleeve pattern pieces.

18A. Mark cutting lines 5/8 inch outside the remaining edges of the pattern pieces.

19A. Cut out the garment pieces along the chalk lines.

20A. Mark the seam lines, hemlines, and notches on the sleeve and godet pieces as you did on the caftan front and back pieces in Step 6. Transfer the sleeve opening dot on the sleeve hemline.

36-INCH FABRIC WITHOUT A ONE-WAY DESIGN

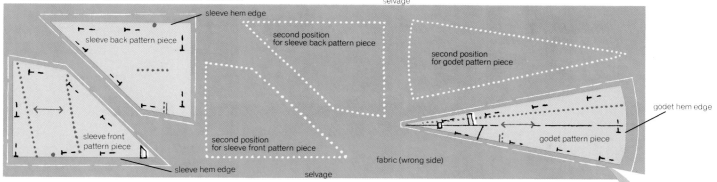

36-INCH FABRIC WITH A ONE-WAY DESIGN

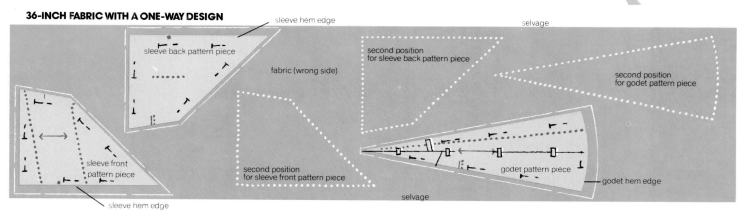

14B. Lay the fabric wrong side down on a flat surface.

15B. Arrange the sleeve and godet pattern pieces on the fabric, as shown. Make sure the grain-line arrows are parallel to the selvages. Pin the pattern pieces in place.

16B-19B. Follow Steps 16A-19A (above). This time mark only the wrong side of the single layer of fabric.

20B. Remove the pins. Turn the pattern pieces over and reposition them on the fabric as indicated by the dotted lines. Then repeat Steps 15B-19B.

ASSEMBLING THE CAFTAN

A PREPARING THE CAFTAN FRONT FOR THE YOKE

1. To reinforce the lower corners of the yoke opening, machine stitch along the seam lines, starting and ending about 1 inch from the corner.

2. Make a diagonal clip at each corner, cutting up to but not into the stitching.

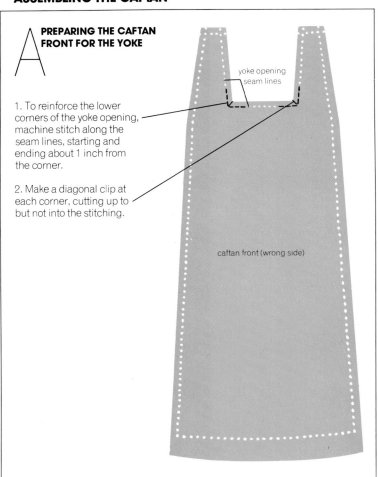

yoke opening seam lines

caftan front (wrong side)

B PREPARING THE YOKE

3. Lay the yoke wrong side up on a flat surface. Place the yoke interfacing, marked side up, over it. Pin.

4. Baste just outside the seam lines, including the slit seam lines. Remove the pins.

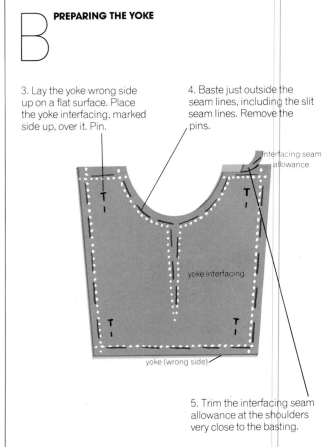

interfacing seam allowance

yoke interfacing

yoke (wrong side)

5. Trim the interfacing seam allowance at the shoulders very close to the basting.

C ATTACHING THE YOKE

6. Place the yoke piece in the yoke opening on the caftan front piece, matching the side and bottom seam lines, as shown.

7. At each lower corner, match the points where the side and bottom seam lines intersect, and insert two pins. The pins should cross each other so that one is along the side seam line and one is along the bottom seam line.

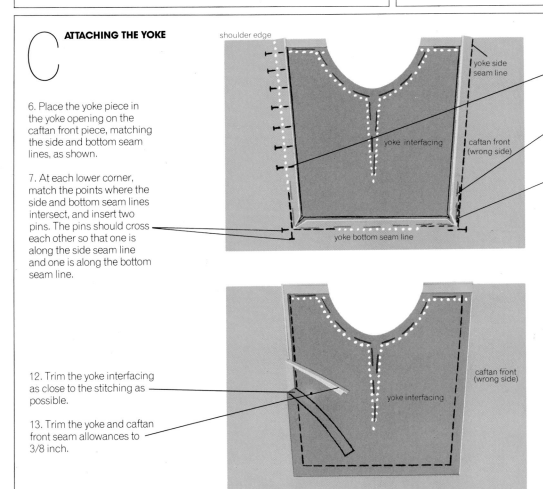

shoulder edge

yoke side seam line

yoke interfacing

caftan front (wrong side)

yoke bottom seam line

8. Match and pin along the side seam lines, and then along the bottom seam line.

9. Baste, then remove the pins except for the crossed ones in each corner.

10. Machine stitch along one of the side seam lines. When you reach the pin, remove it and continue stitching to the corner.

11. At the corner, pivot (Appendix) and remove the other pin. Stitch across the bottom seam line. Sew around the other corner in the same manner. Then stitch the other side seam line. Remove the basting.

12. Trim the yoke interfacing as close to the stitching as possible.

13. Trim the yoke and caftan front seam allowances to 3/8 inch.

yoke interfacing

caftan front (wrong side)

14. Press the seam allowances away from the yoke.

D | CLOSING THE SHOULDER SEAMS

15. Place the caftan front and back pieces together with the wrong sides out. Match the shoulder seam lines and pin.

16. Baste just outside the seam lines, and remove the pins.

17. Machine stitch, and remove the basting.

18. Press open the seams.

19. Finish the raw edges by making a machine zigzag stitch along them or by trimming them with pinking shears.

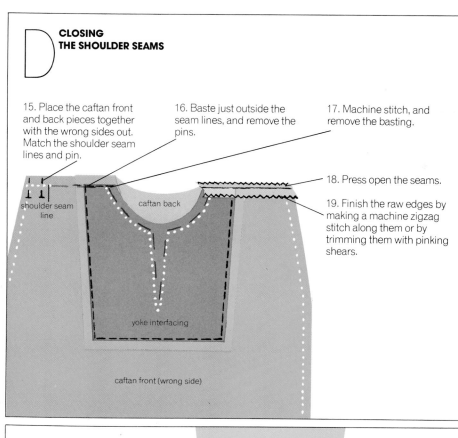

shoulder seam line

caftan back

yoke interfacing

caftan front (wrong side)

E | ATTACHING THE FACINGS

20. To make and attach the neckline facings and to complete the center-front slit, follow the instructions for the faced slit neckline (*pages 51-52, Steps 10-25*).

21. Using a fastening stitch (*Appendix*), attach the yoke facing to the caftan seam allowances at the shoulders, the corners and at the center of the bottom of the yoke.

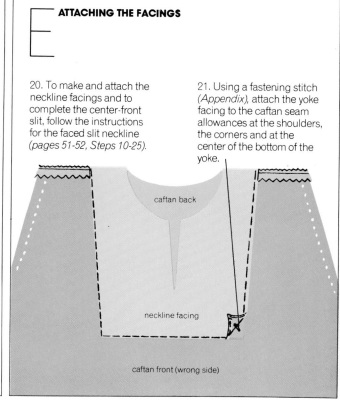

caftan back

neckline facing

caftan front (wrong side)

F | ATTACHING THE GODETS

22. Spread the caftan front, wrong side down, on a flat surface. Place one of the godets, wrong side up, over it. Align the side seam lines.

23. Match the point on the godet where the two side seam lines meet with the underarm dot on the caftan front; pin. Then pin down to the hem, making sure to match the notch marks.

24. Baste just outside the seam line, and remove the pins.

25. Machine stitch, and remove the basting.

26. With the godet wrong side down and extended away from the caftan front, place the caftan back, wrong side up, over it. Then repeat Steps 23-25 to attach the godet to the caftan back.

27. Press the seam allowances away from the godet.

28. Finish the raw edges by making a machine zigzag stitch along them or by trimming them with pinking shears.

29. Attach the other godet in the same manner.

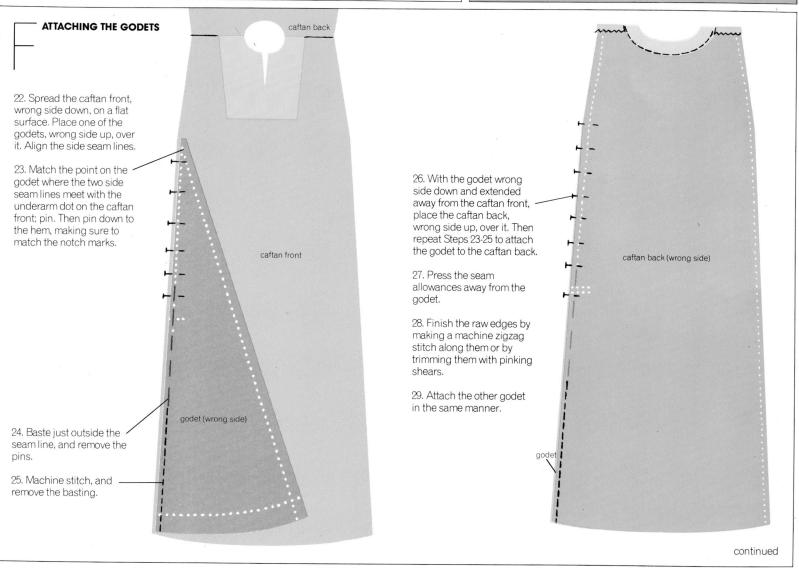

caftan back

caftan front

godet (wrong side)

caftan back (wrong side)

godet

continued

G MAKING THE SLEEVE

30. Place a sleeve front and sleeve back together wrong side out. Match the upper seam lines and pin.

31. Baste just outside the seam line, and remove the pins.

32. Machine stitch, and remove the basting.

33. Press open the seam allowances.

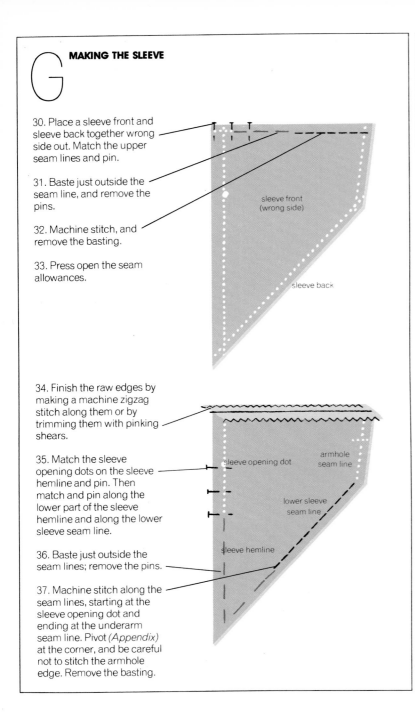

sleeve front (wrong side)

sleeve back

34. Finish the raw edges by making a machine zigzag stitch along them or by trimming them with pinking shears.

35. Match the sleeve opening dots on the sleeve hemline and pin. Then match and pin along the lower part of the sleeve hemline and along the lower sleeve seam line.

36. Baste just outside the seam lines; remove the pins.

37. Machine stitch along the seam lines, starting at the sleeve opening dot and ending at the underarm seam line. Pivot (Appendix) at the corner, and be careful not to stitch the armhole edge. Remove the basting.

sleeve opening dot

armhole seam line

lower sleeve seam line

sleeve hemline

H FINISHING THE SLEEVE

38. Starting 1 inch below the sleeve opening, trim the sleeve hem allowance to 5/8 inch.

39. Clip off the lower corner diagonally and trim the seam allowances at an angle, as shown.

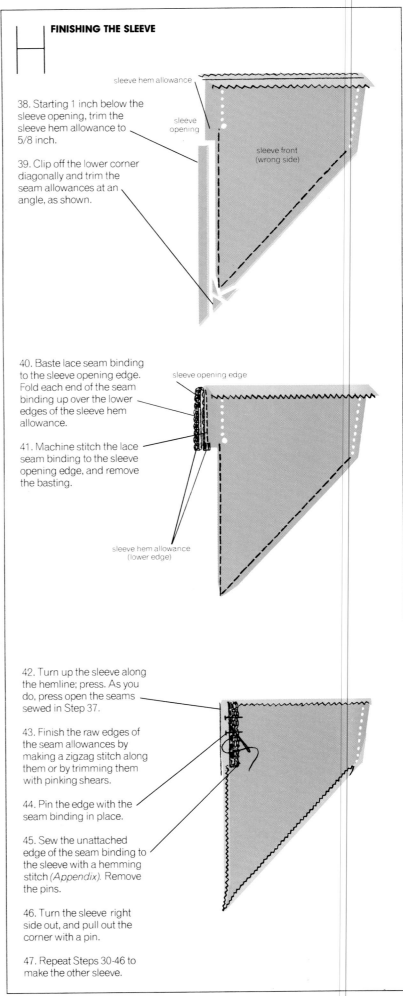

sleeve hem allowance

sleeve opening

sleeve front (wrong side)

40. Baste lace seam binding to the sleeve opening edge. Fold each end of the seam binding up over the lower edges of the sleeve hem allowance.

41. Machine stitch the lace seam binding to the sleeve opening edge, and remove the basting.

sleeve opening edge

sleeve hem allowance (lower edge)

42. Turn up the sleeve along the hemline; press. As you do, press open the seams sewed in Step 37.

43. Finish the raw edges of the seam allowances by making a zigzag stitch along them or by trimming them with pinking shears.

44. Pin the edge with the seam binding in place.

45. Sew the unattached edge of the seam binding to the sleeve with a hemming stitch (Appendix). Remove the pins.

46. Turn the sleeve right side out, and pull out the corner with a pin.

47. Repeat Steps 30-46 to make the other sleeve.

ATTACHING THE SLEEVE

48. With the caftan body wrong side out, insert the sleeve through the armhole. Align the armhole seam lines.

49. Match the lower sleeve seam with the underarm dots on the caftan front and back. Pin on each side of the seam, being careful not to catch the lower sleeve seam allowances or the godet seam allowances.

50. Match the upper sleeve seam with the caftan shoulder seam and pin. Match the notches and pin. Then pin in between.

51. Baste just outside the armhole seam line, and remove the pins.

52. Machine stitch along the armhole seam, starting and ending at the lower sleeve seam. Backstitch twice at each end to strengthen the seam at the underarm. Do not sew over the lower sleeve seam allowances. Remove the basting.

53. Press the seam allowances away from the sleeve.

54. Finish the raw edges by making a machine zigzag stitch along them or by trimming them with pinking shears.

55. Repeat Steps 48-54 to attach the other sleeve.

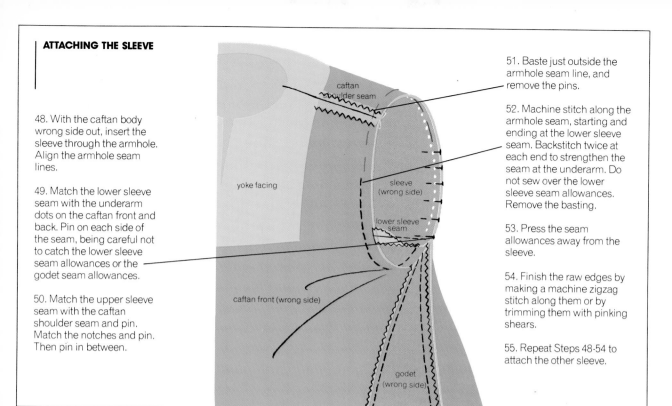

caftan shoulder seam

yoke facing

sleeve (wrong side)

lower sleeve seam

caftan front (wrong side)

godet (wrong side)

HEMMING THE CAFTAN

56. Baste lace seam binding to the hem.

57. Machine stitch the lace seam binding to the hem, and remove the basting.

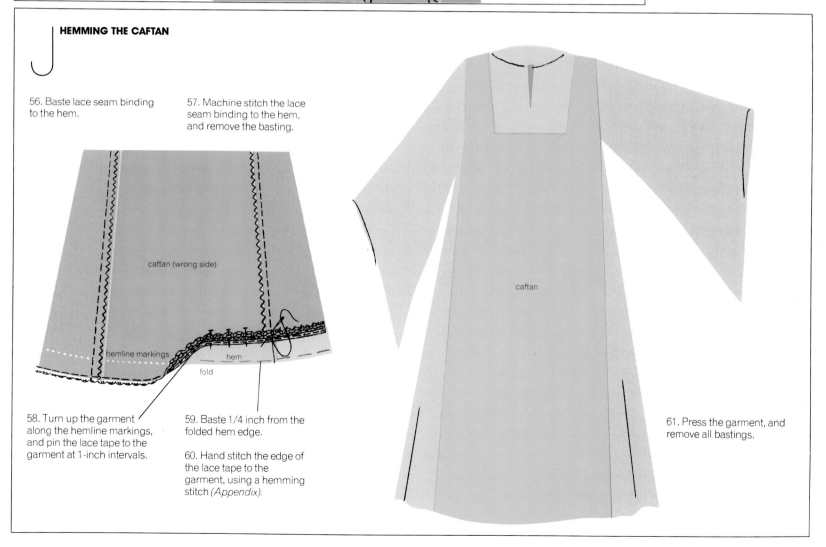

caftan (wrong side)

hemline markings

hem

fold

caftan

58. Turn up the garment along the hemline markings, and pin the lace tape to the garment at 1-inch intervals.

59. Baste 1/4 inch from the folded hem edge.

60. Hand stitch the edge of the lace tape to the garment, using a hemming stitch (Appendix).

61. Press the garment, and remove all bastings.

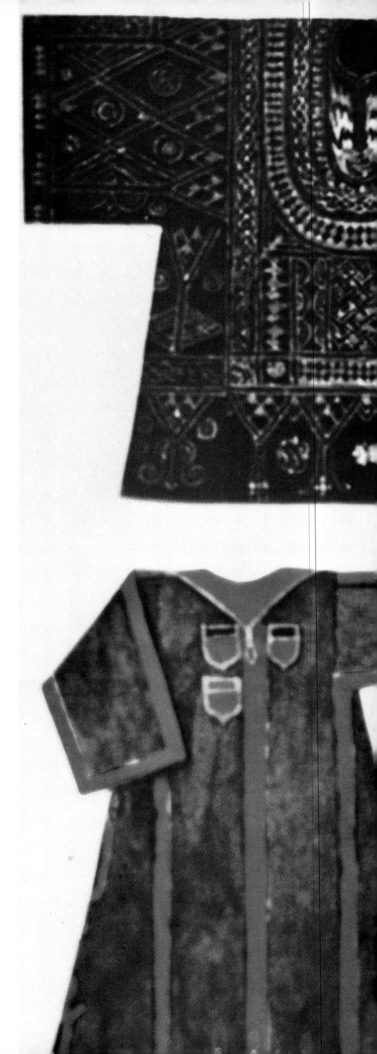

The free and easy dashiki

The African dashiki, with a cut as crisp as a paper doll's tunic, provides a handsome showcase for two or even three subtly patterned but color-related fabrics.

In the version at right the body of the tunic is cut from a large-scale floral batik; the yoke, sleeves and hem from a smaller diagonal print; and a 2-inch band between the yoke and body from a third, still more delicately printed batik.

The base for this garment is a commercial pattern for a shirt-length dashiki with slit front and so-called kimono sleeves. In the revision, the dashiki is lengthened to a mid-thigh length appropriate over pants or as a short dress for beach and country-weekend wear. Also, with comfort in mind, the sleeves have been cropped to elbow length.

Such a combination of fabric and cut as this entails yardage requirements and cutting and sewing plans substantially different from those included in a purchased pattern; directions for adapting the pattern appear overleaf.

Like the authentic dashikis in the background, this version of the classic shirt pulses with color and pattern and keeps its shape simple.

ADJUSTING THE PATTERN

A TAKING YOUR MEASUREMENTS

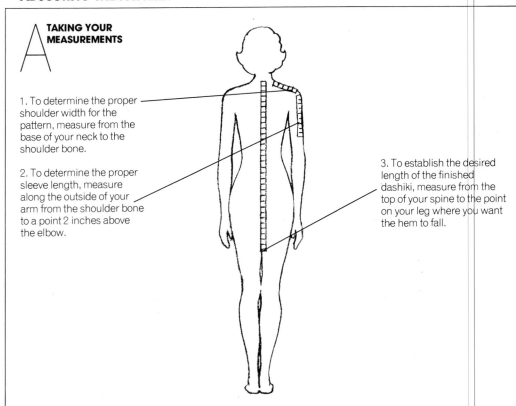

1. To determine the proper shoulder width for the pattern, measure from the base of your neck to the shoulder bone.

2. To determine the proper sleeve length, measure along the outside of your arm from the shoulder bone to a point 2 inches above the elbow.

3. To establish the desired length of the finished dashiki, measure from the top of your spine to the point on your leg where you want the hem to fall.

B ADJUSTING THE LENGTH OF THE PATTERN

4. To lengthen a blouse-length dashiki pattern to dress length, first tape a strip of shelving paper to the bottom of the back pattern piece. Then measure down from the seam line at the neck edge a distance equal to the desired length of the garment determined in Step 3. Make a pencil mark on the attached paper.

5. Measure the distance between the bottom edge of the pattern piece and the mark made in Step 4. Then take that measurement and make a series of pencil marks across the paper, following the curve of the bottom edge of the pattern piece as shown. Connect these marks to create a new hemline.

6. Measure down 2 inches from the new hemline drawn in Step 5, and make pencil marks at intervals across the paper. Connect the marks to make a new cutting line.

7. Extend the pattern's side seam line, side cutting line and center fold line to the new bottom cutting line.

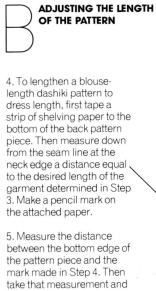

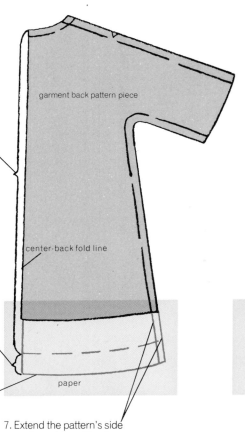

garment back pattern piece

center-back fold line

paper

8. To shorten the sleeve pattern to a point just above the elbow, first measure along the shoulder seam line of the back pattern piece a distance equal to your shoulder width—as determined in Step 1—and mark with a pencil.

9. Next measure from the mark made in Step 8 a distance equal to the desired sleeve length determined in Step 2. Mark with a pencil.

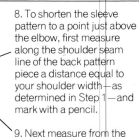

10. Measure the distance between the bottom edge of the sleeve pattern piece and the mark made in Step 9. Then take that measurement and make a series of pencil marks across the paper. Connect these marks to make a new sleeve hemline.

11. Measure down 1 1/4 inches from the new hemline, and make pencil marks at intervals across the pattern piece. Join these marks to make the new cutting line.

12. Cut out the back pattern piece, following the new cutting lines at the hem and sleeve edge.

13. Repeat Steps 4-12 on the front pattern piece.

C — ADDING FLARE TO THE PATTERN

14. Working on the back pattern piece, first tape strips of shelving paper to both sides of the sleeve as shown.

15. Make a pencil mark 1/2 to 1 inch outside the original shoulder seam line at the bottom edge of the sleeve. Then taper a line from that mark into the original seam line at the shoulder mark made in Step 8.

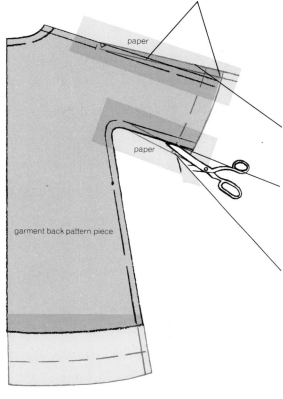

paper

paper

garment back pattern piece

16. Draw a new cutting line 5/8 inch outside the new seam line drawn in the previous step.

17. Repeat Steps 15 and 16 on the lower edge of the sleeve, tapering the new sleeve seam line into the original seam line at the underarm curve.

18. Draw a line extending the bottom of the sleeve pattern out to meet the two new sleeve edges drawn in Steps 16 and 17. Then trim away the excess paper.

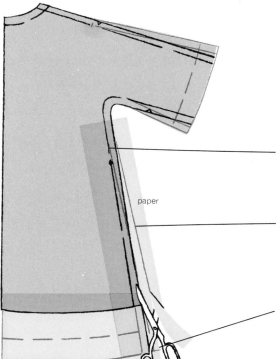

paper

19. Tape strips of paper to the side of the back pattern piece, as shown.

20. Make a pencil mark 1 to 2 inches outside the original side seam line at the bottom of the pattern piece. Then taper a line from that mark into the original seam line at a point 2 inches above the waist.

21. Draw a new cutting line 5/8 inch outside the new seam line drawn in the previous step.

22. Draw a line extending the bottom of the garment out to meet the new side seam line. Then trim away the excess paper.

23. Repeat Steps 14-22 on the front pattern piece.

D — MARKING THE PATTERN FOR THE YOKE

24. Working on the front pattern piece, make a pencil mark on the shoulder seam line 4 inches from the neck seam line.

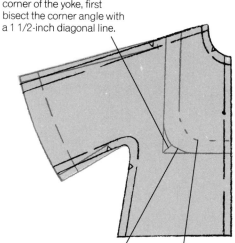

garment front pattern piece

25. On the center front seam line, measure down 3 1/2 inches from the pattern dot indicating the bottom of the neck opening. Mark with a pencil.

26. Align one side of an L square with the shoulder mark made in Step 24 and the other side with the center-front mark made in the previous step. Draw a right angle along the inside edges of the L square, as shown. Then set aside the L square.

27. To round off the lower corner of the yoke, first bisect the corner angle with a 1 1/2-inch diagonal line.

28. Then draw curved lines that taper into the straight lines, about 3 inches from the corner.

29. Draw another line, 1 1/2 inches in from—and parallel to—the curved line.

continued

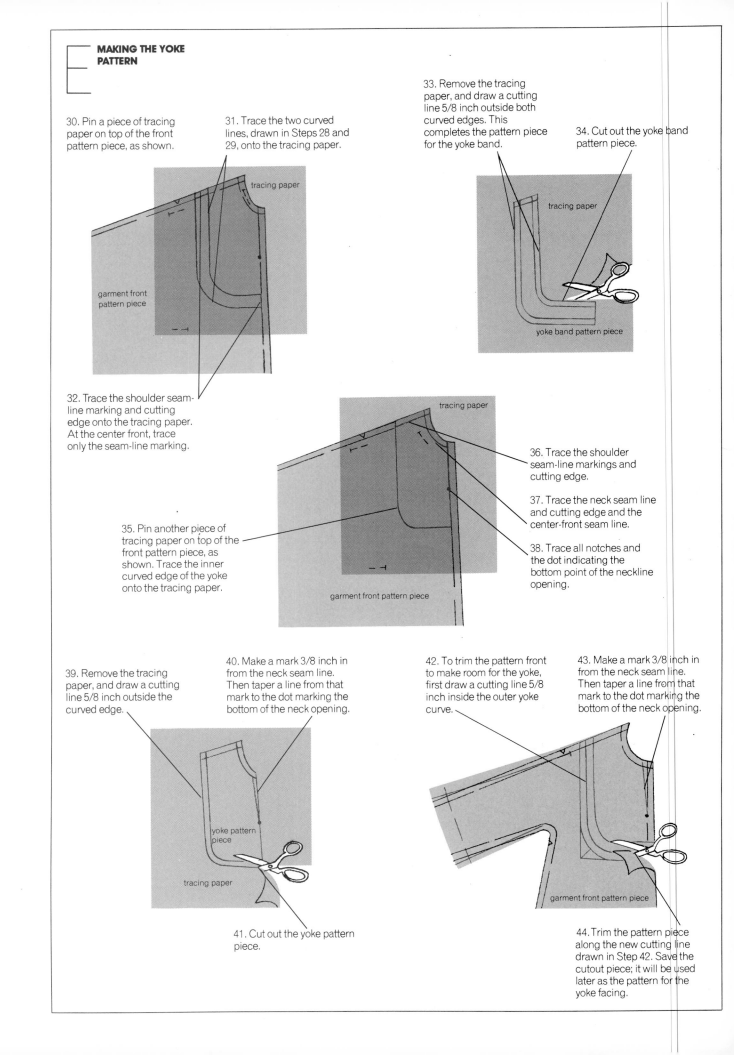

30. Pin a piece of tracing paper on top of the front pattern piece, as shown.

31. Trace the two curved lines, drawn in Steps 28 and 29, onto the tracing paper.

33. Remove the tracing paper, and draw a cutting line 5/8 inch outside both curved edges. This completes the pattern piece for the yoke band.

34. Cut out the yoke band pattern piece.

tracing paper

garment front pattern piece

tracing paper

yoke band pattern piece

32. Trace the shoulder seam-line marking and cutting edge onto the tracing paper. At the center front, trace only the seam-line marking.

tracing paper

35. Pin another piece of tracing paper on top of the front pattern piece, as shown. Trace the inner curved edge of the yoke onto the tracing paper.

36. Trace the shoulder seam-line markings and cutting edge.

37. Trace the neck seam line and cutting edge and the center-front seam line.

38. Trace all notches and the dot indicating the bottom point of the neckline opening.

garment front pattern piece

39. Remove the tracing paper, and draw a cutting line 5/8 inch outside the curved edge.

40. Make a mark 3/8 inch in from the neck seam line. Then taper a line from that mark to the dot marking the bottom of the neck opening.

42. To trim the pattern front to make room for the yoke, first draw a cutting line 5/8 inch inside the outer yoke curve.

43. Make a mark 3/8 inch in from the neck seam line. Then taper a line from that mark to the dot marking the bottom of the neck opening.

yoke pattern piece

tracing paper

41. Cut out the yoke pattern piece.

garment front pattern piece

44. Trim the pattern piece along the new cutting line drawn in Step 42. Save the cutout piece; it will be used later as the pattern for the yoke facing.

F MAKING THE BANDING PATTERN

45. On the front pattern piece, measure up 4 to 5 inches from the hemline of the sleeve, and make a series of pencil marks across the sleeve, following the curve of the sleeve bottom. Connect these marks.

46. Measure up 6 to 8 inches from the hem at the bottom of the pattern piece, and make a series of pencil marks across the garment pattern, following the curve of the bottom edge. Connect these marks.

47. Slash the pattern pieces along the lines drawn in Steps 45 and 46. The cutoff pieces will become the pattern pieces for the hem band and the sleeve band.

48. Tape one end of a strip of shelving paper to the sleeve edge of the pattern piece.

49. Then tape the sleeve band pattern—the piece that was cut off in Step 47 —to the other end of the paper, leaving a 2-inch interval between the two.

50. Draw a line on the paper 5/8 inch beyond the edge of the sleeve and the sleeve band. These lines will become the cutting lines of the sleeve and the band.

51. Extend the shoulder and underarm seam lines and cutting lines to meet the new cutting edges.

52. Repeat Steps 48-51 on the hem edge of the pattern and the hem band pattern piece.

53. Trim away the excess paper.

54. Repeat Steps 45-53 on the back pattern piece.

55. Overlap the front and back sleeve band pattern pieces at the shoulder seam lines. Tape them together to create one pattern piece.

56. Then cut out a duplicate piece, using shelving paper.

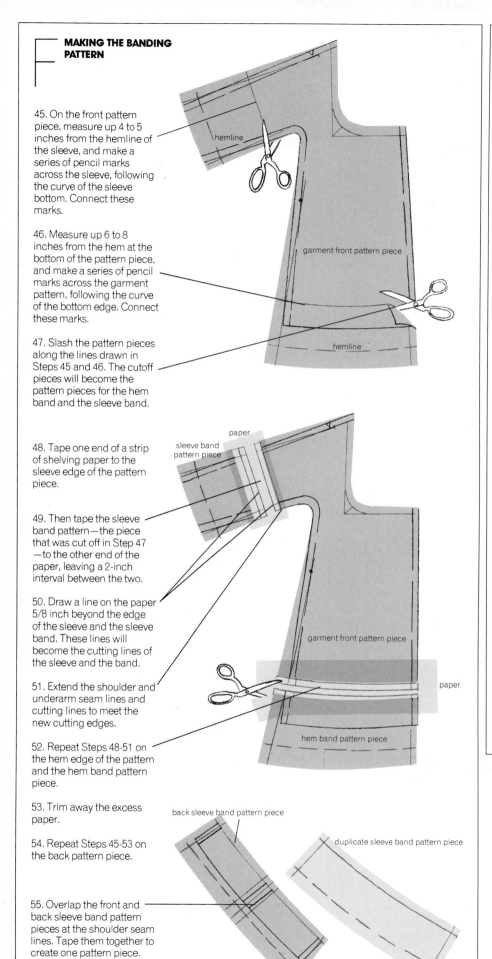

G MAKING THE BACK NECK FACING PATTERNS

57. Pin the front facing pattern piece set aside in Step 44 to the back facing pattern piece at the shoulder; overlap the shoulder seam lines, and align the inside curved edges and seam lines.

58. Measure the distance between the outside edges of the front neck facing and the back neck facing.

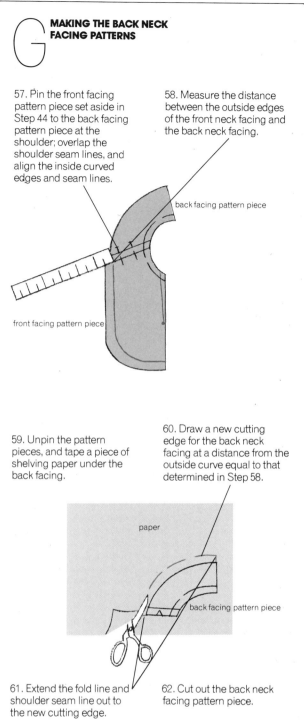

59. Unpin the pattern pieces, and tape a piece of shelving paper under the back facing.

60. Draw a new cutting edge for the back neck facing at a distance from the outside curve equal to that determined in Step 58.

61. Extend the fold line and shoulder seam line out to the new cutting edge.

62. Cut out the back neck facing pattern piece.

125

DETERMINING FABRIC REQUIREMENTS

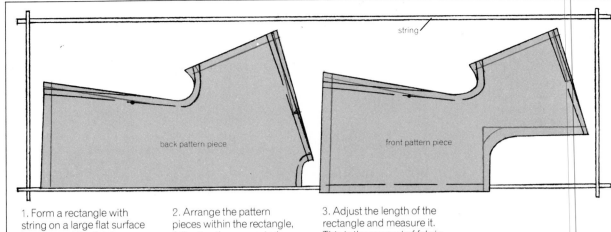

1. Form a rectangle with string on a large flat surface to represent the fabric you intend to use. Make the width of the rectangle equal to the width of the fabric (or a portion of the width as specified for layouts requiring folded fabric).

2. Arrange the pattern pieces within the rectangle, following the suggested layouts below.

3. Adjust the length of the rectangle and measure it. This is the amount of fabric you will need.

CUTTING AND MARKING

 THE DASHIKI FRONT AND BACK PIECES

36- OR 45-INCH FABRIC WITH OR WITHOUT A ONE-WAY DESIGN

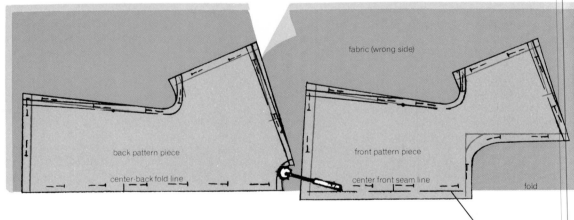

1. Fold the fabric in half lengthwise with the selvage edges together and the wrong sides facing out.

2. Arrange the front pattern piece so that its center-front fold—or seam—line is aligned with the fold in the fabric.

3. Turn over the back pattern piece and place it on the fabric so that its center-back fold—or seam—line is aligned with the fold in the fabric.

4. Pin the pattern pieces in place. Then cut them out.

5. Using dressmaker's carbon paper and a tracing wheel, trace the seam lines on the wrong side of both fabric thicknesses. Transfer the notches and dots onto the seam allowances of the fabric. Then make a 1-inch line down the center-front fold line.

45-INCH FABRIC WITH OR WITHOUT A ONE-WAY DESIGN

6. Fold over one side of the fabric lengthwise, as shown, with the wrong sides facing out, and pin the yoke to the double layer of fabric so that the center front of the pattern is aligned with the fold in the fabric.

7. Pin the back facing, the yoke and the front facing pattern pieces on the fabric so that their center back and front are aligned with the fold in the fabric.

8. Arrange the sleeve band pattern piece and the duplicate made in Step 56, page 125, on the single layer of fabric, as shown. Make sure the overlapping shoulder seam lines are parallel to the selvage edges. Pin the pattern pieces in place.

9. Cut out the pattern pieces.

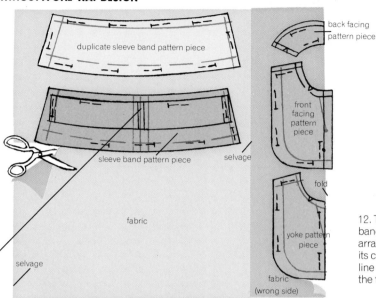

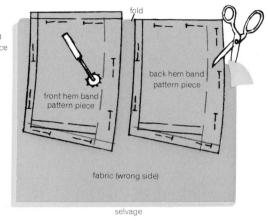

10. Fold the remaining fabric in half lengthwise so that the selvage edges are together and the wrong sides are facing out.

11. Arrange the front hem band pattern piece on this double layer of fabric so that the center front of the pattern is aligned with the fold in the fabric.

12. Turn over the back hem band pattern piece and arrange it on the fabric with its center-back fold or seam line aligned with the fold in the fabric.

13. Pin the pattern pieces in place.

14. Cut out the pattern pieces.

15. With dressmaker's carbon and a tracing wheel, transfer the seam lines, notches and circles to the wrong side of both fabric thicknesses. Make a 1-inch line along the center-front fold line at the bottom of the yoke and front facing pieces.

36-INCH FABRIC WITH OR WITHOUT A ONE-WAY DESIGN

16. Fold over both sides of the fabric so that the selvage edges meet in the center and the wrong sides are facing out.

17. Pin the back and front facing pattern pieces to the fabric so that the center back and front lines are aligned with one folded edge of the fabric.

18. Pin the yoke pattern piece to the other folded edge so that its center front is aligned with the fold in the fabric.

19. Cut out the pattern pieces.

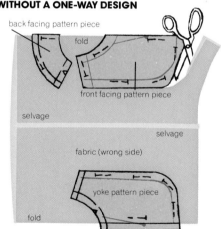

20. Fold the remaining fabric in half lengthwise with the wrong sides facing out.

21. Pin the front hem band pattern piece to the fabric so that its center-front line is aligned with the fold in the fabric.

22. Turn over the back hem band pattern piece and pin it to the fabric so that its center-back line is aligned with the fold in the fabric.

23. Cut out the pattern pieces.

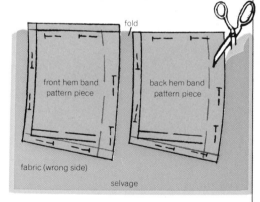

24. Pin the sleeve band pattern piece and the duplicate pattern piece made in Step 56, page 125, to the remaining single layer of fabric. Make sure the overlapping shoulder seam lines at the center of the band are parallel to the selvage edges.

25. Cut out the pattern pieces.

26. With dressmaker's carbon and a tracing wheel, transfer the seam lines, notches and circles to the wrong side of both layers of fabric. Make a 1-inch line along the center-front fold at the bottom of the yoke and front facing pieces.

continued

C THE YOKE BAND

36- OR 45-INCH FABRIC WITH OR WITHOUT A ONE-WAY DESIGN

27. Fold over one side of the fabric lengthwise, as shown, with the wrong sides facing out, and pin the yoke band pattern piece to the double layer of fabric so that the center front seam line of the pattern piece is aligned with the fold in the fabric.

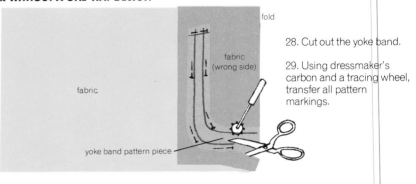

28. Cut out the yoke band.

29. Using dressmaker's carbon and a tracing wheel, transfer all pattern markings.

ASSEMBLING THE GARMENT

A MAKING THE YOKE AND BAND

1. Cut out an interfacing for the yoke, using the yoke pattern piece. With dressmaker's carbon and a tracing wheel, transfer all pattern markings.

2. Lay the yoke wrong side up on a flat surface. Place the yoke interfacing, marked side up, over it. Pin.

3. Baste just outside the seam lines, including the slit seam lines. Remove the pins.

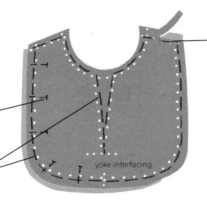

4. Trim the interfacing seam allowance at the shoulders as close as possible to the basting stitches.

5. To prevent the yoke band from stretching as you work, machine stitch just outside the neck seam-line marking.

6. Clip into the curved seam allowance up to, but not into, the machine stitching.

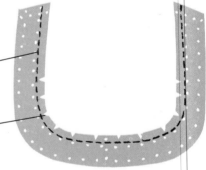

yoke band (wrong side)

7. Lay the yoke wrong side down on a flat surface. Then place the yoke band wrong side up on top of the yoke. Pin the two pieces together at the center front. Then add more pins at 1-inch intervals.

8. Baste just outside the line of machine stitching made in Step 5. Remove the pins.

9. Machine stitch along the seam line and remove the basting.

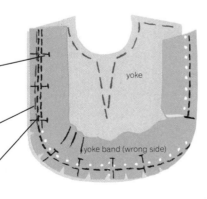

10. With the interfaced side of the yoke turned up and the yoke band folded under the yoke, trim the interfacing close to the machine stitching.

11. Finish both raw seam edges with pinking shears or sew them together with a zigzag stitch.

12. Press the finished seam allowances toward the yoke band—away from the yoke.

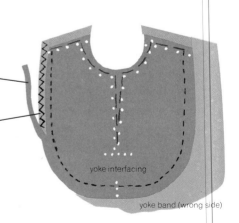

B ATTACHING THE BANDED YOKE TO THE GARMENT

13. To prevent the front neckline from stretching as you work, machine stitch just outside the seam line around the neck edge.

14. Clip into the curved seam allowance up to, but not into, the machine stitching.

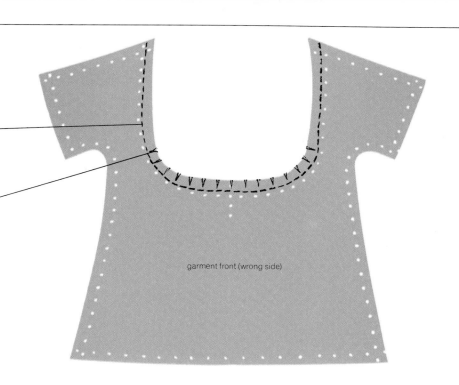

garment front (wrong side)

15. Lay the garment wrong side up on a flat surface. Then place the banded yoke wrong side up on top of the garment. Pin the two pieces together at the center front. Then add more pins at 1-inch intervals.

16. Baste just outside the line of machine stitching made in Step 13 and remove the pins.

17. Machine stitch along the seam line and remove the basting.

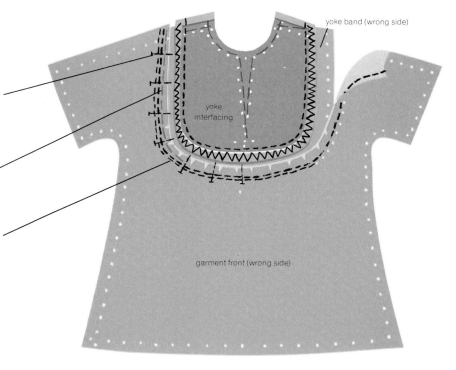

yoke band (wrong side)

yoke interfacing

garment front (wrong side)

18. Finish both raw edges with pinking shears or sew them together with a zigzag stitch.

19. Press the finished seam allowances toward the garment—away from the yoke band.

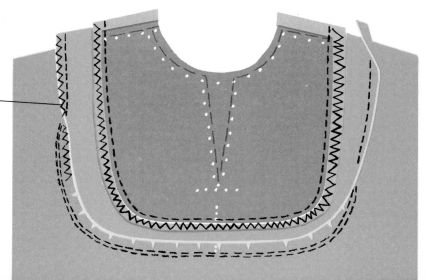

continued

C ATTACHING THE NECKLINE FACING

20. To prevent the back from stretching as you work, machine stitch just outside the seam line.

21. Clip into the curved seam allowance up to, but not into, the machine stitching.

22. With the wrong sides facing out, pin the garment front and back together at the shoulder seams.

23. Baste just outside the seam line and remove the pins.

24. Machine stitch along the seam line and remove the bastings.

25. Finish both raw seam edges with pinking shears or stitch with a zigzag stitch and press open the finished seam.

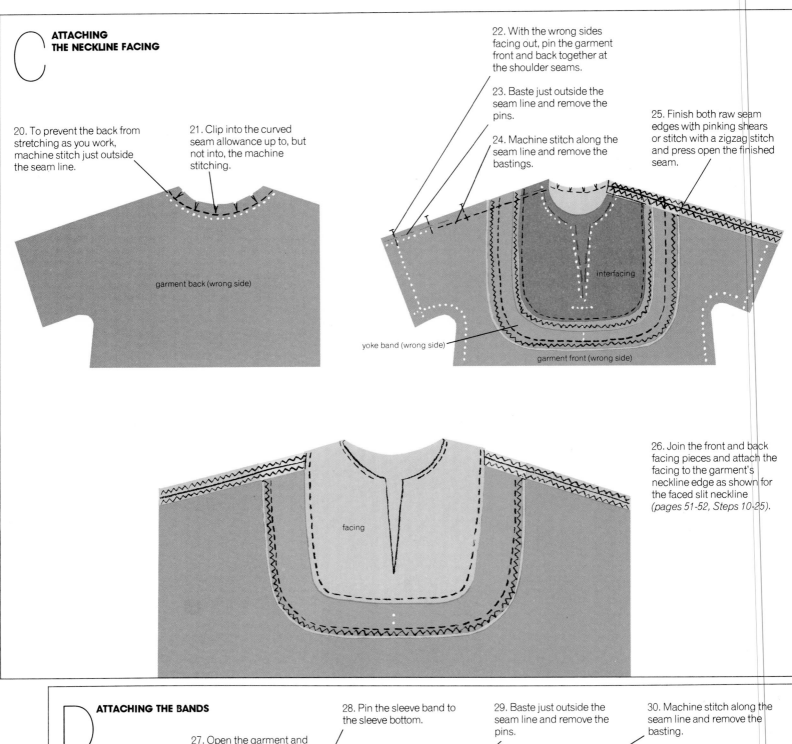

garment back (wrong side)

interfacing

yoke band (wrong side)

garment front (wrong side)

facing

26. Join the front and back facing pieces and attach the facing to the garment's neckline edge as shown for the faced slit neckline (*pages 51-52, Steps 10-25*).

D ATTACHING THE BANDS

27. Open the garment and lay it wrong side up on a flat surface.

28. Pin the sleeve band to the sleeve bottom.

29. Baste just outside the seam line and remove the pins.

30. Machine stitch along the seam line and remove the basting.

31. Finish the raw edge with pinking shears or stitch the seams together with a zigzag stitch.

32. Press the finished seam toward the garment section.

33. Repeat on the other sleeve, and both hem edges.

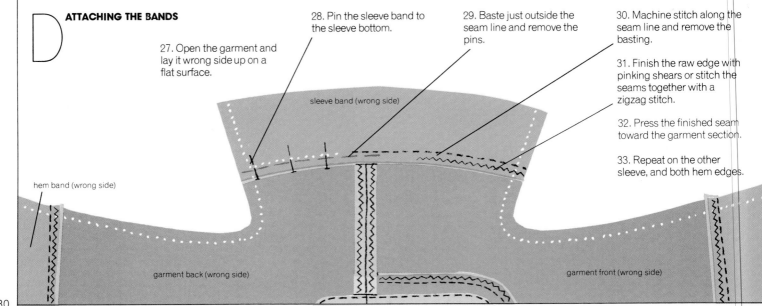

sleeve band (wrong side)

hem band (wrong side)

garment back (wrong side)

garment front (wrong side)

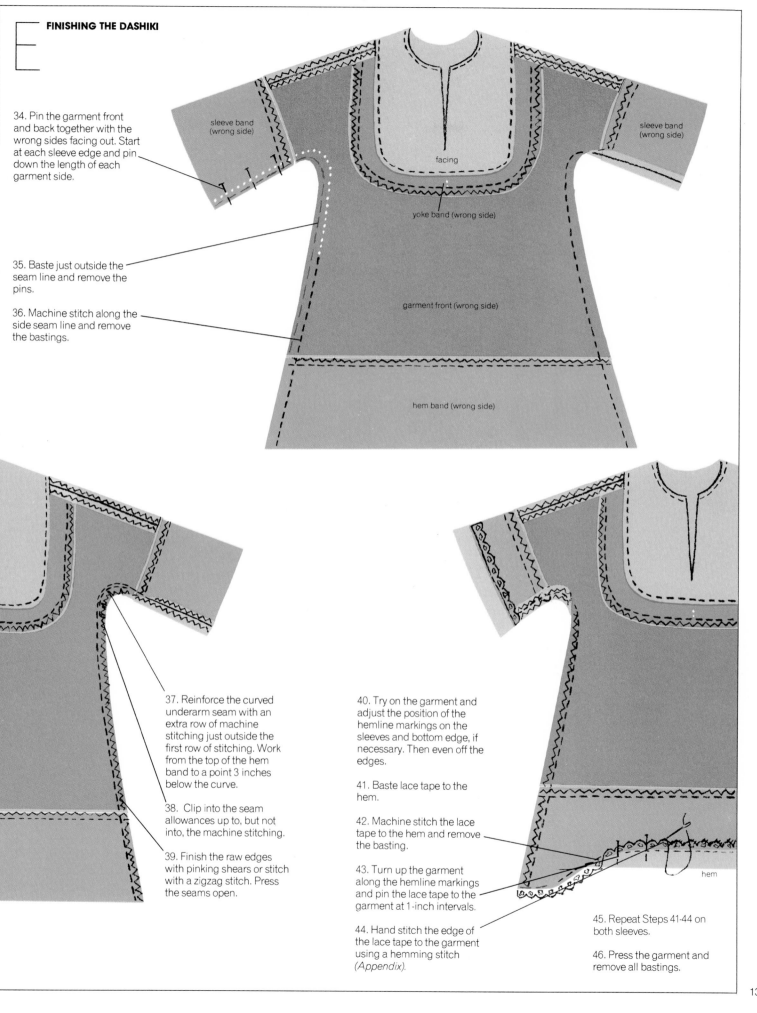

sleeve band (wrong side)

facing

sleeve band (wrong side)

yoke band (wrong side)

garment front (wrong side)

hem band (wrong side)

34. Pin the garment front and back together with the wrong sides facing out. Start at each sleeve edge and pin down the length of each garment side.

35. Baste just outside the seam line and remove the pins.

36. Machine stitch along the side seam line and remove the bastings.

37. Reinforce the curved underarm seam with an extra row of machine stitching just outside the first row of stitching. Work from the top of the hem band to a point 3 inches below the curve.

38. Clip into the seam allowances up to, but not into, the machine stitching.

39. Finish the raw edges with pinking shears or stitch with a zigzag stitch. Press the seams open.

40. Try on the garment and adjust the position of the hemline markings on the sleeves and bottom edge, if necessary. Then even off the edges.

41. Baste lace tape to the hem.

42. Machine stitch the lace tape to the hem and remove the basting.

43. Turn up the garment along the hemline markings and pin the lace tape to the garment at 1-inch intervals.

44. Hand stitch the edge of the lace tape to the garment using a hemming stitch (*Appendix*).

45. Repeat Steps 41-44 on both sleeves.

46. Press the garment and remove all bastings.

hem

A symbol of the good life in China, the chrysanthemum is reflected here in intricate satin stitches.

5
NEEDLEWORK'S GOLDEN AGE

Whenever human beings have found themselves with time on their hands, they have shown an inclination to fill the empty moments by embellishing—walls with paintings, stories with anecdotes, clothes with embroidery.

Excavations of neolithic burial mounds in Europe have revealed scraps of wool or linen beautified by the primitive doodling of a crude bone needle. Friezes on early Egyp-

THE MYSTIQUE OF ORIENTAL STITCHERY

tian palaces and tombs depict men and women wearing what appear to be richly embroidered clothes. The Vedas, venerable Hindu scriptures of India, allude to decorative needlework. And historians of classic Greece rapturously described embroidered Eastern robes: when Alexander the Great conquered Persia in 331 B.C. he was quick to order one for himself.

For these ancients, embroidery was not only a high art but a royal one, a token of status and luxury for sultans, pharaohs and emperors, for whom designs were created out of precious gold and silver threads drawn through sumptuous fabrics. Sometimes the embroidery was further embellished with bright beads, peacock feathers, lustrous pearls and glittering jewels.

Today the home embroiderer creates similar splendors by capturing the spirit of these exotic creations—though without the pearls or beaten gold. As heir to a repertoire of exotic stitches that might have delighted the Caliph of Baghdad himself, a modern needleworker can reproduce what the English poet John Taylor once called,

> "rare patternes (that) have been set
> Beyond the bounds of faithlesse
>   Mahomet,
> From spacious China and those King-
>   domes East. . . ."

The voluptuous colors and textures of these "patternes" can be re-created easily with store-bought floss. And the designs that the seamstresses of Cathay stitched upon the robes of mandarins and their ladies prove adaptable for use on contemporary fashions—like the chrysanthemum shown on page 132.

Such adaptability is the key to the essence of exotic-looking Oriental embroidery, which lies not in the cost of the materials, but in the design. As demonstrated in the evening bag on page 154, those from the Near East prove especially simple to copy. These kinds of rich Turkish embroidery depend on bold, ornate patterns rather than fancy stitchery for their effect.

The basic elements in most of them are flowers, landscapes or geometric forms such as the sultan's three-ringed emblem of royal office. Since the Turks, like the Javanese, were devout Muslims who considered it a sin to accurately depict living creatures, most of their embroidery was stylized. Tulips, for example, became ovals, with two points at the top to represent the petals. In the finished work, the basic designs were filled out with solid masses of colors, in stitches similar to the Arab laid work and brick stitch familiar to embroiderers today, and then overlaid by various couching techniques to give them depth.

Beautiful as it was, each piece of embroidery had built into it one or two purposeful mistakes, put there by superstitious needleworkers to ward off the bad luck that would come from attempts at perfection. But these deliberate gaffes did not alter the exquisite designs of the work. Lady Mary Wortley Montagu, whose husband, Edward, was England's ambassador to Constantinople, wrote in 1718 that she visited the Sultana Hafiten and was served a dinner of 50 dishes of meat. "The knives were of gold, the hafts set with diamonds. But the piece of luxury that grieved my eyes was the tablecloth and napkins, . . . embroidered with silks and gold . . . as finely wrought as the finest handkerchiefs . . . of this country."

But not of any country. For the very finest embroidery in the world came from the highest of its ancient civilizations—China. The Imperial needlecrafters developed an extraordinary lexicon of delicate and complex designs. While the Turkish embroiderers sought to stylize motifs by simplifying

objects into their basic design elements, the Chinese went to extraordinary lengths to reproduce nature realistically. And they succeeded superbly. With refined colors and delicate stitches like the shaded satin stitch, the Chinese embroiderer was able to capture the tiniest details in a bird's plumage *(opposite)*.

The Empress Dowager of China, Tz'u Hsi, contemporary of Queen Victoria, was so fond of embroidered gowns that she maintained a vast workshop of artisans at her Summer Palace outside Peking. There, consummate needlecrafters would cut a design out of paper, tack it onto the fabric and embroider over it, leaving the paper to lend the needlework body. Alternatively, they first painted the basic design onto the fabric, stretched it taut, and then worked backward and forward with satin stitches so that there would be no wrong side to the embroidery.

Tz'u Hsi's self-indulgent pleasure in ornate clothing may be unparalleled in all history. She owned several thousand robes, and one of her greatest delights was inspecting her wardrobe. Another was sitting in her pleasure gardens: she once embezzled the entire budget that China had appropriated for helping modernize its navy and squandered it on a huge marble boat installed in a pond. No amount of exquisite work was too excessive for her tastes.

The vain Empress took little interest in the complex tradition of the Imperial Court's symbolic robes—apparently because the

Chinese robes with embroidered symbols are shown clockwise from the top: a dragon for imperial power, a phoenix for tranquillity, a crane for top civil status.

Emperor's dragon robe

First-rank mandarin

Empress' phoenix robe

Badges of rank among Chinese mandarins featured a range of creatures, including the silver pheasant *(left)*, denoting the fifth civil rank; a leopard *(top)*, the third military rank; and a horned dragon with a lion's body *(above)*, indicating a judge.

official royal color, yellow, did not flatter her sallow complexion. Her distaste for this particular type of regalia, however, was virtually unique among members of the Chinese dynasties and their adherents. Never did a civilization devote such passion and genius to the elaboration of official insignia as did China. In fact, the most imaginative of all Chinese embroideries are, literally, status symbols, such as the ornate insignia of office shown on these pages.

The Emperor and Empress were too exalted for emblems: their entire robes were covered with embroidery. They were much too godlike to wear insignia made up of replicas of living birds and beasts. For them, the symbols were mythological: a dragon embellished the Emperor's robes *(pages 136-137)*, the phoenix was the special perquisite of the Empress.

Among mere mortals, the nine ranks of civil officials were each designated by a different bird; the stately crane represented the highest rank, and the tiny paradise flycatcher, the lowest. The nine ranks of military officers were symbolized by animals ranging in ferocity from lion to sea horse.

For contemporary embroiderers, who can re-create such symbols as pleasurable and exotic decorations, the classic Chinese motifs are surprisingly simple to render. Most Chinese embroidery was done with techniques that are as easy to master and as popular in the West now as they were in the East: the satin stitch, stem stitch, chain stitch and split stitch. And the designs themselves, like the peacock-and-flower border on pages 150-151, grace Western garb with delicate Eastern elegance.

Eastern modes in embroidery

In Asia, where the embroiderer's art is at its richest, even the basic stitches used to create outlines, fill in blocks of color and form accents are superlative examples of needlework refinement.

Shown here and on the following pages are an assortment of these Oriental stitches and techniques —11 in all—chosen for their versatility and for the range of textures and shadings they create. For example, scroll stitches done in series become ornate, wavy lines; a row of coral stitches shows up as a perky sequence of knotted dots and dashes; and a series of Pekingese stitches forms a string of airy loops.

Other stitches, such as the complex whipped spider web, are so ornamental they can be used singly to produce isolated decorative notes.

Couching, too, can create especially appealing effects. In couching, thread or yarn is laid across a section of fabric and tied down at intervals with tacking stitches. The result is a pretty accent for outlining motifs and forming borders, and is especially effective in making fillers.

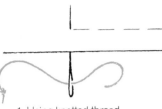

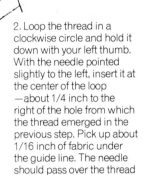

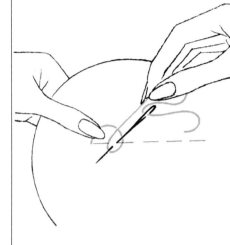

1. Using knotted thread, bring the needle up from the wrong side of the fabric at the left-hand end of the guide line for the design. Pull the thread through.

2. Loop the thread in a clockwise circle and hold it down with your left thumb. With the needle pointed slightly to the left, insert it at the center of the loop —about 1/4 inch to the right of the hole from which the thread emerged in the previous step. Pick up about 1/16 inch of fabric under the guide line. The needle should pass over the thread at both sides of the loop.

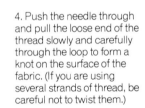

3. Holding only the start of the loop with your left thumb, grasp the loose end of the thread between your right thumb and forefinger and pull the loop tightly around the needle.

4. Push the needle through and pull the loose end of the thread slowly and carefully through the loop to form a knot on the surface of the fabric. (If you are using several strands of thread, be careful not to twist them.)

5. Make similar stitches from left to right until the guide line is covered. Space the knots evenly. After making the last stitch, push the needle through to the wrong side of the fabric just beside the final knot. Then secure the stitch (*Ending Off, Appendix*).

6. If you are making more than one row of scroll stitches, center the knots on each successive row between the knots on the previous row to form a pattern. End off each row as you did in Step 5.

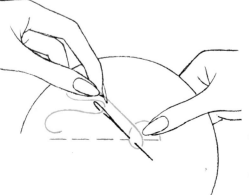

IF YOU ARE LEFT-HANDED...
Follow Steps 1-6, but proceed from right to left across the guide line. Make a counterclockwise loop and hold it in place with your right thumb. Point the needle slightly to the right as you insert it and pull the thread with your left thumb and forefinger to form the knot. The angle and direction of the stitches will be reversed.

THE PEKINGESE STITCH: For filling an area with a feathery texture

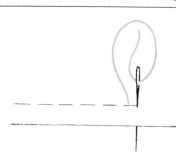

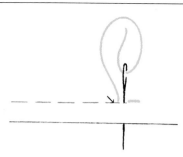

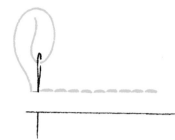

1. To make a row of backstitches, which will form the foundation for the distinctive loops of the Pekingese stitch, thread an embroidery needle and knot the end. Bring the needle up from the wrong side of the fabric about 1/8 inch from the right-hand end of the guide line for the design. Pull the thread through. Then insert the needle at the end of the guide line and pull the thread through to the wrong side.

2. Bring the needle up 1/8 inch to the left of the hole from which the thread emerged in the previous step *(arrow)*. Pull the thread through and insert the needle just to the left of the original hole. Then pull the thread through to the wrong side of the fabric:

3. Working from right to left, make a row of even backstitches across the guide line by repeating Step 2. If you want to use a contrasting color for the loops, secure the last stitch on the wrong side *(Ending Off, Appendix)*.

4. To make the loops, change to a blunt-ended tapestry needle. Using knotted thread in the new color—or the same thread used for the backstitches —bring the needle up from the wrong side of the fabric just below the end of the last backstitch you made.

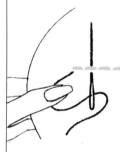

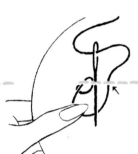

5. Make a small counterclockwise loop with the thread, just below the row of backstitches. Hold the loop in place with your left thumb. Slip the needle —from bottom to top— under the second backstitch from the end. Be careful not to catch the fabric or the thread.

6. Continuing to hold the loop down with your thumb, pull the needle through and slip it—from top to bottom —under the first backstitch on the left. Bring the needle out so that it passes over the thread of the loop. Pull the thread gently through the backstitch, holding and guiding the loop with your thumb until the loop is the desired size.

7. To form the second loop, repeat Step 5, but slip the needle under the third backstitch *(arrow)*. Then repeat Step 6, but slip the needle under the second backstitch just to the right of the thread of the first loop. Pull the loops evenly so that the upper part of each is close to the top of the backstitches and the lower part extends the desired length below the backstitches.

8. Continue making a series of uniform loops across the row until you reach the last backstitch at the right-hand end of the design. Make a loop as in Step 5, but insert the needle to the wrong side of the fabric just below the end of the last backstitch and secure the stitch *(Ending Off, Appendix)*.

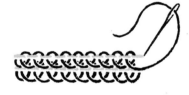

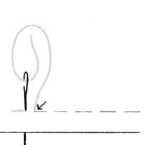

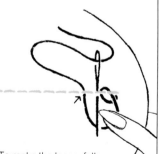

9. To make more than one row, sew a second row of backstitches about 1/4 inch above the first row so that the second row of loops —and each successive row —will slightly overlap the backstitches on the previous row. Then make the loops. Be sure they are the same size as in the first row.

IF YOU ARE LEFT-HANDED...
1. To make the backstitches, follow Steps 1-3, but proceed from left to right.

2. To make the loops, follow Steps 4-9, but proceed from right to left, making clockwise loops and holding them in place with your right thumb.

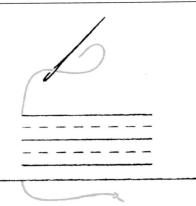

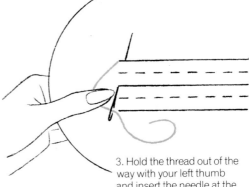

1. To mark the guide lines for the stitches in the area of the design to be filled, draw parallel horizontal pencil lines separated by a distance equal to the desired length of the stitches. Then draw a line of dashes midway between them.

2. Using knotted thread, bring the needle up from the wrong side of the fabric at the left-hand edge of the uppermost solid line. Pull the thread through.

3. Hold the thread out of the way with your left thumb and insert the needle at the left-hand edge of the second solid line, but do not pull the thread through. Point the needle to the right. Bring it out on the top line, leaving a space equal to the width of the thread you are using between the needle and the hole from which it emerged in the previous step. Pull the thread through to form the first stitch.

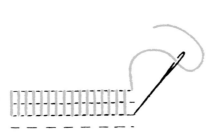

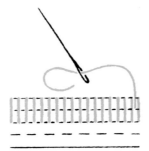

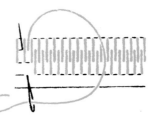

4. Make similar stitches until you reach the right-hand edge of the top line, by repeating Step 3. To complete the last stitch in the row, insert the needle on the second solid line and pull the thread through to the wrong side.

5. To make the second row, bring the needle up on the uppermost line of dashes in the space between the two last stitches of the previous row. Pull the thread through.

6. Working from right to left, and between the lines of dashes, repeat Steps 3 and 4; this time point the needle to the left and keep the thread out of the way to the right.

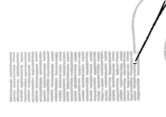

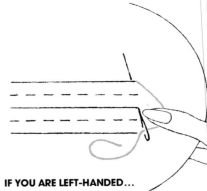

7. To make the third row, bring the needle up from the wrong side through the hole (made in Step 3) that forms the bottom of the first stitch (arrow). Then repeat Steps 3 and 4 between the bottom of the stitches on the first row and the third solid line. Make as many rows of stitches as your design requires.

8. After you finish the bottom row, fill in the spaces between the threads by making a series of stitches half as long as the stitches in the previous rows. Complete the last stitch. Secure it on the wrong side (Ending Off, Appendix). Then reknot the thread and fill in the spaces between the threads of the top row in the same manner.

IF YOU ARE LEFT-HANDED...
Follow Steps 1-8, but begin the first row of stitches at the upper right-hand corner of the design and proceed from right to left. In Step 3, hold the thread out of the way with your right thumb and point the needle to the left, as shown above. Make the second row of stitches from left to right.

THE CORAL STITCH: For outlining and solidly filling an area with a beaded texture

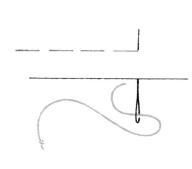 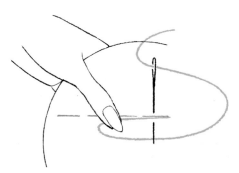 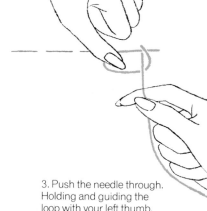

1. Using knotted thread, bring the needle up from the wrong side of the fabric at the right-hand end of the guide line for the design. Pull the thread through.

2. Turn the thread to the left and hold it just below the guide line with your left thumb. Make a counterclockwise loop and insert the needle vertically just above the guide line and about 1/4 inch to the left of the hole from which the thread emerged in Step 1. Pick up about 1/16 inch of fabric. Bring the needle out through the loop so that it passes under the thread at the top and over the thread at the bottom.

3. Push the needle through. Holding and guiding the loop with your left thumb, pull the thread gently with your right thumb and forefinger until a small knot is formed.

  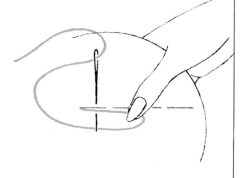

4. Make similar stitches from right to left along the guide line until the design is completed by repeating Steps 2 and 3. Space the knots evenly, and pick up the same amount of fabric for each stitch. When you have completed the last stitch, push the needle through to the wrong side of the fabric just beside the last knot and secure the stitch (*Ending Off, Appendix*).

5. If you are making more than one row of coral stitches, center the knots on each successive row between the knots on the previous row to form a pattern. End off each row as you did in Step 4.

IF YOU ARE LEFT-HANDED...
Follow Steps 1-5, but proceed from left to right. Make a clockwise loop and hold it down with your right thumb. Make each successive stitch to the right of the previous stitch.

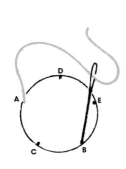

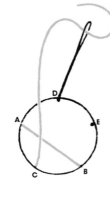

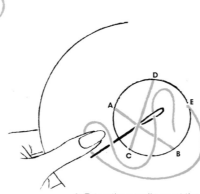

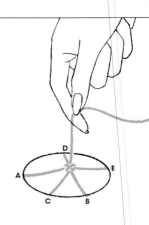

1. To make the spokes for the stitch, begin by marking five evenly spaced points just inside the circular guide line. Using a blunt-ended tapestry needle and knotted thread, bring the needle up from the wrong side of the fabric at a mark on the left-hand side of the circle (point A in this drawing). Pull the thread through and insert the needle at a mark on the right-hand side (point B).

2. Pull the thread through to the wrong side of the fabric. Bring the needle up again at a mark on the lower part of the circle (point C). Pull the thread through; then insert the needle at one of the upper marks (point D). Pull the thread through to the wrong side. Be careful not to pull the threads so tight that they pucker the fabric.

3. Bring the needle up at the remaining mark (point E) and pull the thread through. Make a clockwise loop with the thread just below the circle, as shown, and hold the loop in place with your left thumb. Slip the needle —from right to left—under the crossed threads at the center of the circle. Then bring the needle through the loop so that it passes under the top thread and over the bottom thread.

4. Draw the thread through the loop; then pull it straight up to form a tiny knot at the center of the circle. Make sure the five spokes are of equal length before you pull the knot tight.

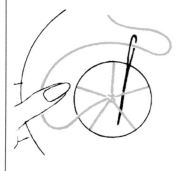

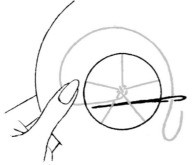

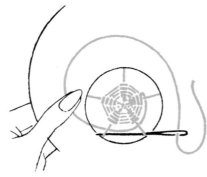

5. To cover the spokes, begin by making a clockwise loop with the thread to the left of the circle. Hold the loop out of the way with your left thumb and slip the needle under the two spokes at the right-hand side of the circle. Pull the thread under the spokes; do not catch the fabric or the thread of the spokes.

6. Now make another clockwise loop with the thread and hold it out of the way with your left thumb. Slip the needle under two spokes again; this time the second spoke it passed under in the previous step and the spoke to the left of that one. Pull the thread under the spokes so that it wraps fairly tightly around the right-hand spoke.

7. Work around the circle in a clockwise direction, repeating Step 6. As you progress, turn the work in a counterclockwise direction, and push the threads covering the spokes toward the center of the circle.

8. When all the spokes are completely covered with thread, carry the thread back over the last spoke. Then insert the needle to the wrong side of the fabric at the tip of the spoke. Pull the thread through and secure the stitch (Ending Off, Appendix).

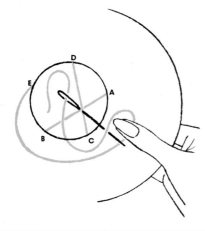

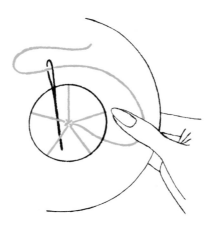

IF YOU ARE LEFT-HANDED...
1. To form the spokes, follow Steps 1-4, but reverse the direction in which you make them as shown by the letters in the drawing at left. Make a counterclockwise loop with the thread and hold it down with your right thumb. Slip the needle from left to right under the spokes.

2. To cover the spokes, follow Steps 5-8, but make a counterclockwise loop with the thread and hold it out of the way with your right thumb. Work around the circle in a counterclockwise direction, turning the work in the opposite direction as you proceed.

RAISED NEEDLE WEAVING: For decorative leaves and petals

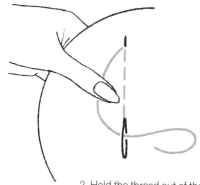

1. To make the two vertical stitches that will form the foundation for the weaving, use a blunt-ended tapestry needle with knotted thread. Begin by bringing the needle up from the wrong side of the fabric at the top end of the guide line for the design. Pull the thread through.

2. Hold the thread out of the way with your left thumb. Insert the needle to the wrong side of the fabric at the bottom end of the guide line. Bring the needle up again just next to the hole from which the thread emerged in the previous step and pull the thread through.

3. Insert the needle at the bottom of the guide line just beside the hole through which the thread was inserted in Step 2 (arrow). Pull the thread through. Then bring the needle up at the top of the guide line just above the two parallel foundation stitches and pull the thread through. Be careful not to pull the thread so tight that it puckers the fabric.

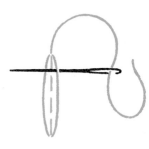
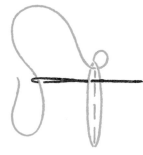

4. To make the weave, keep the thread out of the way above the foundation stitches and slip the needle —from right to left—under the right-hand foundation stitch without catching the threads or the fabric. Pull the thread under the stitch.

5. Keep the thread out of the way again, and slip the needle—from left to right —under the left-hand foundation stitch. Pull the thread under the stitch, again taking care not to catch any fabric or thread.

6. Weave the thread over and under the foundation stitches by repeating Steps 4 and 5. Keep the tension uniform so that the covering threads are smooth and even. From time to time, push the stitches toward the top of the work so that they are closely packed.

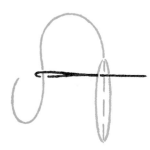

7. When the foundation stitches are completely covered, insert the needle at the bottom of the guide line. Pull the thread through to the wrong side of the fabric and secure it (Ending Off, Appendix).

IF YOU ARE LEFT-HANDED...
1. To make the foundation stitches, follow Steps 1-3. Then, to begin the weave, follow Step 4, but keep the thread out of the way to the left and slip the needle under the left-hand foundation thread—from left to right—as shown above.

2. To complete the weave, insert the needle—from right to left—under the right-hand foundation stitch. Then follow Steps 5-7.

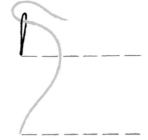

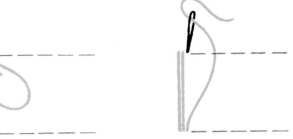

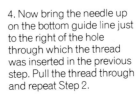

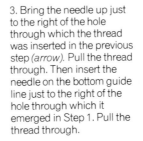

1. To make the parallel vertical stitches that will form the foundation for the tying stitches, use one or more strands of thread and knot the ends. Bring the needle up from the wrong side of the fabric at the left-hand end of the bottom guide line for the design. Pull the thread through.

2. Insert the needle on the top guide line at a point directly opposite the hole from which the thread emerged in the previous step. Pull the thread through.

3. Bring the needle up just to the right of the hole through which the thread was inserted in the previous step (arrow). Pull the thread through. Then insert the needle on the bottom guide line just to the right of the hole through which it emerged in Step 1. Pull the thread through.

4. Now bring the needle up on the bottom guide line just to the right of the hole through which the thread was inserted in the previous step. Pull the thread through and repeat Step 2.

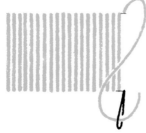

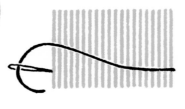

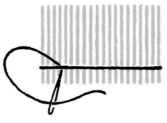

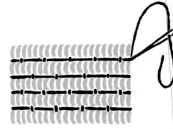

5. Continue to make parallel vertical stitches by repeating Steps 2-4 until the area is covered. Space the stitches closely and keep the tension even. If you want to use thread of contrasting color for the tying stitches, bring the thread through to the wrong side of the fabric as you make the last vertical stitch and secure it (Ending Off, Appendix).

6. To make the horizontal rows of tying stitches, use thread of the same or of a contrasting color knotted at the end. For the first row —which should be a distance above the bottom guide line equal to the desired spacing between the rows—bring the needle up Just to the right of the last vertical stitch you made. Pull the thread through. Then insert the needle at a point directly opposite the hole from which it emerged, just to the left of the first vertical stitch you made (Step 2). Pull the thread through to the wrong side of the fabric to form a horizontal stitch.

7. To make the first small tying stitch, count over from three to four vertical stitches. Bring the needle up between the stitches, just above the horizontal stitch. Be careful not to catch any threads of the previous stitches. Pull the thread through.

8. Insert the needle just below the horizontal stitch. Pull the thread through so that it holds down the horizontal stitch. Repeat until you have made a series of evenly spaced tying stitches across the horizontal thread.

9. Continue to make rows of tying stitches by repeating Steps 6-8 until the entire area is covered. Space the horizontal stitches evenly, and center the small tying stitches on each successive row between the stitches on the previous row. Secure the last tying stitch on the wrong side of the fabric (Ending Off, Appendix).

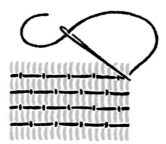

IF YOU ARE LEFT-HANDED...
Follow Steps 1-9, but note that the angle of the needle will be different, as shown.

BOKHARA COUCHING: For filling in a large area

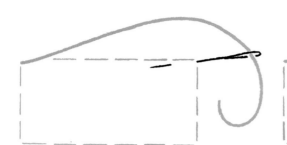

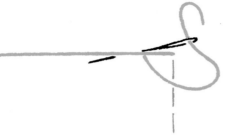

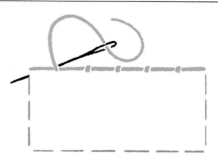

1. To make the horizontal stitch that will form the foundation for the first row of tying stitches, use a strand of thread knotted at the end. Bring the needle up from the wrong side of the fabric at the left-hand end of the uppermost guide line for the design. Pull the thread through.

2. Insert the needle at the right-hand end of the guide line. Without pulling the thread through, point the needle slightly to the left and bring it up just below the guide line, about 1/4 inch from the end.

3. To make the tying stitches, first pull the thread through. Then, with the needle again pointed slightly to the left, insert it just above the horizontal stitch, directly opposite the hole from which the thread just emerged. Do not pull the thread through. Leaving a space equal to the desired interval between tying stitches, bring the needle up on the left just below the horizontal stitch. Pull the thread through.

4. To finish the first row, make small, evenly spaced tying stitches across the horizontal thread by repeating Step 3. As you make the last tying stitch, bring the point of the needle up on the left-hand edge of the design just below the end of the horizontal thread, leaving a space equal to the desired interval between rows. Pull the thread through.

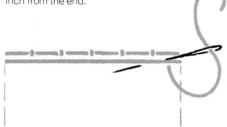

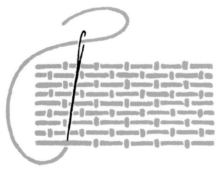

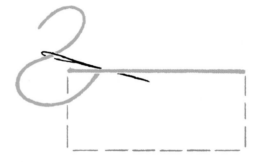

5. To make the next row, make the horizontal stitch and the tying stitches as you did in Steps 2-4, centering the tying stitches between the stitches on the previous row.

6. Make as many rows of stitches as your design requires by repeating Steps 2-5. On the last row, pull the thread through to the wrong side of the fabric as you make the last tying stitch and secure the stitch (Ending Off, Appendix).

IF YOU ARE LEFT-HANDED...
Follow Steps 1-6, but reverse the direction in which you make the stitches, and point the needle slightly to the right as you insert it. In Step 1, bring the needle up at the right-hand end of the guide line and insert it at the left-hand end. In Steps 3 and 4, work from left to right as you make the small tying stitches.

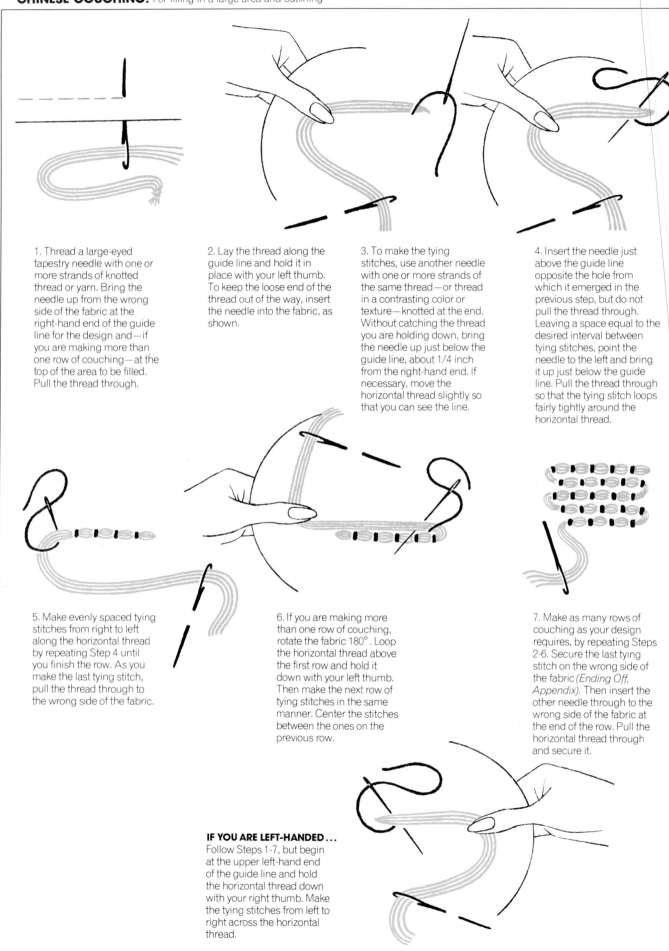

1. Thread a large-eyed tapestry needle with one or more strands of knotted thread or yarn. Bring the needle up from the wrong side of the fabric at the right-hand end of the guide line for the design and—if you are making more than one row of couching—at the top of the area to be filled. Pull the thread through.

2. Lay the thread along the guide line and hold it in place with your left thumb. To keep the loose end of the thread out of the way, insert the needle into the fabric, as shown.

3. To make the tying stitches, use another needle with one or more strands of the same thread—or thread in a contrasting color or texture—knotted at the end. Without catching the thread you are holding down, bring the needle up just below the guide line, about 1/4 inch from the right-hand end. If necessary, move the horizontal thread slightly so that you can see the line.

4. Insert the needle just above the guide line opposite the hole from which it emerged in the previous step, but do not pull the thread through. Leaving a space equal to the desired interval between tying stitches, point the needle to the left and bring it up just below the guide line. Pull the thread through so that the tying stitch loops fairly tightly around the horizontal thread.

5. Make evenly spaced tying stitches from right to left along the horizontal thread by repeating Step 4 until you finish the row. As you make the last tying stitch, pull the thread through to the wrong side of the fabric.

6. If you are making more than one row of couching, rotate the fabric 180°. Loop the horizontal thread above the first row and hold it down with your left thumb. Then make the next row of tying stitches in the same manner. Center the stitches between the ones on the previous row.

7. Make as many rows of couching as your design requires, by repeating Steps 2-6. Secure the last tying stitch on the wrong side of the fabric *(Ending Off, Appendix)*. Then insert the other needle through to the wrong side of the fabric at the end of the row. Pull the horizontal thread through and secure it.

IF YOU ARE LEFT-HANDED...
Follow Steps 1-7, but begin at the upper left-hand end of the guide line and hold the horizontal thread down with your right thumb. Make the tying stitches from left to right across the horizontal thread.

SATIN STITCH COUCHING: For filling in a large area and outlining

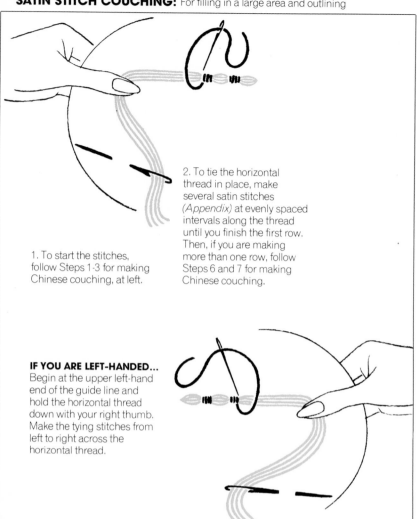

1. To start the stitches, follow Steps 1-3 for making Chinese couching, at left.

2. To tie the horizontal thread in place, make several satin stitches (*Appendix*) at evenly spaced intervals along the thread until you finish the first row. Then, if you are making more than one row, follow Steps 6 and 7 for making Chinese couching.

IF YOU ARE LEFT-HANDED... Begin at the upper left-hand end of the guide line and hold the horizontal thread down with your right thumb. Make the tying stitches from left to right across the horizontal thread.

CROSS-STITCH COUCHING: For filling in a large area and outlining

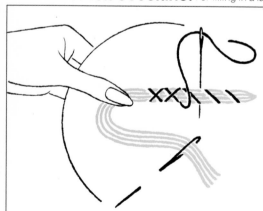

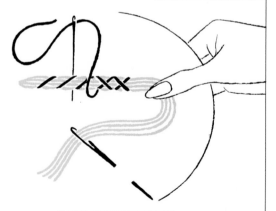

1. To start the stitches, follow Steps 1-3 for making Chinese couching, at left.

2. To tie the horizontal thread in place, make evenly spaced cross-stitches (*Appendix*) until you finish the first row. Then, if you are making more than one row, follow Steps 6 and 7 for making Chinese couching. Make either half or full cross-stitches, as desired, but if you choose full cross-stitches, secure the last stitch of each row on the wrong side of the fabric.

IF YOU ARE LEFT-HANDED... Begin at the upper left-hand end of the guide line and hold the horizontal thread down with your right thumb. Make the tying stitches from left to right across the horizontal thread.

Borders with a delicate air

A proud peacock and fragile sprays of spring blossoms form a border design done in the subtle style of the finest Chinese embroidery. The muted colors—whites, grays, greens, ecru and black—blend together in an interplay of stitches that creates softly shaded and realistic tones.

These stitches, like the satin stitch used for the leaves, are so decorative that Oriental needlecrafters dubbed them "needle painting." The feathery Pekingese stitch used on the peacock's body once commanded twice the price of work executed in more conventional stitches.

In China, a border design such as this is traditionally applied to the hem and sleeve of a robe like the one shown here. For Western wear, such designs can be applied in the same way—or as exotic edging for a skirt, an overblouse or a scarf. Complete instructions for executing these trimmings appear overleaf.

Instructions for embroidering the border designs

To make the embroidered border designs, you will need several embroidery needles (Sizes 7 or 8) and a blunt-ended tapestry needle (Size 18 or 22). Each design requires two skeins of six-strand cotton embroidery thread in white, and one skein each of ecru, light and medium green, light and medium gray, and black. Use a 4-inch screw hoop to secure the work. If the area of the garment on which you are embroidering does not fit inside the hoop, baste a piece of extra fabric to the edge while you are working.

These designs are most successfully worked on heavier fabric, such as satin, crisp taffeta or linen. If you are applying the embroidery to a finished garment, be sure to open the hems before you begin the work. Restitch the hems in place when the embroidery is completed. If the embroidery is to be worked on a garment in progress, measure the length of the sleeve and the garment so that the designs are positioned correctly. Add 2 inches of fabric beyond the edges so that the work fits inside the hoop.

The designs may be used singly or combined and extended to make borders, such as the ones shown in the photograph on the preceding pages. If you use them around the bottom of sleeves, reverse the diagrams when you transfer the border designs onto the garment fabric.

Transferring the design: Follow the instructions given in the Appendix.

Selecting colors and stitches: Thread colors needed for the border designs are shown in the chart below. These can be matched to the color photograph of the border designs on the preceding pages. Instructions for making the stitches are given on pages 140-149 or in the Appendix. The placement of the stitches is keyed by letter on the diagrams opposite.

Use three strands of embroidery thread in your needle when making most of the stitches. When making the whipped spider-web stitch, use the full six strands. To avoid constant rethreading of your needle, keep several needles threaded in the colors you are using.

Stitching the design: To make the peacock design, begin by working the flower petals in white, light gray and ecru. Work the dark gray flower centers, then the leaves in light and medium green. Using white, light gray and black, make the peacock's head and wings; outline the wings in light gray, then make the markings or eyes in the tail feathers of the bird using light and dark gray. Fill in the white tail feathers, then the white feathers on the body. Work the peacock's legs in ecru, and embroider the dark gray and ecru branches last.

To make the floral border design, begin by working the flower petals in white, light gray and ecru; then embroider the dark gray flower centers. Next work the buds of the flowers in white, light and dark gray and ecru; then make the leaves in light and medium green. Embroider the branches in dark gray.

Pressing the finished work: Place the embroidery wrong side up over a soft towel. Cover the work with a dry, lightweight press cloth; then press lightly with a steam iron.

white

ecru

light green

medium green

light gray

dark gray

black

All flower petals in the diagram above are worked in brick and satin stitches; the flower centers in the whipped spider-web stitch; the leaves, the peacock's head and wings and the eyes on the tail in the satin stitch; the feathers at the crown, the outline of the wings, the tail feathers and the legs in the stem stitch; the body feathers in the Pekingese stitch; and the branches in uneven rows of scroll and coral stitches. Each area is keyed by letter to the right. When making brick stitches in curved areas, the stitches at the edges must be uneven to follow the curve.

A satin stitch
B stem stitch
C brick stitch
D whipped spider-web stitch
E Pekingese stitch
F scroll stitch
G coral stitch

All flower petals in the diagram above are worked in brick and satin stitches; the flower centers in the whipped spider-web stitch; the leaves and buds in satin stitches; the flower stems in the stem stitch; and the branches in uneven rows of scroll and coral stitches. Each area is keyed by letter at right. When making brick stitches in curved areas, the edge stitches must be uneven to follow the curve.

A satin stitch
B stem stitch
C brick stitch
D whipped spider-web stitch
E Pekingese stitch
F scroll stitch
G coral stitch

A purse full of Turkish treasures

A blaze of flowers embroidered in a characteristic Turkish design gives Near Eastern excitement to this Western evening bag. Gold and silver threads sparkle among the vivid yarns. And the flowers themselves glitter like precious jewels in a ring of golden twine. The motif of this purse was adapted from one of the versatile embroideries the Turks called towels. Made by harem women, these much-prized needleworks served as head coverings, handkerchiefs and ceremonial napkins. Lavishly embroidered, they produced a rich, textured effect, like the one shown here.

In this modern adaptation, the central flower, created with brick stitches *(page 142)*, resembles a tapestry, and clusters of French knots provide an extra dimension to the design. Gold threads tacked down by the so-called couching technique create a maximum of ornate display with a minimum of costly thread.

Complete instructions for making the purse appear overleaf.

Instructions for embroidering the purse

To make the Turkish purse—which should be embroidered before it is assembled—you will first need 1/4 yard of heavy or mediumweight pale beige linen fabric, several crewel embroidery needles (Sizes 3 or 4), a large tapestry needle (Size 18) and the following yarns: 2 one-ounce skeins of Persian wool or crewel yarn in dark red and medium green, and 1 skein each of the other yarn colors indicated on the chart at right; 1 small ball or card of metallic crochet yarn in gold and silver; and approximately 1 yard of bone-colored raffia. You will also need about three dozen pale green sequins, measuring 1/4 inch in diameter.

In order to reinforce, stiffen and line the purse, you will need 1/4 yard each of wool felt; heavy, nonwoven interfacing material; and a sturdy, but lightweight lining fabric of your choice. To finish the purse, use a 7-inch-long nylon zipper in light beige, and 2 yards of gold cord with tassels at both ends.

Transferring the design: Draw the design in the center of a 9-by-12-inch piece of the linen, following the instructions given in the Appendix. To prevent fraying, finish the edges of the fabric with hand overcast stitches (Appendix) or machine zigzag stitches.

Selecting colors and stitches: Choose the yarn colors from those shown in the chart at right. These can be matched to the colors in the photograph of the purse on the preceding pages. Instructions for making the embroidery stitches are given on pages 140-149 or in the Appendix. The placement of the stitches is keyed by letter on the diagram opposite. For the majority of the stitches, use one strand of Persian wool or crewel yarn in your needle, but when making the French knots and raised needle weaving, use two strands of yarn, worked as one. For most of the large, couched flower stems, use a strand of raffia together with five strands of very dark green yarn, tied down with gold. Work the stem at the center in raffia and silver, tied down with gold. To avoid constant rethreading, keep several needles threaded in the colors you are using. Use a small screw hoop to secure the work.

Stitching the design: Begin by working the seven large stems using dark green, gold and silver yarn, and strands of raffia. Then work the large flower petals at the center of the design, using pale and medium pink, and light and dark red. Next make the petals of the blue flower at the upper right-hand corner of the design; then the petals of the pink and orange flowers at each side of the large central flower. Now make the six gold and silver leaves at the bottom of the design. Fill in the gold centers of the pink and orange flowers, and make the gold stitches around the leaf below the central flower stem. Outline the petals and the leaves where indicated, using dark green yarn. Make the light- and medium-green leaves at the top. Fill in the remaining areas, making the French knots and raised needle weaving after you have completed all other stitches. Apply the sequins last.

Assembling the purse: Cut out the purse front to measure 7 1/2 inches from top to bottom and 9 1/2 inches across at the widest point, leaving 1 inch of extra fabric at the top and 1/2 inch around the curved edge. Using the front as a guide, cut out the back, two pieces of interfacing, two pieces of lining and one piece of felt. Pin and baste the felt to the wrong side of the front. Using thread in a color that matches the linen, make tiny, invisible hand basting stitches around the embroidered motifs. Sew through both the fabric and the felt. Place a piece of the interfacing over the felt, and machine baste the three pieces together, sewing on the seam line. Trim the seam allowances of the felt and the interfacing close to the stitching line.

Attach the remaining piece of interfacing to the wrong side of the back, as you did for the front. Place the front and the back together, wrong sides out. At the top, make 5/8 inch of machine stitching at each end; then stitch a centered zipper at the opening. For an elegant touch, apply the zipper by hand using the prick stitch (Appendix).

Open the zipper. Match the front and back seam lines, and machine stitch around the curved edges. Remove all bastings; trim the seam allowances, and clip around the curves. Turn the purse right side out. Machine stitch the lining pieces, wrong sides out, as you stitched the purse. Insert the lining and attach the top edges to the zipper tape with hemming stitches (Appendix). Center the cord around the curved edge. Fasten it to the fabric with hemming stitches, using the same thread you used for the tiny basting stitches.

light blue	medium pink
medium blue	light red
dark blue	dark red
light green	light orange
medium green	dark orange
very dark green	gold
pale pink	silver

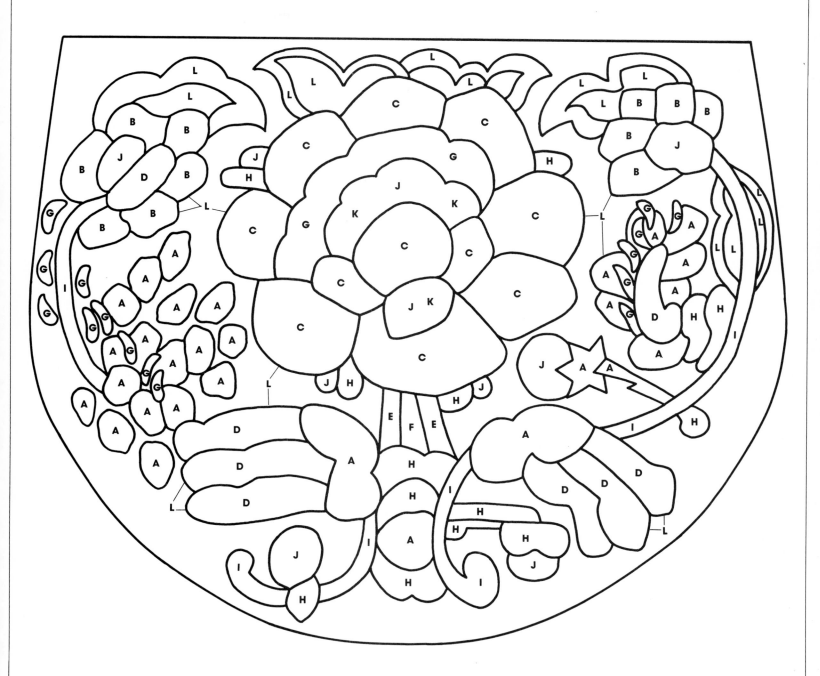

Each area is keyed by letter at right. Work the stems in satin stitch or cross-stitch couching. Make the large flower petals at the center using brick stitches, and the majority of the petals on the three small flowers in Arab laid work or Bokhara couching. Cover the gold and silver leaves and the gold centers of the small flowers with Chinese couching. Now outline the motifs with stem stitches and fill in the leaves at the top of the design with the same stitches, spacing them very close together. Use satin stitches or Arab laid work to make most of the remaining leaves. Work the gold stamens of the large flower and the rest of the leaves and petals in raised needle weaving. Make the small flower clusters and buds in French knots. To attach the sequins, pull the thread through the hole at the center, then make French knots over them. When making stitches in curved areas, the stitches at the edges will have to be slightly uneven to conform to the bend of the curve.

A Arab laid work
B Bokhara couching
C brick stitch
D Chinese couching
E cross-stitch couching
F half cross-stitch couching
G raised needle weaving
H satin stitch
I satin stitch couching
J French knots
K sequins with French knots
L stem stitch

6
PROVOCATIVE LOOK IN CROCHET

During the autumn of 1971, a Manhattan chain store courted a mini-pandemonium simply by posting a sign: "We have wool today!" Quickly, the yarn counter began to bustle and continued to do so until the wool ran out, snapped up by needlecrafters for whom the crocheting of exotic garments in bright wools had become a passion. After centuries of serving as a grandmotherly technique for turning out nice little things

REJUVENATION OF A FINE OLD CRAFT

from cotton string—napkins, antimacassars and handkerchiefs—crochet had lost its thin-lipped propriety, and blossomed into a sexy-looking fashion vehicle.

When the demand for crochet materials took off in the late 1960s, stores chronically ran short of wool and other yarns, and stocks of crochet hooks vanished. Avid crocheters were reduced to unraveling old sweaters and begging hooks from friends.

The supply of wool did not entirely catch

up with demand until 1973, by which time sales of craft yarns had climbed from 39 million pounds a year to 115. And sales of crochet hooks had tripled. This boom was instigated primarily by youngsters who discovered that the stitches and patterns grandmother executed in miniature could be worked in a larger scale with bigger hooks to form filigrees and thick-nubbled textures with all manner of exotic potential. They discarded the traditional tiny crochet hooks (00 in the numbered system used to classify sizes, though longer, is not much larger than a darning needle and forms about four to eight stitches in a linear inch) and took up letter-coded modern hooks that yield super stitches. With a Size K, for example, a hook 1/4 inch in diameter and a standard length of almost 6 inches, two to four stitches fill an inch. Giant 1/2-inch-thick hooks lettered Q make even more daringly open patterns.

Colors and textures beyond the prim imaginings of the antimacassar crowd were needed to match the bold new stitches. Brilliant hues appeared, like those inventively combined in the paisleys on pages 162-163. And in addition to the worsteds used in these paisleys, crocheters began exploring the possibilities of yarns with other textures, such as fuzzy mohairs, shiny rayons, nubby bouclés and velvety chenilles.

Among the first garments to be widely made and worn when the crochet fad began were hats—often little skullcaps shaped like those of Muslim pilgrims, but created in every color of the rainbow. Then fringed ponchos became the rage, and finally vests. The vests were hip length at first, but got shorter and shorter until, having earned the name "rib ticklers," they stopped just below the bust.

A netlike stitch called filet, which traditionally had been used as background for other stitches, turned out to look absolutely smashing by itself—see-through, and simple to make. And it spurred crocheters to try ever more outré crocheted fashions. Not just vests and caps, but bikinis and blouses and capelets too. Homey styles like cardigan sweaters and A-line dresses became exotic when done in openwork.

Amateur crocheters were quickly followed by professionals. A pioneer designer was Mady Gerrard, who had learned to crochet at the age of five in her native Hungary. She began commercial production in 1970 in four New York boutiques—which did $45,000 worth of business in the first five months. Now expanded to employ more than 20 crocheters, Mrs. Gerrard produces everything from dresses to men's sweaters.

Another designer using crochet is Dorothy Leeds, who has created bare-waisted and openwork evening wear with single chain stitches. And artist Janet Lipkin Decker has scrambled a welter of stitches in the elaborately ruffled, padded and beaded bib fronts she makes for boutiques.

The beauty of crochet, however, is that the merest novice can, after only a few days' practice, undertake projects such as these. By mastering something as basic as the double crochet stitch, for example, it is possible to proceed confidently to make the seductive harem outfit on pages 176-177.

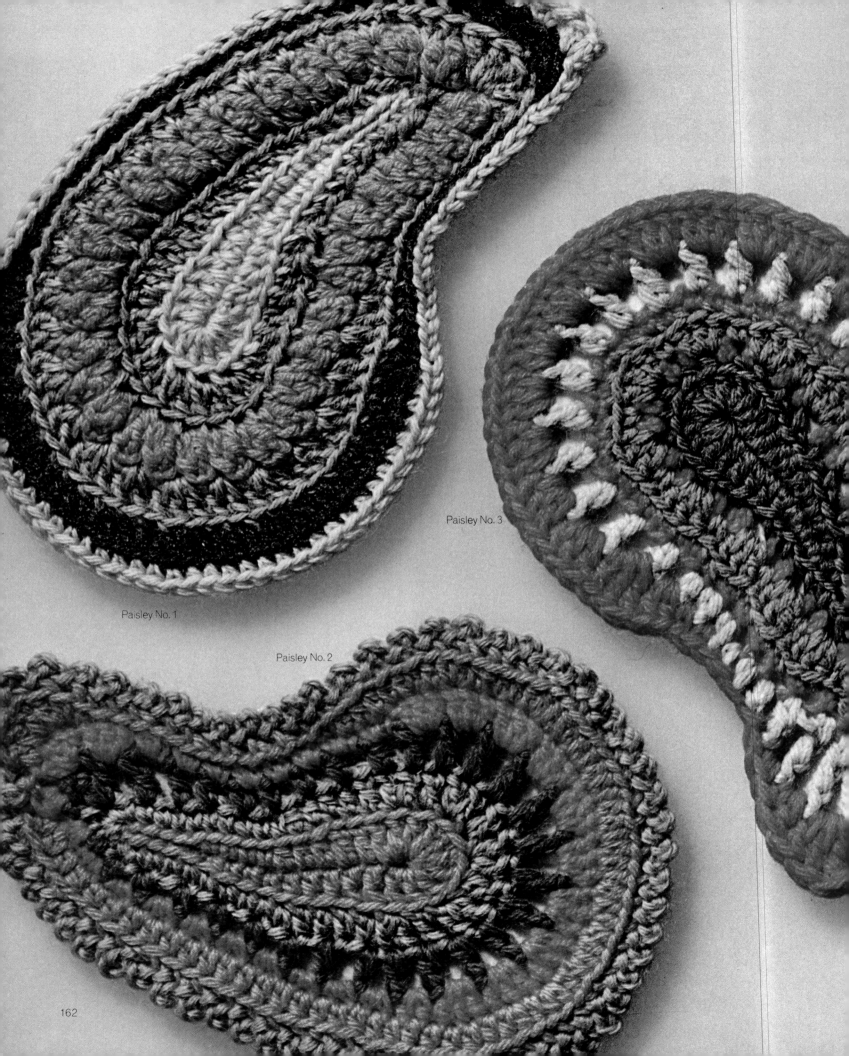

Paisley No. 1

Paisley No. 2

Paisley No. 3

162

Embryos of intriguing garments

The colorful shapes curling across these pages are contemporary crocheted versions of the centuries-old Indian fabric designs called paisleys. Each crocheted paisley is made up of six concentric rounds worked with a variety of basic stitches—the chain, single, double, half-double and triple crochet, and the slip stitch. Combining the stitches in different ways produces such distinctive accents as the fat lilac mounds, called popcorns, in Paisley No. 1 and the lively blue picot edging that frames Paisley No. 4.

A group of paisleys sewed together can create a dramatic afghan or shawl or a unique overblouse like the one on pages *168-169.* Even one or two paisleys used as appliqués can enliven a skirt or sweater.

Detailed directions for each of these designs (labeled here as paisley variations 1-4 for easy reference) begin overleaf. Left-handed crocheters, working from left to right instead of right to left, should remember that their paisleys will curve in the opposite direction to those pictured here.

Paisley No. 4

Instructions for crocheting the paisleys

The instructions given below are for crocheting the paisley designs that are pictured on the preceding pages. The paisleys were made with a Size E aluminum crochet hook and yarn of knitting worsted weight. Directions for all the crochet stitches used can be found in the Appendix.

PAISLEY VARIATION No. 1 ROUND ONE: Using color A (pink, in the picture on the preceding pages), make a foundation chain of 16. Make 1 slip stitch in each of the first 5 chains, 1 single crochet stitch in each of the next 4 chains, 1 half double crochet stitch in each of the next 3 chains, and 1 double crochet stitch in each of the next 2 chains. Make 10 double crochet stitches in the last chain; this will form a semicircle. Do not turn the work around but continue now to crochet along the opposite side of the foundation chain *(drawing 1)* by making 1 double crochet stitch in each of the next 2 chains, 1 half double crochet stitch in each of the next 3 chains, 1 single crochet in each of the next 4 chains, then 1 slip stitch in each of the last 5 chains. Com-

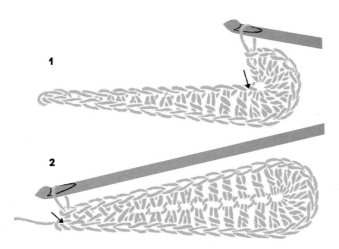

plete this round by making a slip stitch in the first slip stitch of this round *(drawing 2)*. Fasten off.

ROUND TWO: Using color B (green), and working through the back loops of the stitches only, make 1 single crochet stitch in the stitch that joined the first and last stitches of round 1 *(drawing 3)* and in each of the next 8 stitches. Then make 1 half double crochet stitch in each of the next 5 stitches, 1 double crochet stitch in each of the next 4 stitches, 2 double crochet stitches in each of the next 7 stitches, 1 double crochet stitch in each of the next 4 stitches, 1 half double crochet stitch in each of the next 2 stitches, and 1 single crochet stitch in each of the last 12 stitches. Com-

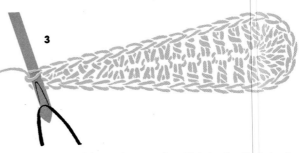

plete this round by making a slip stitch in the first single crochet stitch of this round. Fasten off.

ROUND THREE: Attach color C (lilac) in the stitch that joined the first and last stitches of the previous round and chain 3. Working through the back loops of the stitches only, make 2 double crochet stitches in the stitch that joined the first and last stitches of round two. Remove the hook from the loop and insert the hook into the space made

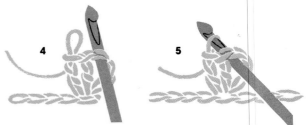

by the 3 chains made at the beginning of the row *(drawing 4)*. Pick up the dropped loop with the hook *(drawing 5)* and draw it through; then chain 1. This sequence results in a popcorn stitch at the start of a row. (For all popcorns that do not occur at the beginning of a round, follow this sequence—make 3 double crochet stitches in the same stitch, then remove the hook, insert it in the space created by the chain 1 that preceded the 3 double crochet stitches. Now pick up the dropped loop and draw it through; then chain 1. This completes a popcorn stitch occurring in midrow.) After the first popcorn stitch made at the start of this round, repeat the following sequence—skip 1 stitch and work a popcorn in the next stitch—9 times, then work a popcorn in each of the next 13 stitches. Then repeat this sequence—skip 1 stitch and work a popcorn in the next stitch—10 times. Complete this round by making a slip stitch in the first space of the round. Fasten off.

ROUND FOUR: Attach color D (gray) between the first and last popcorn stitches of the previous round, and chain 3. Work 3 triple crochet stitches in the stitch that joined the first and last stitches of the previous round. Then make 3 triple crochet stitches in the space made by the chain stitch that completed the first popcorn stitch of the preceding row. Make 3 double crochet stitches in the next space, 2 half double crochet stitches in each of the next 10 spaces, and 2 double crochet stitches in each of the next 2 spaces. Then repeat the following sequence—make 3 double crochet stitches in the next space and 2 double crochet stitches in the following space—5 times. Make 3 double crochet stitches in the next space, 2 half double crochet stitches in the next space, 2 single crochet stitches in the next space, 1 slip stitch in each of the next 6 spaces and 1 single and 1 half double crochet stitch in the last space. Complete the round by making a slip stitch in the third chain of the round. Fasten off.

ROUND FIVE: Using color E (brown) and working through the back loops of the stitches only, make 1 single crochet stitch in the stitch that joined the first and last stitches of the previous row. Make 1 double and 1 half double crochet stitch in each of the next two stitches, then make 1 half double crochet stitch in each of the next 3 stitches, 1 single crochet stitch in each of the next 19 stitches, 1 half double crochet stitch in each of the next 2 stitches, and 1 double crochet stitch in the next stitch. Then repeat the following sequence—make 2 double crochet stitches in the next stitch and 1 double crochet stitch in the following stitch—14 times. Next make 1 half double crochet stitch in the next stitch, 1 single crochet stitch in each of the next 3 stitches, and 1 slip stitch in each of the last 11 stitches. Complete the round by making a slip stitch in the first single crochet stitch of this round. Fasten off.

ROUND SIX: Attach color A (pink) in the stitch that joined the first and last stitches of the previous round and chain 2. Make 1 double crochet stitch in the joining stitch. Then make 2 half double crochet stitches in each of the next 3 stitches, 2 single crochet stitches in the next stitch, 1 slip stitch in each of the next 26 stitches, 1 single crochet stitch in each of the next 38 stitches, and 1 slip stitch in each of the next 10 stitches. Next repeat the following sequence—make 2 slip stitches in the next stitch and 1 slip stitch in the following stitch—5 times. Then make 1 slip stitch in the first chain stitch of this round and conclude with a half double crochet stitch in the same stitch. Fasten off.

PAISLEY VARIATION No. 2 ROUND ONE: Using color A (lilac, in the picture on the preceding pages), make a foundation chain of 16. Make 1 slip stitch in each of the first 5 chains, then make 1 single crochet stitch in each of the next 4 chains, 1 half double crochet stitch in each of the next 3

chains, and 1 double crochet stitch in each of the next 2 chains. Make 10 double crochet stitches in the last chain; this will form a semicircle. Do not turn the work but continue now to crochet along the opposite side of the foundation chain (drawing 1, opposite) by making 1 double crochet stitch in each of the next 2 chains, 1 half double crochet stitch in each of the next 3 chains, 1 single crochet in each of the next 4 chains, then 1 slip stitch in each of the last 5 chains. Complete with a slip stitch in the first slip stitch of this round (drawing 2, opposite). Fasten off.

ROUND TWO: Using color B (gray), and working through the back loops of the stitches only, make 1 single crochet stitch in the stitch that joined the first and last stitches of round 1—and in each of the next 9 stitches. Then make 1 half double crochet stitch in each of the next 4 stitches and repeat the following sequence—make 2 double crochet stitches in the next stitch and 1 double crochet stitch in the following stitch—5 times. Make 1 half double crochet stitch in each of the next 4 stitches, then 1 single crochet stitch in each of the last 11 stitches. Complete this round by making a slip stitch in the first single crochet stitch of this round. Fasten off.

ROUND THREE: Using color C (taupe), make 1 single crochet stitch in the stitch that joined the first and last stitches of round two. Then repeat the following sequence—chain 1, skip 1 stitch and make 1 single crochet stitch in the next stitch—6 times. Next repeat this sequence—chain 1, skip 1 stitch and make 1 half double crochet stitch in the next stitch—twice. Then, repeat the following sequence—chain 1 and make 1 double crochet stitch in the next stitch—12 times. Chain 1, make 1 half double crochet stitch in the next stitch, chain 1, skip 1 stitch, and make 1 half double crochet stitch in the next stitch. Next repeat this sequence—chain 1, skip 1 stitch, make 1 single crochet stitch in the next stitch—twice. Then repeat the following sequence—chain 1, skip 1 stitch, make 1 half double crochet stitch in the next stitch—3 times. Then repeat this sequence—chain 1, skip 1 stitch, make 1 double crochet stitch in the next stitch—twice. Chain 1, make 1 double crochet stitch in the last stitch and chain 1. Complete this round by making a slip stitch in the first single crochet stitch of this round. Fasten off.

ROUND FOUR: Attach color D (orange) in the first space and chain 2. Then make 1 double crochet stitch in this space. Next make 2 single crochet stitches in each of the next 10 spaces, 2 half double crochet stitches in the next space, 3 double crochet stitches in each of the next 10 spaces, 2 half double crochet stitches in the next space, 2 single crochet stitches in each of the next 6 spaces, 2 half double crochet stitches in the next space, and 3 double crochet stitches in the last 2 spaces. Finish with a slip stitch in the second chain of the round. Fasten off.

ROUND FIVE: Attach color A (lilac) in the stitch that joined the first and last stitches of the preceding round and chain

1. Make 1 half double crochet stitch in this and in each of the next 25 stitches. Then repeat the following sequence —make 2 half double crochet stitches in the next stitch and 1 half double crochet stitch in the following stitch—13 times. Make 1 half double crochet stitch in each of the next 2 stitches, 1 single crochet stitch in the next stitch, 1 slip stitch in each of the next 15 stitches, 1 single crochet, 1 half double crochet and 1 double crochet in the next stitch, 2 double crochet in the next stitch and 1 half double crochet stitch in the last stitch. Complete this round by making a slip stitch in the first chain of this round. Fasten off.

ROUND SIX: Using color E (gold), make 1 slip stitch in the stitch that joined the first and last stitches of the preceding round. Working in the back loops of the stitches only, repeat the following sequence—chain 3 and make 1 slip stitch in the next stitch—around the paisley, skipping a stitch where necessary to have the paisley lie flat. End with chain 3. Complete this round by making a slip stitch in the first slip stitch of this round. Fasten off.

PAISLEY VARIATION No. 3 ROUND ONE: Using color A (turquoise, in the picture on pages 162-163), make a foundation chain of 16. Make 1 slip stitch in each of the first 5 chains, then make 1 single crochet stitch in each of the next 4 chains, 1 half double crochet stitch in each of the next 3 chains, and 1 double crochet stitch in each of the next 2 chains. Make 10 double crochet stitches in the last chain to form a semicircle. Do not turn the work but now crochet along the opposite side of the foundation chain (drawing 1, page 164) by making 1 double crochet stitch in each of the first 2 chains, 1 half double crochet stitch in each of the next 3 chains, 1 single crochet stitch in each of the next 4 chains, and 1 slip stitch in each of the last 5 chains. Join the last stitch to the first stitch of the round (drawing 2, page 164) with another slip stitch. Fasten off.

ROUND TWO: Using color B (orange), make 1 single crochet stitch in the stitch that joined the first and last stitches of round one (drawing 3, page 164). Working through the back loops only of the stitches for the rest of round two, repeat the following sequence—chain 1, skip 1 stitch and make 1 single crochet stitch in the next stitch—8 times. Now repeat the next sequence—chain 1 and make 1 single crochet stitch in the next stitch—8 times. Then repeat this sequence—chain 1, skip 1 stitch and make 1 single crochet stitch in the next stitch—7 times. Chain 1. Complete this round by making a slip stitch in the first single crochet stitch of the round. Fasten off.

ROUND THREE: Attach color C (avocado) in the first space, and chain 2; then make 2 double crochet stitches in this same space. Now repeat the following sequence for the entire round—make 1 single crochet stitch in the next space and 3 double crochet stitches in the following space. End with 1 single crochet, 3 double crochet and 1 single crochet stitch in the last space. Complete by making a slip stitch in the second chain of this round. Fasten off.

ROUND FOUR: Using color B (orange) and working through the back loops of the stitches only, make 1 single crochet stitch in the stitch that joined the first and last stitches of round three—and in each of the next 16 stitches. Then repeat the following sequence—make 2 single crochet stitches in the next stitch and 1 single crochet stitch in the following stitch—7 times. Next make 1 single crochet stitch in each of the next 6 stitches, 1 single crochet stitch in every other stitch 6 times, 2 half double crochet stitches in the next stitch, 3 double crochet stitches in the next stitch, and 1 single crochet stitch in the last stitch. Complete this round by making a slip stitch in the first single crochet stitch of this round. Fasten off.

ROUND FIVE: Using color D (light blue), make 1 single crochet stitch in the stitch that joined the first and last stitches of round four. Then repeat the following sequence—chain 1, skip 1 stitch, make 1 single crochet in the next stitch—4 times. Now repeat the next sequence—chain 1, skip 1 stitch, make 1 half double crochet stitch in the next stitch—twice, and the following sequence—chain 1, skip 1 stitch, make 1 double crochet stitch in the next stitch—14 times. Chain 1, skip 1 stitch, make 1 half double crochet stitch in the next stitch, chain 1 and skip 1 stitch. Then repeat the following sequence—make 1 single crochet stitch in the next stitch and chain 1—5 times, then make 1 half double crochet stitch in the next stitch, chain 1, make 1 double crochet stitch in the next stitch, chain 1, make 1 triple crochet stitch in the next stitch, chain 1, make 3 triple crochet stitches with a chain 1 between each in the next stitch, chain 1, make 1 double crochet stitch in the next stitch, chain 1, and make 1 half double crochet stitch in the next stitch. Next repeat the following sequence—chain 1 and make 1 single crochet stitch in the next stitch—twice, then chain 1. Complete by making a slip stitch in the first single crochet stitch of this round. Fasten off.

ROUND SIX: Using color E (burnt orange), make 1 single crochet stitch that joined the first and last stitches of round five. Then repeat the following sequence—make 2 single crochet stitches in the next space—8 times, then make 2 half double crochet stitches in the next space. Next repeat the following sequence—make 3 double crochet stitches in the next space—12 times. Then make 2 half double crochet stitches in the next space, 1 single crochet stitch in each of the next two spaces, 1 slip stitch in each of the next 4 spaces, 2 single crochet stitches in the next space, 1 single and 1 half double crochet stitch in the next space, 3 triple crochet stitches in the next space, 2 double crochet and 1 half double crochet stitch in the next space, 2 single crochet stitches in each of the next 2 spaces, 1 single crochet in each of the next 2 spaces. Finish with a slip stitch in the first single crochet stitch of the round. Fasten off.

PAISLEY VARIATION No. 4 ROUND ONE: With color A (gold, in the picture on page 163), make a foundation chain of 16. Make 1 slip stitch in each of the first 5 chains, 1 single crochet stitch in each of the next 4 chains, 1 half double crochet stitch in each of the next 3 chains, and 1 double crochet in each of the next 2 chains. Make 10 double crochet stitches in the last chain to form a semicircle. Do not turn the work, but continue to crochet along the opposite side of the foundation chain *(drawing 1, page 164)*, with 1 double crochet stitch in each of the next 2 chains, 1 half double crochet stitch in each of the next 3 chains, 1 single crochet stitch in each of the next 4 chains, then 1 slip stitch in each of the last 5 chains. Finish with a slip stitch in the first slip stitch of the round. Fasten off.

ROUND TWO: Attach color B (avocado) in the stitch that joined the first and last stitches of round one and chain 3. Working through the back loops of the stitches only, make 2 double crochet stitches in the joining stitch. Remove the hook from the loop and insert the hook into the space made by 3 chains made at the beginning of the row *(drawing 4, page 164)*. Pick up the dropped loop with the hook *(drawing 5, page 164)* and draw it through; then chain 1. This sequence results in a popcorn stitch at the start of a row. (For all popcorns that do not occur at the beginning of a round, follow this sequence—make 3 double crochet stitches in the same stitch, then remove the hook, insert it in the space created by the chain 1 preceding the 3 double crochet stitches; now pick up the dropped loop and draw it through; then chain 1. This completes a popcorn stitch occurring in mid-row.) After the first popcorn stitch made at the start of this round, repeat the following sequence—skip 1 stitch and work a popcorn in the next stitch—8 times, then work a popcorn in each of the next 8 stitches. Now repeat the following sequence—skip 1 stitch and work a popcorn in the next stitch—7 times. Work a popcorn in the first popcorn of this round, and chain 1. Finish with a slip stitch in the space created by the chain 1 that followed the first popcorn stitch. Fasten off.

ROUND THREE: Using color C (blue), make 1 single crochet stitch in the first space. Chain 1 and make 2 single crochet stitches with a chain 1 between them in the next space. Then repeat the following sequence—chain 1 and make 1 single crochet stitch in the next space—6 times. Now repeat the next sequence—chain 1 and make 2 single crochet stitches with a chain 1 between them in the next space—9 times. Next repeat this sequence—chain 1 and make 1 single crochet in the next space—8 times. Chain 1 and make 1 single crochet stitch in the space created by the first chain 1 of this round. Then chain 1. Complete this round by making a slip stitch in the first single crochet stitch of this round. Fasten off.

ROUND FOUR: Attach color D (turquoise) in the first space and chain 3. Then make 1 double crochet stitch in this same space. Chain 1 and make 3 triple crochet stitches with a chain 1 between each of them in the next space. Chain 1 and make 1 double crochet stitch in the next space. Chain 1 and make 1 half double crochet stitch in the next space. Chain 1 and make 1 single crochet stitch in the next space. Next make 1 slip stitch in the next space.

Chain 1 and make 1 single crochet stitch in the next space. Then repeat the following sequence—chain 1 and make 1 double crochet stitch in the next space—29 times, and chain 1. Complete this round by making a slip stitch in the third chain at the beginning of the round. Fasten off.

ROUND FIVE: Attach color E (olive) in the first space and chain 2. Make 1 double crochet stitch in the same space. Then make 2 double crochet stitches in the next space, 3 triple crochet and 1 double crochet stitch in the next space, and 1 half double and 1 single crochet stitch in the next space. Slip stitch over the next 6 spaces; add slip stitches if needed to keep the paisley flat. Then make 1 single crochet stitch in the next space, 1 half double and 1 double crochet stitch in the next space, 2 double crochet stitches in the next space, 3 double crochet stitches in the next space, 2 double crochet stitches in each of the next 3 spaces, 3 double crochet stitches in each of the next 5 spaces, 2 double crochet stitches in each of the next 5 spaces, 1 double crochet stitch in the next space, and 2 half double crochet stitches in each of the last 11 spaces. Finish with a slip stitch in the second chain of the round. Fasten off.

ROUND SIX: Attach color D (turquoise) to the stitch that joined the first and last stitches of the previous row. Working through the back loops of the stitches only, chain 3 and make a slip stitch in the first chain to make what is called a picot *(drawings 6 and 7)*. Skip 1 stitch and make 1 slip stitch in the next stitch. Now repeat the following sequence for the entire round—make 1 picot, skip 1 stitch, and make 1 slip stitch in the next stitch. Complete this round by making a slip stitch in the first chain of this round. Fasten off.

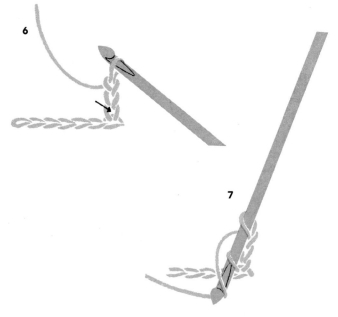

6

7

A blouse from a swirl of paisleys

Particolored paisleys, in the colors of a peacock's plume, coil together into an overblouse that slips over the head and drapes the upper body in Oriental intrigue.

Thirty-eight matched paisleys—each of them crocheted as a separate unit—make up the blouse. Fitting the paisleys' curves together requires careful planning *(overleaf),* but the resulting design appears to flow in a whimsical and spontaneous manner that flatters any figure. When completed, the overblouse can complement a formal gown. Yet it is casual enough to wear with pants or a softly swinging skirt.

Instructions for making the paisley overblouse

The crocheting instructions that follow are for the paisley overblouse shown on the preceding pages. The instructions for the paisleys are on pages 164-167; the basic crochet stitches are in the Appendix.

CROCHETING THE PAISLEY OVERBLOUSE

The following instructions are for crocheting a small size (8-10) overblouse; the changes necessary to make medium (12-14) and large (16-18) sizes follow in parentheses, in that order. You will need 3 (6,8) ounces of knitting worsted weight yarn in color A (gold in the blouse pictured on the preceding pages); 8 (10,12) ounces of color B (avocado); 4 (6,8) ounces of color C (blue); 8 (10,12) of color D (turquoise); and 4 (4,8) ounces of color E (olive). Use a Size E aluminum crochet hook for the small size, F for medium and G for large. Sew the paisleys together with a tapestry needle. Before you begin to make the overblouse, crochet a 4-by-4-inch sample swatch in a single crochet stitch to check the gauge—that is, the number of stitches and rows you are getting to the inch. For this project, the gauge is 5 stitches and 6 rows to the inch for a Size E crochet hook; 9 stitches to 2 inches and 5 rows to the inch for a Size F hook; and 4 stitches and 4 rows to the inch for a Size G hook. Measure the swatch with a firm ruler. If the required gauge calls for more stitches to the inch, change to a smaller size hook; if it calls for fewer stitches, use a larger hook. This change of hook size should also adjust the row-to-the-inch gauge. If not, try the next size hook.

Making the individual paisleys: Crochet 38 identical paisleys, following the detailed instructions for Paisley Variation No. 4 on pages 166-167.

Joining the paisleys: Place the paisleys wrong side down on a flat surface according to the diagram opposite, using eight paisleys for each sleeve and 22 for the back and front together. Maintaining this arrangement, move the paisleys close together so that their concave and convex areas touch in several places. Using yarn of the color of the outside edge of each paisley (color D, turquoise), sew the paisleys together through the adjoining tips of the picots—that is, the little triangles that frame each paisley. Then ease together any small openings that remain between the paisleys and sew them in the same fashion. Do not pull the yarn too tightly.

Note: If you are left-handed, the paisleys will curve in a direction opposite to that pictured in the diagram. The placement of the paisleys should, however, be the same.

Finishing the sleeve edge: With color B (avocado), add a narrow border along the armhole and underarm edge of the sleeve as follows: with the sleeve wrong side down, start at the top center and make 1 slip stitch in the first picot. Chain 1 and make a slip stitch in the next picot; repeat until you are within two picots of where the first two paisleys are joined. Chain 1, then make 1 half double crochet stitch in the next picot, chain 1, make 1 double crochet stitch in the next picot, chain 1 and make 1 triple crochet stitch in the space in the seam where the paisleys were joined. Chain 1, make 1 triple crochet stitch in the space directly after the space in the seam where the paisleys were joined. Chain 1 and make 1 triple crochet stitch in the space on the other side of the previous stitch. Chain 1, make 1 double crochet stitch in the next picot, chain 1 and make 1 half double crochet stitch in the next picot. Repeat this sequence around the outside of the sleeve, eliminating only the initial slip stitch. Fasten off.

Attaching the sleeve trim: Attach avocado yarn to one bottom corner of the sleeve and work a filet trim as follows: chain 5, skip 2 stitches, then repeat the following sequence—make 1 double crochet stitch in the next stitch, chain 2, skip 2 stitches—across the bottom of the sleeve, ending with 1 double crochet stitch in the last stitch. Fasten off. With a tapestry needle and avocado yarn, weave the underarm seam together for 8 inches, starting at the bottom edge of the sleeve and working up toward the sleeve cap. Complete the other sleeve in the same manner.

Finishing the overblouse: Sew the side of the blouse together from bottom to top by stitching with color D (turquoise) through the picot tips where they meet. Leave an opening at the top sufficient to fit the entire unseamed portion of the sleeve cap in place. Work a filet border around the neck edge and bottom edge of the overblouse as you did across the bottom of the sleeve. Then weave the sleeves to the front and back of the blouse with color D and fasten off. Block the finished overblouse by placing it on a flat surface, covering it with a damp cloth, and pressing it lightly with a warm iron. Do not pin the overblouse to the pressing surface or let the iron rest long in one area lest you leave marks. Enlarge or reduce the size of the overblouse if necessary by dampening it slightly, then pushing or stretching it to the desired size as you lay it out.

CROCHETING ALTERNATE VERSIONS OF THE OVERBLOUSE

The overall instructions for the alternate versions—using different paisley designs—are the same as those for the pictured version described above.

Making the individual paisleys: Crochet 38 identical paisleys following the detailed instructions for Paisley Variations Nos. 1, 2 or 3 on pages 164-166.

Joining the paisleys: Although Paisley Variations Nos. 1, 2 or 3 will curve in an opposite direction to those in the diagram opposite, the paisleys should be placed wrong side down in exactly the same order as shown. Use eight paisleys for each sleeve and 22 for the back and front strip. Maintaining this arrangement, move the paisleys close together so that their concave and convex areas touch in several places. Using yarn of the color of the outside edge of

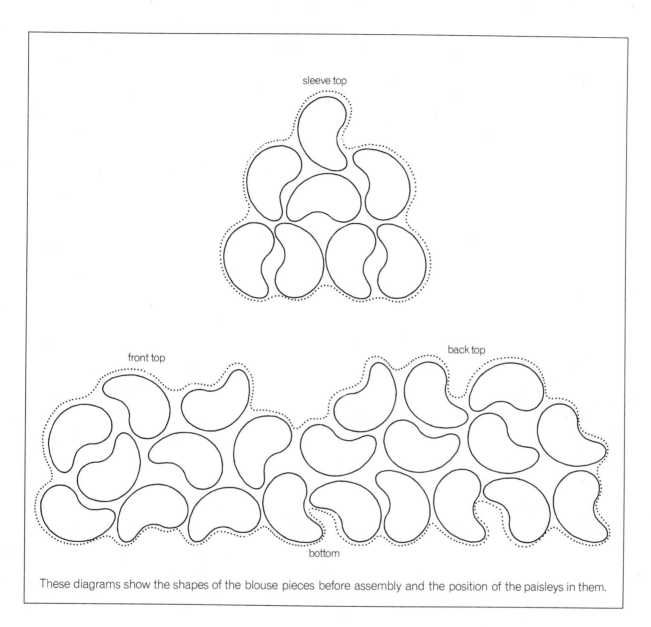

These diagrams show the shapes of the blouse pieces before assembly and the position of the paisleys in them.

each paisley, sew the paisleys together through all of the outside stitches that meet.

Finishing the sleeve edge: With yarn of another color in the paisley, add a narrow border along the armhole and underarm edge of the sleeve as follows: with the sleeve wrong side down, start at the top center and make 1 slip stitch in the center stitch. Then chain 1, skip 1 stitch and make a slip stitch in the next stitch. Repeat this sequence to within 4 stitches of where the first two paisleys are joined. Then chain 1, skip 1 stitch and make 1 half double crochet stitch in the next stitch. Chain 1, skip 1 stitch and make 1 double crochet stitch in the last stitch before the next paisley. Chain 1, make 1 triple crochet stitch in the stitch that is in the seam where the paisleys are joined. Chain 1, make 1 double crochet stitch in the next stitch, chain 1 and make 1 half double crochet stitch in the next stitch. Repeat this sequence around the side and top edges of the sleeve. Fasten off.

Attaching a sleeve trim: Make a filet trim for the sleeve as you did for Variation No. 4 above.

Finishing the overblouse: Sew the side of the blouse together from bottom to top by stitching with yarn the color of the outside edge of each paisley through the outside stitches. Leave an opening at the top sufficient to fit the entire unseamed portion of the sleeve cap in place. Work a filet border around the neck edge and bottom edge of the overblouse as you did across the bottom of the sleeve in Variation No. 4. Then sew the sleeves to the front and back of the blouse with the same color used to make the sleeve trim, and fasten off.

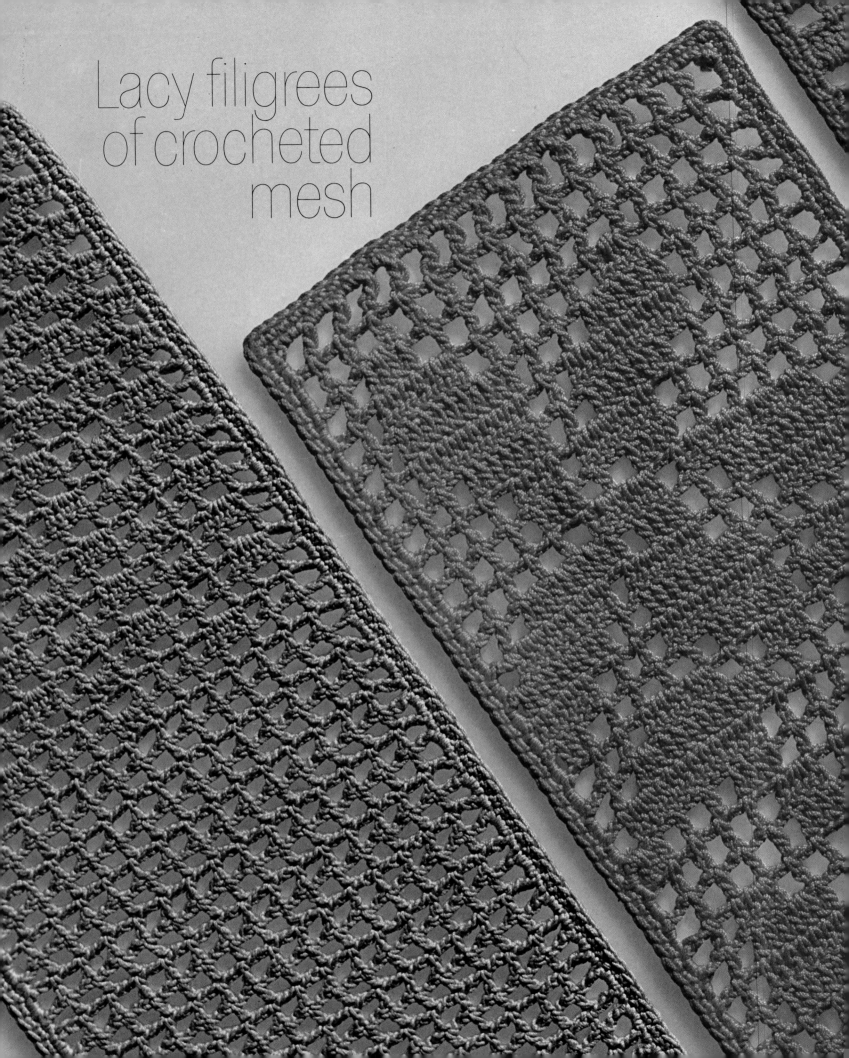

Lacy filigrees
of crocheted
mesh

Airy as lace and intricate as a filigree, the filet mesh crochet swatches shown here are examples of patterns that can be turned out for projects ranging from pillowcase trim to clothing. In filet, blocks of double crochet stitches are interspersed with open spaces to form a design. The design is governed by the number of stitches in a block —from two to eight or more—and by the number of spaces that are left open between the blocks.

In simple combinations of blocks and spaces, filet creates a network pattern *(far left)*. More complicated combinations can produce a floral or a geometric design *(center and above)*. Instructions for all three patterns appear on the following pages.

Instructions for the mesh patterns

The following instructions are for crocheting the filet patterns on the preceding pages. The swatches were made with a Size F aluminum hook and a mediumweight cotton thread. Variations can be achieved with different sizes of hooks and types of yarns.

THE GRADED FILET PATTERN: Make a foundation chain of 45 stitches; then chain 3 more to turn. For a wider swatch, make a foundation chain of any multiple of 45 plus 3, and repeat the sequence given for each row as many times as necessary. *Row 1:* Make a row of double crochet stitches; chain 3 and turn. *Row 2:* Make a row of double crochet stitches; chain 5 and turn. *Row 3:* Make 1 double crochet stitch in the third stitch of the previous row, skipping the first 2 stitches to create an open space *(drawing 1)*. Make a double crochet stitch in each of the next 3 stitches *(drawing 2)*. Chain 2, skip 2 stitches to leave another open space; then make a double crochet stitch in the next stitch *(drawing 3)*. Repeat the sequence of chain 2, skip 2 stitches and double crochet 1 to make a space; then double crochet 3. End the row with a space; chain 3 and turn. *Row 4:* Make 2 double crochet stitches in the hole created by the last space of the previous row; then make a double crochet stitch in the next stitch *(drawing 4)*. Follow this with a space, that is, chain 2, skip 2 stitches and make a double crochet in the next stitch. Make 2 double crochet stitches in the hole created by the space below, then make a double crochet stitch in the next stitch to create a block. Repeat the sequence of 1 block and 1 space across the row. End by making 2 double crochet stitches in the last hole created by the space below. Then make a double crochet stitch in the last stitch of the row. Chain 5 and turn. *Rows 5-14:* Repeat rows 3 and 4. *Row 15:* Make 3 spaces, then 1 block as in row 4; repeat this sequence across the row, ending with 3 spaces. Chain 5 and turn. *Row 16:* Make 1 space, then 1 block as in row 4 and 3 spaces. Repeat the sequence of 1 block and 3 spaces across the row, ending with 1 block and 1 space. Chain 5 and turn. *Rows 17-24:* Repeat rows 15 and 16. *Row 25:* Make 7 spaces, then 1 block as in row 4; repeat this sequence across the row, ending with 7 spaces. Chain 5 and turn. *Row 26:* Make 3 spaces, 1 block as in row 4; then 7 spaces, 1 block; repeat this sequence across the row, ending with 3 spaces. Chain 5 and turn. *Row 27:* Repeat row 25. *Row 28 to completion of pattern:* Make a row of spaces. Chain 5 and turn.

THE GEOMETRIC FILET PATTERN: Make a foundation chain of 45, then chain 3 more to turn. For a wider swatch, make a foundation chain of any multiple of 45 plus 3, and repeat the sequence given for each row as many times as necessary. *Row 1:* Make a row of double crochet stitches; chain 3 and turn. *Row 2:* Make a row of double crochet stitches; chain 5 and turn. *Rows 3 and 4:* Make a double crochet stitch in the third stitch of the previous row, skipping the first 2 stitches to create an open space. Chain 2, skip 2 stitches and make a double crochet stitch in the next stitch to create another space. Repeat this sequence across the row; chain 3 and turn. *Row 5:* Make 2 double crochet stitches in the last space of the previous row and 1 double crochet stitch in the next stitch to create a block; then make 2 spaces. Follow with 1 block and 1 space and repeat this 1 block-1 space sequence across the row, ending with 1 block, 2 spaces, 1 block. Chain 5 and turn. *Row 6:* Make 1 space, 1 block, 2 spaces, 1 block, 5 spaces, 1 block, 2 spaces, 1 block, 1 space. Repeat this sequence across the row. Chain 5 and turn. *Row 7:* Make 2 spaces, 1 block, 2 spaces, 1 block, 1 space, 1 block, 1 space, 1 block, 2 spaces, 1 block, 2 spaces. Repeat this sequence across the row, ending with 2 spaces, 1 block, 2 spaces. Chain 5 and turn. *Row 8:* Make 3 spaces, 1 block, 2 spaces, 1 block, 1 space, 1 block, 2 spaces, 1 block, 3 spaces. Repeat this sequence across the row; chain 5 and turn. *Row 9:* Make 4 spaces, 1 block, 2 spaces, 1 block, 2 spaces, 1 block, 4 spaces. Repeat this sequence across the row; chain 5 and turn. *Row 10:* Make 3 spaces, 1 block, 2 spaces, 3 blocks, 2 spaces, 1 block, 3 spaces. Repeat this sequence across the row; chain 5 and turn. *Row 11:* Make 2 spaces, 1 block, 2 spaces, 5 blocks, 2 spaces, 1 block, 2 spaces. Repeat this sequence across the row; chain 5 and turn. *Row 12:* Make 1 space, 1 block, 2 spaces, 7 blocks, 2 spaces, 1 block, 1 space. Repeat this sequence across the row; chain 3 and turn. *Row 13:* Make 1 block, 2 spaces, 9 blocks, 2 spaces, 1 block. Repeat this sequence across the row; chain 5 and turn. *Row 14:* Repeat row 12. *Row 15:* Make 1 block, 1 space, 1 block, 2 spaces, 5 blocks, 2 spaces, 1 block, 1 space, 1 block. Repeat this sequence across the row; chain 5 and turn. *Row 16:* Repeat row 10. *Row 17:* Make 1 block, 1 space, 1 block, 1 space, 1 block, 2 spaces, 1 block, 2 spaces, 1 block, 1 space, 1 block, 1 space, 1 block. Repeat this sequence across the row; chain 5 and turn. *Row 18:* Repeat row 10. *Row 19:* Repeat row 15. *Row 20:* Repeat row 12. *Row 21:* Repeat row 13. *Row 22:* Repeat row 12. *Row 23:* Repeat row 15. *Row 24:* Repeat row 10. *Row 25:* Repeat row 17. *Row 26:* Repeat row 10. *Row 27:* Repeat row 15. *Row 28:* Repeat row 12. *Row 29:* Repeat row 13. *Row 30:* Repeat row 12. *Row 31:* Repeat row 11. *Row 32:* Repeat row 10. *Row 33:* Repeat row 9. *Row 34:* Repeat row 8. *Row 35:* Repeat row 7. *Row 36:* Repeat row 6. *Row 37:* Repeat row 5. *Rows 38 and 39:* Repeat rows 3 and 4. *Row 40 to completion of pattern:* Repeat rows 3-39.

THE FLORAL FILET PATTERN: Make a foundation chain of 45, then chain 3 more to turn. For a wider swatch, make a foundation chain of any multiple of 45 plus 3, and repeat the sequence given for each row as many times as necessary. *Row 1:* Make a row of double crochet stitches; chain 3 and turn. *Row 2:* Make a row of double crochet stitches; chain 5 and turn. *Rows 3 and 4:* Make a double crochet stitch in the third stitch, skipping the first 2 stitches of the previous row to create a space. Make another space by chaining 2, then skipping 2 stitches and making a double crochet stitch in the next stitch. Repeat this sequence across the row; chain 5 and turn. *Row 5:* Make a double crochet stitch in the third stitch, skipping the first 2 stitches of the previous row to create a space. Make another space by chaining 2, skipping 2 stitches and making a double crochet stitch in the next stitch. Then make 2 double crochet stitches in the last space of the previous row and 1 double crochet stitch in the next stitch to create a block. Follow with 12 spaces. Repeat this sequence of 2 spaces, 1 block, 12 spaces across the row, chain 5 and turn. *Row 6:* Make 2 spaces as at the beginning of row 5, then make 3 more spaces, 1 block, 5 spaces, 2 blocks, 2 spaces. Repeat the sequence of 5 spaces, 1 block, 5 spaces, 2 blocks, 2 spaces across the row; chain 5 and turn. *Row 7:* Make 2 spaces as at the beginning of row 5, then make 3 blocks, 3 spaces, 2 blocks, 5 spaces. Repeat the sequence of 2 spaces, 3 blocks, 3 spaces, 2 blocks, 5 spaces across the row; chain 5 and turn. *Row 8:* Make 2 spaces as at the beginning of row 5, then make 3 more spaces, 3 blocks, 2 spaces, 3 blocks, 2 spaces. Repeat the sequence of 5 spaces, 3 blocks, 2 spaces, 3 blocks, 2 spaces across the row; chain 5 and turn. *Row 9:* Make 2 spaces as at the beginning of row 5, then make 1 more space, 2 blocks, 2 spaces, 2 blocks, 6 spaces. Repeat the sequence of 3 spaces, 2 blocks, 2 spaces, 2 blocks, 6 spaces across the row; chain 5 and turn. *Row 10:* Make 2 spaces as at the beginning of row 5, then make 5 more spaces, 2 blocks, 1 space, 1 block, 4 spaces. Repeat the sequence of 7 spaces, 2 blocks, 1

space, 1 block, 4 spaces across the row; chain 5 and turn. *Row 11:* Make 2 spaces as at the beginning of row 5, then make 2 more spaces, 1 block, 2 spaces, 1 block, 7 spaces. Repeat the sequence of 4 spaces, 1 block, 2 spaces, 1 block, 7 spaces across the row; chain 5 and turn. *Row 12:* Make 2 spaces as at the beginning of row 5, then make 1 more space, 4 blocks, 1 space, 2 blocks, 5 spaces. Repeat the sequence of 3 spaces, 4 blocks, 1 space, 2 blocks, 5 spaces across the row; chain 5 and turn. *Row 13:* Make 2 spaces as at the beginning of row 5, 3 blocks, 1 space, 1 block, 2 spaces, 5 blocks, 1 space. Repeat this sequence across the row; chain 3 and turn. *Row 14:* Make 5 blocks, 3 spaces, 2 blocks, 1 space, 3 blocks, 1 space. Repeat this sequence across the row; chain 3 and turn. *Row 15:* Make 3 blocks, 2 spaces, 3 blocks, 7 spaces. Repeat this sequence across the row; chain 5 and turn. *Row 16:* Make 2 spaces as at the beginning of row 5, then make 1 more space, 2 blocks, 2 spaces, 3 blocks, 3 spaces, 2 blocks. Repeat the sequence of 3 spaces, 2 blocks, 2 spaces, 3 blocks, 3 spaces, 2 blocks across the row; chain 3 and turn. *Row 17:* Make 1 block, 5 spaces, 2 blocks, 1 space, 4 blocks, 2 spaces. Repeat this sequence across the row; chain 5 and turn. *Row 18:* Make 1 space as at the beginning of row 5, 4 blocks, 2 spaces, 1 block, 2 spaces, 2 blocks, 3 spaces. Repeat this sequence across the row; chain 5 and turn. *Row 19:* Make 2 spaces as at the beginning of row 5, 4 blocks, 4 spaces, 1 block, 3 spaces, 1 block. Repeat this sequence across the row; chain 5 and turn. *Row 20:* Make 2 spaces as at the beginning of row 5, then make 3 more spaces, 1 block, 4 spaces, 4 blocks, 1 space. Repeat the sequence of 5 spaces, 1 block, 4 spaces, 4 blocks, 1 space across the row; chain 3 and turn. *Row 21:* Make 1 block, 3 spaces, 1 block, 3 spaces, 2 blocks, 1 space, 1 block, 3 spaces. Repeat this sequence across the row; chain 5 and turn. *Row 22:* Make 2 spaces as at the beginning of row 5, 3 blocks, 1 space, 2 blocks, 1 space, 1 block, 5 spaces. Repeat this sequence across the row; chain 5 and turn. *Row 23:* Make 2 spaces as at the beginning of row 5, then make 3 more spaces, 1 block, 1 space, 1 block, 3 spaces, 3 blocks, 1 space. Repeat the sequence of 5 spaces, 1 block, 1 space, 1 block, 3 spaces, 3 blocks, 1 space across the row; chain 3 and turn. *Row 24:* Make 1 block, 2 spaces, 1 block, 4 spaces, 1 block, 3 spaces, 1 block, 2 spaces. Repeat this sequence across the row; chain 5 and turn. *Row 25:* Make 2 spaces as at the beginning of row 5, 2 blocks, 2 spaces, 1 block, 2 spaces, 1 block, 5 spaces. Repeat this sequence across the row; chain 5 and turn. *Rows 26-34:* Repeat rows 7-15. *Row 35:* Make 2 blocks, 3 spaces, 3 blocks, 7 spaces. Repeat this sequence across the row; chain 5 and turn. *Row 36:* Make 2 spaces as at the beginning of row 5, then make 5 more spaces, 2 blocks, 5 spaces, 1 block. Repeat the sequence of 7 spaces, 2 blocks, 5 spaces, 1 block across the row; chain 5 and turn. *Row 37:* Make 2 spaces as at the beginning of row 5, then make 5 more spaces, 1 block, 7 spaces. Repeat the sequence of 7 spaces, 1 block, 7 spaces across the row; chain 5 and turn. *Rows 38 and 39:* Repeat rows 3 and 4. *Rows 40 to completion of pattern:* Repeat rows 3-39.

Harem-style from top to bottom

A bravura bit of filet crochet, this two-piece halter dress has been worked in cotton yarn with a nice dress-up luster. The pattern combines rows of daringly open filet mesh with tightly knotted double crochet stitches to provide a little support and modesty here, a touch of the seraglio there.

The floor-length skirt is made without a waistband; it rests at the hip—and fits there like a second skin. The slit up the left side to the top of the leg gives freedom of movement. The halter top snaps at the midriff and neckband, leaving most of the back prettily open.

Instructions for crocheting the filet dress

The instructions that follow are for crocheting the skirt and halter pictured on pages 176-177. Instructions for making the graded filet mesh pattern are on page 174 and the double crochet stitch needed to work the design is explained in the Appendix.

The skirt described here is size 8; the changes in the number of stitches necessary for sizes 10, 12, 14 and 16 follow in that order, in parentheses. To complete the skirt you will need 21 (23,25,27, 29) 100-yard balls of mediumweight cotton thread; an aluminum crochet hook, Size F; 4 snaps to close the waistband; and a 6-inch skirt zipper.

Directions for the halter are for a small size (30-32). The change for medium (34-36) and large (38-40) follow in parentheses in that order. For the halter you will need 4 (6,8) 100-yard balls of the same thread used in the skirt; an aluminum crochet hook, Size F; and 4 snap fasteners to fasten the neckband and the strips across the back.

If you wish to make the headband that complements the outfit, you will need five 100-yard balls of the same yarn.

CHECKING THE GAUGE

To be sure that the hook and yarn you select will provide the right number of stitches and rows per inch so that the filet skirt and halter come out the proper size, crochet a sample swatch before beginning the actual project. The swatch should measure at least 4 by 4 inches, and be made with the yarn and hook size recommended in the pattern—in this case, mediumweight cotton thread and a Size F aluminum hook. Lay the swatch on a flat surface and count the number of stitches to the inch. Measure with a firm ruler, not a tape measure. The required gauge for the filet skirt and halter is 5 1/2 double crochet stitches and 3 double crochet rows to the inch. If your sample has too few stitches to the inch, change to a smaller hook. If it has too many stitches, use a larger hook. This change of hook size will also probably adjust the row-to-the-inch gauge. If it does not, try the next size hook.

In working filet patterns, the more blocks (or units of double crochet stitches) in a row, the more the work will spread out; the more spaces, the more the work will draw in. In places where several rows of spaces occur between other pattern rows, you can most successfully adjust the gauge on a straight piece of filet work by changing to a larger or smaller hook. To adjust the gauge when shaping a garment, you can increase the number of spaces in the row.

THE LONG FILET SKIRT

The waistband and skirt top: Chain 129 (141, 153, 165, 177), then crochet 3 rows of double crochet stitches. Make the waistband tab by slip stitching across 9 stitches; then double crochet across the remaining 120 (132,144,156,168) stitches. On the next row, increase 1 stitch in every 10th (11th,12th,13th,14th) stitch across the row; you will now have 132 (144,156,168,180) stitches. Crochet 3 rows of double crochet stitches; then increase 6 stitches evenly spaced on the fourth row. Repeat this increase every fourth row twice more; then repeat it every other row until there are 204 (216,228,240,252) stitches. Double crochet across 1 row, then on the next row increase 18 stitches evenly spaced; you will have 222 (234,246,258,270) stitches.

First pattern section: *Row 1:* Work 1 double crochet stitch in each of the first 8 stitches. To make a space, chain 2, skip 2 stitches; then make 1 double crochet stitch in each of the next 4 stitches. Continue to make similar spaces across the row, until 8 stitches remain. Then make 1 double crochet in each of these last 8 stitches; chain 2, turn. *Row 2:* Work 1 double crochet stitch in each of the first 8 stitches. Then make 2 double crochet stitches in the first hole created by the space in the previous row and 1 double crochet in the next stitch. Make 1 space (chain 2, skip 2 stitches, 1 double crochet in the next stitch), 1 block (2 double crochet stitches in the hole created by the space below) and 1 double crochet stitch in the next stitch. Repeat 1 space, 1 block until you are 8 stitches from the end of the row; make 1 double crochet stitch in each of the last 8 stitches. Chain 2 and turn. Working the first 8 and last 8 stitches of each row in double crochet stitches throughout the garment, work the remaining stitches of the rows as follows: *Row 3:* Make 1 space, 1 block; repeat this sequence across the row, ending with 1 space. *Row 4:* Make 1 block, 1 space across the row, ending with 1 block. *Rows 5-12:* Repeat rows 3 and 4.

Second pattern section: Remembering to double crochet the first 8 and last 8 stitches in each row, work the remaining stitches as follows: *Rows 1-10:* Make 3 spaces, 1 block; repeat across the row, ending with 1 space.

Third pattern section: Remembering to keep the first 8 and last 8 stitches in each row as double crochet stitches, work the remaining stitches of each row as follows: *Row 1:* Make 7 spaces, 1 block; repeat across the row, ending with 5 (1,5,1,5) spaces. *Row 2:* Make 1 (5,1,5,1) space, 1 block, 7 spaces; repeat across the row, ending with 3 spaces. *Rows 3-8:* Repeat rows 1 and 2 three times.

Fourth pattern section: Still keeping the first 8 and last 8 stitches of each row as double crochet, work the remaining stitches in each row as follows: *Row 1:* Work across the row making spaces only. *Row 2:* Still making only spaces, increase 4 spaces at even intervals across the row. (To increase a space, chain 2, make a double crochet stitch in the next space, then chain 2 and make a double crochet stitch in the next stitch.) Increase 4 spaces at even intervals, on every 10th row thereafter, until the entire skirt measures 5 1/2 inches less than the desired length.

Repeat the third pattern section for 8 rows. On the ninth row, work 1 double crochet swatch in each stitch and 2 double crochet stitches in each space. On the 10th row, decrease 1 double crochet stitch in every third stitch across the row. Continue double crochet stitches for 3 inches.

Finishing the skirt: Work 1 row of single crochet stitches along the full length of each side edge. Leaving a 6-inch opening just below the waistband tab made in row 2 tab, sew the side seam up to the point where the first pattern section begins. Insert a zipper; then sew snap fasteners on the tab and waistband.

THE FILET HALTER

The body section: Chain 130 (154,178), then crochet 3 rows of double crochet stitches. On the fourth row, slip stitch across 5 stitches, double crochet to within the last 5 stitches, chain 2 and turn. Continuing to work in the double crochet stitch, decrease 1 stitch at the beginning and end of the next row *(see below);* simultaneously, start the first pattern section as on the skirt and work that pattern for 6 rows. Start and end the first row with 1 block and decrease 1 block or 1 space (whichever occurs at the beginning and end of subsequent rows) at each end of every row.

When you have completed 6 rows of the first pattern section, work 4 rows of the second pattern section and then 2 rows of the third pattern section, continuing to decrease 1 space or 1 block at the beginning and end of every row. When these 6 rows have been completed, work 4 rows of the fourth pattern section without decreasing.

Note: To decrease at the beginning of a row, slip stitch across the first block or space; then chain 5 if the next stitch is to be a space, or chain 2 if it is to be a block. Work the pattern to the end of a row. To decrease at the end of a row, work to within the last space or block, chain 5 and turn if the next stitch is a space, or chain 2 if it is a block.

The neck shaping: Still working in the fourth pattern section, work across 9 (10,11) spaces, chain 1 and turn. Working on these stitches only, decrease 1 space at the beginning of the next row—the neck edge. Repeat this decrease at the neck edge on every row until only 1 space remains. Fasten off.

Return to the row where the neck shaping began. Skip the center 3 (5,7) spaces, attach the yarn and work the other side of the halter to correspond to the completed side.

The finishing touches: To make the neckband, chain 15, work a row of single crochet stitches around the neck, then chain another 15. Working on these stitches in a double crochet stitch, decrease 6 stitches at even intervals around the front portion of the neck. On the second row, decrease 2 stitches, one at either side of the center front. Fasten off. Work 1 row of single crochet stitches along each side edge of the halter, spacing them so that the halter lays flat. Sew 2 snap fasteners at the bottom band of the halter, and 2 at the back of the neckband.

THE HEADBAND

Chain 36. Make 12 spaces in the row, chain 5 and turn. Repeat this row until the strip measures 60 inches. Fasten off.

BLOCKING THE FINISHED WORK

Lay each garment out flat, cover it with a damp cloth, and press it firmly with a warm iron. Do not pin the garment to the pressing surface or let the iron rest long in one area. To enlarge or reduce the size of the garment if necessary, wet it slightly, then push or stretch it as you lay it out.

GLOSSARY

ADJUSTMENT LINE: A double line printed on a pattern piece to indicate where the piece may be lengthened or shortened.

BACKSTITCH: To reinforce a seam at the beginning or end, by making several machine stitches back over the seam line.

BASTE: To stitch pieces of fabric together temporarily, or to indicate pattern markings on both sides of a piece of fabric.

BIAS: A line running diagonal to the threads in a woven fabric. (A 45° bias is called a true bias.)

BIAS TAPE: A folded strip of nylon, rayon or cotton, cut diagonally to its fabric threads, i.e., on the bias, so that the strip will stretch smoothly to cover curved and straight edges of a garment piece. Double-folded bias tape is called bias binding; commonly made of cotton or a cotton synthetic blend, it is used to bind raw edges.

CLIP: A small straight cut made into a seam allowance—often up to the line of stitching—to help the seam lie flat around curves and at corners.

CORDED TUBING: Cord covered with bias-cut fabric strips, sewed and turned inside out, so that the seam allowances of the fabric are invisible. Corded tubing can be sewed onto fabric or used to make such fasteners as loops and frogs.

CORDING: Cord covered with bias-cut fabric strips so that the seam allowances of the fabric are to the outside, permitting them to be stitched into garment seams.

CROCHETING: The process of making fabric by using a hook to knot strands of yarn into a series of connected loops.

DART: A stitched fabric fold, tapering to a point at one or both ends; used to shape fabric around curves.

DRESSMAKER'S CARBON: A marking paper, available in a range of colors, used to transfer pattern markings to fabric.

DRILL CLOTH: Durable linen or cotton twill fabric of varying weights, commonly used for work clothes.

EMBROIDERY: The decoration of fabric or leather executed with a needle and thread, often in several colors and a wide variety of stitches.

FACING: A piece of fabric—usually cut from the same cloth as the garment—that is sewed along the raw edge of an opening such as a neckline and then turned to the inside to give the edge a smooth finish.

FILET: Square-mesh net or lace that can be made by crocheting.

FRINGE: Lengths of yarn or buttonhole twist attached and knotted along a fabric edge.

FROGS: Fasteners made from braid or corded tubing; frogs are made in pairs in the shape of cloverleaves, one ending in a loop and the other with a button.

GRADING: The act of trimming each seam allowance within a multilayer seam (one containing the fabric, facing, etc.) to a different width so as to reduce bulk and make the seam lie flat.

GRAIN: The direction of threads in a woven fabric. The warp—threads running from one cut end to the other—forms the lengthwise grain. The woof, or weft—threads running across the lengthwise grain from one finished edge to the other—forms the crosswise grain.

HOOP: A pair of circular frames, one fitting snugly around the other, to hold fabric taut while embroidering.

MACHINE STITCH: To stitch permanent seams—or finish edges—by machine.

NOTCH: A V- or diamond-shaped marking made on the edge of a garment piece as an alignment guide; intended to be matched with a similar notch or group of notches on another piece. Also, a triangular cut made into the seam allowance of a curved seam to help it lie flat.

PIVOT: A technique for machine sewing angular corners by stopping the machine with the needle down at the apex of a corner, raising the presser foot, pivoting the fabric and then lowering the presser foot before continuing to stitch again.

PLAIN WEAVE: A weave in which the yarns are interlaced in a checkerboard fashion.

POMPON: A decorative ball made of a number of strands of yarn tied in the middle, with the loose ends fluffed out to form a ball.

PRESSER FOOT: The part of a sewing machine that holds down fabric while it is being advanced under the needle. An all-purpose, or general purpose, foot has two prongs of equal length and is used for most stitching. A straight-stitch foot has one long and one short prong and can be used for straight stitching and stitching fabrics of varying thicknesses. A zipper foot has only one prong and is used to stitch zippers and cording.

PRESSING CLOTH: A piece of fabric, preferably cotton drill cloth, that is placed between the iron and the garment when pressing.

SEAM: The joint between two or more pieces of fabric, or the line of stitching that makes a fold in a single fabric piece, e.g., a dart.

SEAM ALLOWANCE: The extra fabric—usually about 5/8 inch—that extends outside a seam line.

SELVAGE: The lengthwise finished edge in woven fabric.

STAY STITCH: A line of machine stitches, sewed at a gauge of 12 stitches to the inch, along the seam line of a garment piece before the seam is stitched. Stay stitching prevents curved edges from stretching, and acts as a guide for folding an edge precisely.

TAILOR TACKS: Hand stitches taken through a pattern piece and fabric with large loops of thread that are clipped when the pattern and fabric layer or layers are separated, leaving the thread ends in the fabric as markings; used on cloth that cannot be easily marked or might be damaged by chalk or carbon.

TASSEL: A decorative cluster of fringing, secured at one end and then attached to a garment.

TRACING WHEEL: A small wheel attached to a handle, used with dressmaker's carbon paper to transfer pattern markings to fabric.

TRIM: To cut away excess fabric in a seam allowance after a seam has been stitched.

UNDERSTITCHING: A line of machine stitches sewed next to a seam, attaching the seam allowance to the facing to keep the seam from showing on the finished garment.

WARP: See GRAIN

WEFT: See GRAIN

WOOF: See GRAIN

ZIGZAG STITCH: A serrated line of machine stitching used as decoration or to prevent raveling of raw edges.

ZIPPER FOOT: A presser foot with only one prong used to stitch zippers and cording.

BASIC STITCHES

The diagrams below and on the following pages show how to make the elementary hand stitches, crocheting and embroidery stitches referred to in this volume.

THE FASTENING STITCH

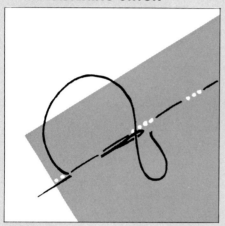

To end a row with a fastening stitch, insert the needle back 1/4 inch and bring it out at the point at which the thread last emerged. Make another stitch through these same points for extra firmness. To begin a row with a fastening stitch, leave a 4 inch loose end and make the initial stitch the same way as an ending stitch.

THE OVERCAST STITCH

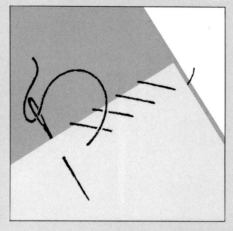

Draw the needle, with knotted thread, through from the wrong side of the fabric 1/8 to 1/4 inch down from the top edge. With the thread to the right, insert the needle under the fabric from the wrong side 1/8 to 1/4 inch to the left of the first stitch. Continue to make evenly spaced stitches over the fabric edge and end with a fastening stitch.

THE CATCH STITCH

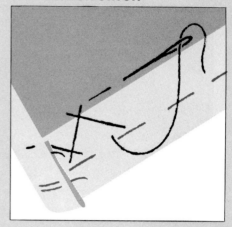

Working from left to right, anchor the first stitch with a knot inside the hem 1/4 inch down from the edge. Point the needle to the left and pick up one or two threads on the garment directly above the hem, then pull the thread through. Take a small stitch in the hem only (not in the garment), 1/4 inch down from the edge and 1/4 inch to the right of the previous stitch. End with a fastening stitch.

THE SLIP STITCH

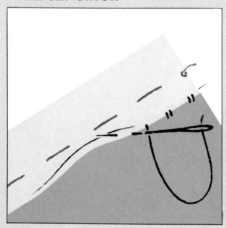

Fold under the hem edge and anchor the first stitch with a knot inside the fold. Point the needle to the left. Pick up one or two threads of the garment fabric close to the hem edge, directly below the first stitch, and slide the needle horizontally through the folded edge of the hem 1/8 inch to the left of the previous stitch. End with a fastening stitch.

THE HEMMING STITCH

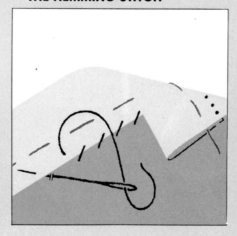

Anchor the first stitch with a knot inside the hem; then pointing the needle up and to the left, pick up one or two threads of the garment fabric close to the hem. Push the needle up through the hem 1/8 inch above the edge; pull the thread through. Continue picking up one or two threads and making 1/8-inch stitches in the hem at intervals of 1/4 inch. End with a fastening stitch.

THE PRICK STITCH

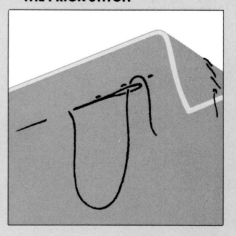

Using a knotted thread, draw the needle up from the bottom layer of fabric and pull it through. Insert the needle to the right three or four threads, and bring it out 1/4 to 3/8 inch to the left of where it last emerged. Continue the process, ending with a fastening stitch on the bottom layer of fabric.

1. Form a loose slipknot around the crochet hook, about 1 inch from the end of the yarn. Grasp the yarn attached to the ball with the tip of the hook and pull the yarn through the slipknot with the tip of the hook, as shown.

2. Hold the hook in your right hand much like a pencil. Place the yarn from the ball around the left little finger, then up and over the left index finger. Grasp the free end of the yarn between the thumb and middle finger of the left hand.

3. With your left index finger, bring the yarn from the back to the front of the hook and catch it under the tip of the hook.

4. Pull the tip of the hook through the loop on the hook, bringing the yarn with it to create the first chain stitch in the foundation chain. Repeat Steps 1-4 to form a chain of the desired length.

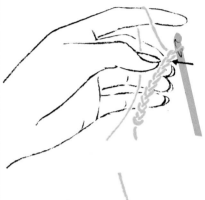

1. To single crochet the first row after a foundation chain, insert the hook through the second chain stitch from the hook (arrow)—do not count the loop on the hook.

2. With two loops now on the hook, bring the yarn over the hook from back to front and catch it under the tip as shown. Then draw the yarn caught under the tip through the loop closest to the tip.

3. Bring the yarn over the hook again and draw it through both of the loops that were on the hook; there is now only a single loop on the hook. Insert the crochet hook into the next chain stitch and repeat Steps 1 and 2. At the end of each row, chain one stitch if the next row is to be worked in single crochet, two stitches for a double crochet pattern, and three stitches for a triple crochet pattern.

4. Turn the work to crochet back across the previous row. Insert the hook through both loops of the second stitch from the edge, as shown, and all subsequent stitches on this and all rows after the foundation chain.

THE DOUBLE CROCHET STITCH

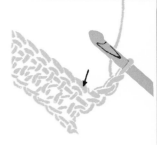

1. To double crochet the first row of stitches after a foundation chain, chain 2 and count back to the third chain stitch from the hook (arrow)—do not count the loop on the hook. Swing the yarn over the hook from back to front, then insert the hook through this third chain stitch.

2. Bring the yarn over the hook again and draw it through the loop closest to the tip. Bring the yarn over the hook again and draw it through the two loops closest to the tip.

3. Bring the yarn over the tip again and draw it through the remaining two loops on the hook. At the end of each row, chain one stitch if the next row is to be worked in single crochet, two stitches for double crochet and three stitches for triple crochet.

4. Turn the work to crochet back across the previous row. Bring the yarn over the hook and insert the hook through both loops of the second stitch from the edge (arrow) on this and all rows after the first.

THE HALF DOUBLE CROCHET STITCH

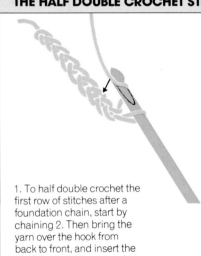

1. To half double crochet the first row of stitches after a foundation chain, start by chaining 2. Then bring the yarn over the hook from back to front, and insert the hook through the second chain stitch from the hook (arrow).

2. With 3 loops now on the hook, bring the yarn over the hook again.

3. Catch the yarn under the tip of the hook, and draw it through the loop closest to the tip.

4. Bring the yarn over the hook again, and draw it through all 3 loops remaining on the hook.

5. Repeat the stitch in each succeeding chain across the row. At the end of the row, chain 2, and turn.

6. To crochet the second row, bring the yarn over the hook, insert the hook into the first stitch and make a half double crochet stitch, following Steps 2-4. Then continue to make half double crochet stitches in each succeeding stitch across the row. At the end of the row, chain 2, and turn. Continue repeating row 2.

THE TRIPLE CROCHET STITCH

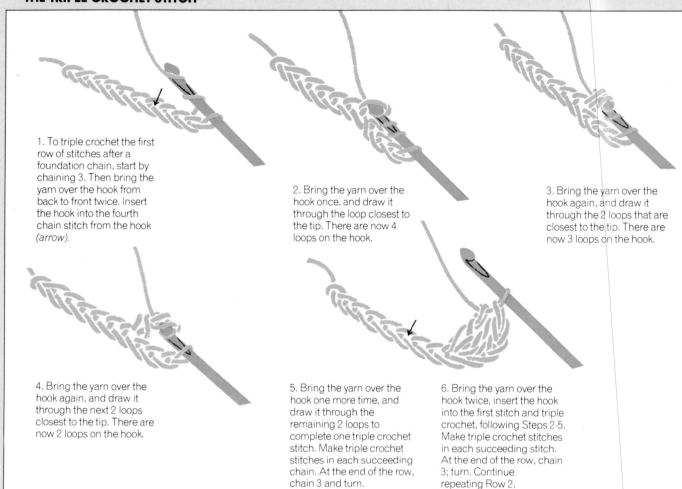

1. To triple crochet the first row of stitches after a foundation chain, start by chaining 3. Then bring the yarn over the hook from back to front twice. Insert the hook into the fourth chain stitch from the hook (arrow).

2. Bring the yarn over the hook once, and draw it through the loop closest to the tip. There are now 4 loops on the hook.

3. Bring the yarn over the hook again, and draw it through the 2 loops that are closest to the tip. There are now 3 loops on the hook.

4. Bring the yarn over the hook again, and draw it through the next 2 loops closest to the tip. There are now 2 loops on the hook.

5. Bring the yarn over the hook one more time, and draw it through the remaining 2 loops to complete one triple crochet stitch. Make triple crochet stitches in each succeeding chain. At the end of the row, chain 3 and turn.

6. Bring the yarn over the hook twice, insert the hook into the first stitch and triple crochet, following Steps 2-5. Make triple crochet stitches in each succeeding stitch. At the end of the row, chain 3; turn. Continue repeating Row 2.

DECREASING STITCHES, SINGLE CROCHET

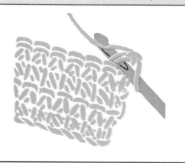

1. To decrease in a row of single crochet stitches, insert the hook into both loops of a stitch. Bring the yarn over the hook and draw it through the two loops closest to the tip; this leaves two loops on the hook.

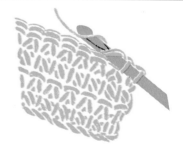

2. Insert the hook through both loops of the next stitch. Bring the yarn over the hook and draw it through the two loops closest to the tip. Bring the yarn over the hook again and draw it through the three remaining loops on the hook.

DECREASING STITCHES, DOUBLE CROCHET

1. To decrease in a row of double crochet stitches, bring the yarn over the hook and insert it through both loops of a stitch. Bring the yarn over the hook again, as shown, and draw it through the two loops closest to the tip. Then bring the yarn over the hook again and insert it through both loops of the next stitch.

2. Again bring the yarn over the hook and draw it through the two loops closest to the tip, as shown; there are now five loops on the hook. Bring the yarn over the hook again and draw it through the two loops now closest to the tip. Repeat the process until there are three loops remaining on the hook. Then pull the yarn through the three remaining loops.

INCREASING STITCHES

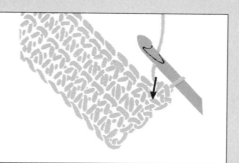

To increase stitches, work one stitch—either a single, double or triple crochet, as called for in the instructions—then insert the crochet hook back into the same loop or loops *(arrow)* and repeat the stitch.

THE SLIPSTITCH FOR JOINING CROCHETED PIECES

1. Align the edges of the pieces to be joined. Insert the hook from front to back through both loops of the first stitch at the end of each piece. Then place a strand of yarn over the hook, and draw it through all 4 loops, leaving a loop on the hook.

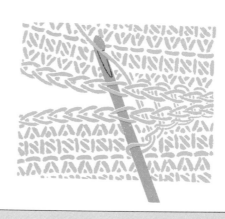

2. Insert the hook through both loops of the next pair of stitches. Bring the yarn over the hook, and draw it—in one motion—through these stitches as well as through the loop on the hook. Repeat until the pieces are joined.

FASTENING OFF

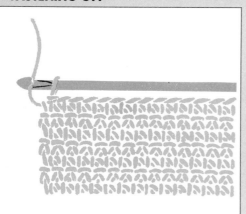

Cut the yarn from the ball, leaving a 2-inch-long end. Pull this end through the loop on the hook to secure it and weave it through one or two nearby stitches.

JOINING YARN

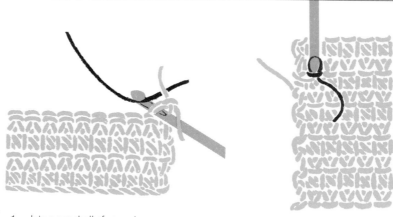

1. Join a new ball of yarn at the beginning of a row by drawing it through the first loop; leave a 1-inch-long end. Join a new color at the end of a row, working the last two loops on the hook with the new yarn.

2. When you have crocheted two or three rows, weave the loose ends of the yarn through nearby stitches with the crochet hook.

EMBROIDERY/ THE SATIN STITCH

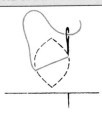 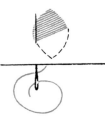 

1. Using a knotted thread, bring the needle up from the wrong side of the material held in the hoop; then, at the angle desired, insert it down to the wrong side at a point diagonally across the design.

2. Bring the needle straight up from the wrong side just above the first hole and insert it above the hole made in Step 1.

3. Repeat Step 2 until the top is filled. Then bring the needle from the wrong side just below the filled part and make diagonal stitches until the bottom is filled. Secure the last stitch on the wrong side (Ending Off, *below*).

THE FRENCH KNOT

 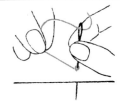 

1. Using a knotted thread, bring the needle up from the wrong side of the material held in the hoop. Put down the hoop and loop the thread once around the needle.

2. Holding the looped thread taut with one hand, push the needle tip into—or just next to—the hole made in Step 1. Slide the loop down to the fabric. Then push the needle through to the wrong side of the fabric.

3. Bring the needle up from the wrong side at a point that suits your design, and repeat Steps 1 and 2. Secure the last stitch on the wrong side (Ending Off, *below*).

THE STEM STITCH

 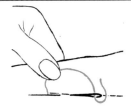 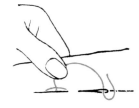

1. Using a knotted thread, bring the needle up from the wrong side of the material held in the hoop.

2. With your left thumb, hold the thread away from the needle. Point the needle to the left, but take a stitch to the right of the hole made in Step 1. The needle should emerge midway between the beginning of this stitch and the hole made in Step 1

3. Pull the thread through taut and take another stitch to the right the same size as the one made in Step 2. Continue making similar stitches along the design and secure the last stitch on the wrong side (Ending Off, *below*).

THE CHAIN STITCH

1. Using a knotted thread, bring the needle up from the wrong side of the material held in the hoop. Pull it through and loop the thread from left to right.

2. With your left thumb, hold the thread in a loop of the desired size and insert the needle in the hole from which it emerged in Step 1. Keeping the loop under the needle point, bring the needle out directly below. Pull the needle through.

3. Again loop the thread and hold it. Insert the needle in the hole from which it last emerged and bring it out through the loop. Complete the design and anchor the last stitch by inserting the needle below its loop. Secure on the wrong side (Ending Off, *below*).

THE CROSS-STITCH

1. Using a knotted thread, bring the needle up from the wrong side of the fabric at the lower right corner of the design. Then insert the needle down at the upper left end of the first diagonal line; bring it out as shown. Continue this diagonal pattern for one row.

2. At the end of the row, turn and go back over the row, bringing the needle up at the lower left corner of each diagonal line, and inserting it down at the upper right, making a series of "X"s. Secure the last stitch on the wrong side (*Ending Off, below*).

ENDING OFF

On the wrong side of the material, slide the needle underneath the nearest 3 or 4 consecutive stitches and pull it through. Snip off the excess thread.

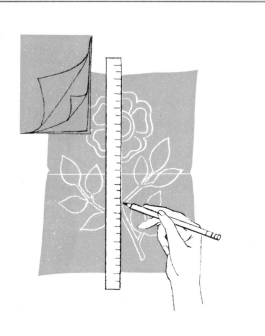

1. Tape the drawing, print or photograph to be traced to a table top or board. Center a sheet of tracing paper over the design and tape it at the top.

2. Trace the design with a fine-tipped black pen. If you are making a tracing for needlepoint be sure the line is strong enough to be seen through the canvas.

3. Remove the tracing and fold it into quarters.

4. Unfold it and lightly mark the fold lines with a ruler and pencil.

ENLARGING OR REDUCING A DESIGN

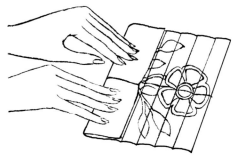

1. Trace the design onto a square piece of paper—it must be square to preserve proportions in rectangular designs—and fold the tracing in half across its width, then across its length. Unfold and fold it in quarters and eighths across its width and length to make a grid with eight squares on each side. (For an elaborate design, the paper may be folded into a 16-square grid.) With a ruler and pencil draw lines along the fold marks.

2. Identify horizontal and vertical coordinates as on a map, by penciling letters (A to H) along the top and numbers (1 to 8) down the side.

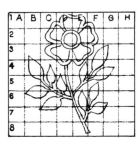

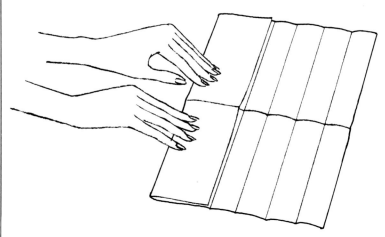

3. Cut a sheet of drawing paper into a square approximately the size you want the embroidery or needlepoint to be.

4. Fold it just as you folded the original and pencil in the same lines and coordinates.

5. Using the coordinates to locate matching squares, copy the design freehand, square by square.

6. Transfer the enlarged or reduced design to the fabric as shown on page 196.

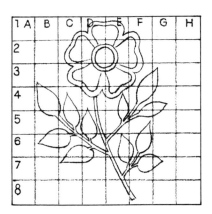

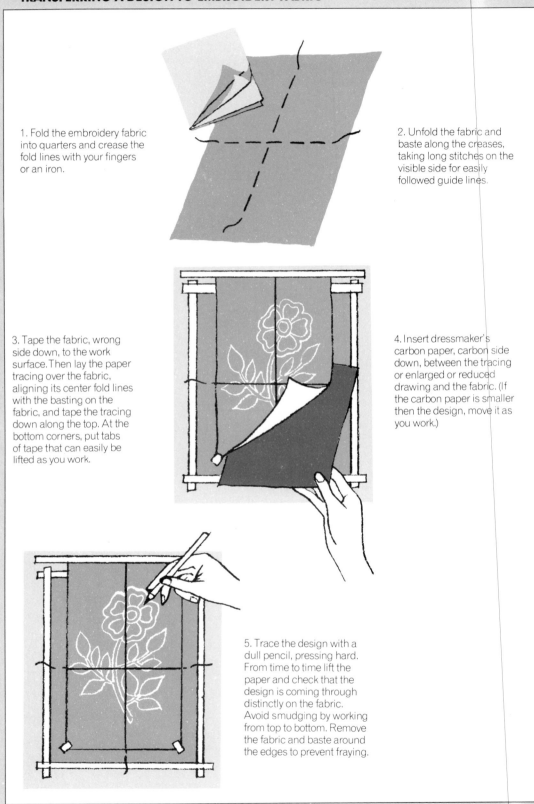

1. Fold the embroidery fabric into quarters and crease the fold lines with your fingers or an iron.

2. Unfold the fabric and baste along the creases, taking long stitches on the visible side for easily followed guide lines.

3. Tape the fabric, wrong side down, to the work surface. Then lay the paper tracing over the fabric, aligning its center fold lines with the basting on the fabric, and tape the tracing down along the top. At the bottom corners, put tabs of tape that can easily be lifted as you work.

4. Insert dressmaker's carbon paper, carbon side down, between the tracing or enlarged or reduced drawing and the fabric. (If the carbon paper is smaller then the design, move it as you work.)

5. Trace the design with a dull pencil, pressing hard. From time to time lift the paper and check that the design is coming through distinctly on the fabric. Avoid smudging by working from top to bottom. Remove the fabric and baste around the edges to prevent fraying.

CREDITS

Sources for the illustrations in this book are shown below. Credits from left to right are separated by semicolons, from top to bottom by dashes.

Cover—Fabric design courtesy of Far Eastern Fabrics Inc., New York City. 6,7—Alen MacWeeney. 11—Culver Pictures except left, Ira L. Hill, copied by Frank Lerner, courtesy Dance Collection, The New York Public Library at Lincoln Center, Astor, Lenox, and Tilden Foundations. 14 through 19—Alen MacWeeney. 20,21—Ryszard Horowitz. 25—Lisa Larsen, TIME-LIFE Picture Agency, © 1972 Time Incorporated. 28 through 33—Ryszard Horowitz. 36,37—Ann Spanos Kuhn, garment courtesy Giorgio di Sant'Angelo. 40—Drawing by Steven Stipelman. 41 through 47—Drawings by John Sagan. 48—Drawing by Steven Stipelman. 49 through 53—Drawings by Carolyn Mazzello. 54—Drawing by Steven Stipelman. 55 through 59—John Sagan. 60—Drawing by Steven Stipelman. 61,62,63—Drawings by Raymond Skibinski. 66—The Bettmann Archive. 68,69—Enrico Ferorelli, courtesy The Metropolitan Museum of Art, New York (2); Enrico Ferorelli, courtesy Museum of the City of New York; Enrico Ferorelli, opera coat from the private collection of Umberto Tirelli. 70—Drawing by Steven Stipelman. 71,72,73—Drawings by Raymond Skibinski. 74—Drawing by Steven Stipelman. 75 through 79—Drawings by Carolyn Mazzello. 80—Drawing by Steven Stipelman. 81,82,83—Drawings by Raymond Skibinski. 84—Drawing by Steven Stipelman. 85,86,87—Drawings by Raymond Skibinski. 88,89—Silhouette photo by Tasso Vendikos, background photo by Jay Maisel. 93,94,95—Drawings by John Sagan. 96,97—Tasso Vendikos, background photo by Paulus Leeser, from the book *Costume Patterns and Designs* by Max Tilke, courtesy Verlag Ernst Wasmuth. 98 through 107—Drawings by Raymond Skibinski. 108,109—Tasso Vendikos, background photo by Paulus Leeser, from the book *Costume Patterns and Designs* by Max Tilke, courtesy Verlag Ernst Wasmuth. 110 through 119—Drawings by John Sagan. 120,121—Tasso Vendikos, background photo by Paulus Leeser, from the book *Costume Patterns and Designs* by Max Tilke, courtesy Verlag Ernst Wasmuth. 122 through 131—Drawings by Carolyn Mazzello. 132,133—Ken Kay. 136,137—The George Crofts Collection, Royal Ontario Museum, Toronto, except bottom left, Paulus Leeser, courtesy Hartman Rare Art, New York. 138,139—Paulus Leeser, courtesy Private Collection, Brooklyn, New York. 140 through 149—Drawings by John Sagan. 150,151—Ryszard Horowitz. Embroidery by Lucy Ciancia. 152—Chart by Pat Byrne. 153—Drawings by Nick Pliakis. 154,155—Ken Kay. Embroidery by Toni Scott. 156—Chart by Pat Byrne. 157—Drawing by Nick Pliakis. 158,159—Tasso Vendikos. 162,163—Ken Kay. Crochet by Annette Feldman. 164,167—Drawings by John Sagan. 168,169—Tasso Vendikos. Crochet by Annette Feldman. 171—Drawing by Pat Byrne. 172,173—Ken Kay. Crochet by Annette Feldman. 174—Drawing by John Sagan. 176,177—Richard Noble. Crochet by Annette Feldman. 181 through 186—Drawings by John Sagan. 187—Drawings by Raymond Skibinski—Drawings by John Sagan. 188—Drawings by Raymond Skibinski.

ACKNOWLEDGMENTS

For their help in the preparation of this book the editors would like to thank the following individuals: Helen Barer; Margaret Bertin, Metropolitan Museum of Art; Susan Costello; Michael Durham; Dr. Joanne B. Eicher; Del Pitt Feldman; Audrey C. Foote; Sara Penn; Fumi Schmidt; Toni Scott; Pat Sukhaprayura; Takako Ueno; Madeleine Walker; Mrs. Diana Vreeland.

The editors would also like to thank the following: Beng Sole Trading Corporation; Brooks-Van Horn Costume Company; Jerry Brown Imported Fabrics, Inc.; Butterick Fashion Marketing Company; China Seas, Inc.; Ernst/Reiko Designs, Inc.; Far Eastern Fabrics, Inc.; Henri Bendel Inc.; India Nepal Handloom House; Lady Continental Shoes; The McCall Pattern Company; Maskit Design, Ltd.; Rivitz of Boston; Scovill, Sewing Notions Division.

 # INDEX

Numerals in italics indicate an illustration of the subject mentioned.